Farewell
To Revolution

Farewell
To Revolution
Marxist Philosophy
and the Modern World

S.F.Kissin

St. Martin's Press
New York

792770

Copyright © 1978 by S. F. Kissin

All rights reserved.   For information, write:
St. Martin's Press, Inc., 175 Fifth Avenue, New York, N.Y. 10010
Printed in Great Britain
Library of Congress Catalog Card Number 78–18948
ISBN 0–312–28267–2
First published in the United States of America in 1978

Library of Congress Cataloging in Publication Data

Kissin, S. F.
   Farewell to revolution.

   Includes bibliographical references and index.
   1. Communism—1945-   2. Communist revisionism.   3. Dialectical
materialism.   4. Russia—Foreign relations—1945-   I. Title.
HX44.K5155   1978   335.43   78–18948
ISBN 0–312–28267–2

Contents

To my sister Lilly

Preface

The four essays in this book deal with aspects of Marxist theory and practice. All of them except 'Diamat and Dogma' are concerned primarily with what could be called post-Marxian Marxism, i.e. with developments which occurred after the death of Marx and Engels and which deviated, to a varying extent, from the original teachings and from the policies Marx and Engels might have envisaged or approved. These three studies describe and assess the changes the doctrine has undergone in the writings, speeches and actions of twentieth-century Marxists. The process, which is still going on, has always been closely bound up with actual events in the world of social and economic reality, and with the practical exigencies of government or party politics.

This interaction of theoretical and practical developments is particularly striking in the themes of the two essays devoted to topical issues. 'Farewell to Revolution' examines the gradual conversion (unavowed but undeniable) of the bulk of the Moscow-oriented world communist movement to revisionism since the Second World War. This essay is based on a Fabian pamphlet published early in 1972, which incidentally foreshadowed the rise of 'Euro-communism' – without, of course, mentioning the phrase, which had not yet been coined. The other topical study, 'The Decline and Fall of the Soviet Empire', tries to show how the leadership of the USSR, right from the start and at an ever faster pace as time went on, abandoned its world-revolutionary ideals in the conduct of international affairs and embraced the traditional power policies pursued by its tsarist predecessors – and by statesmen all over the world. Elaborate propagandistic manoeuvres were initiated to disguise the true motivation of Soviet foreign policy and to provide the requisite theoretical justification of actions which were no different, in essence, from what Marxist-Leninist literature had always described and denounced as typical examples of 'imperialist' and 'colonialist' behaviour.

The longest essay in this volume, 'Marxism and Marxianity', purports to analyse the transformation of the Marxist system, during the course of the present century, into a religious creed.

Marxism started off as a scientific theory. Marx's main work, *Das Kapital*, is a sober and erudite analysis of nineteenth-century capitalism, its genesis, its dynamics and its prospects. Karl Marx did not indulge in Utopian prophecy and did not elaborate on the physiognomy of the future society which he thought would replace the 'bourgeois' society of his time.

How, since about the turn of the century, Marxism has absorbed certain irrational and religious elements, and has thus been turned into 'Marxianity', is the subject of that study. In this context the term Marxism denotes the world-wide movement, comprising the parties, groups, factions, etc., in and out of power, which describe themselves as Marxist or Marxist-Leninist, as well as their ideologies, principles and policies. Marxists in this sense are the pro-Moscow, pro-Peking and non-aligned communists (i.e. not aligned with either Moscow or Peking), the Trotskyists and other adherents of the extreme Left who, rightly or wrongly, claim ideological descent from Marxist philosophy.

Religion, in the sense in which comparison with Marxism becomes possible, is the actual historical phenomenon, not religious emotions in the abstract, such as Freud's 'oceanic feeling' or the 'sensation of the mystical' which, according to Einstein, is at the centre of true religiousness. The question is whether, and to what extent, Marxism is a religion like one of the major universal creeds, Buddhism, Christianity and Islam. Its characterization as a world religion would obviously not be precluded by the fact that, as a movement, it comprises a multiplicity of divergent views and antagonistic groupings and tendencies: fragmentation and inter-necine conflicts and rivalries are typical of most of the higher and especially of the three great world religions.

'Diamat and Dogma', the only essay in this volume which does not specifically investigate post-Marxian developments, was originally conceived as a chapter in the study on Marxism as a religious creed. And, indeed, the lack of rationality in Marxist dialectics, as expounded by Engels and some twentieth-century communists, has some marginal bearing on the issue of Marxianity, Marxist theory turned religion. But the case regarding the religious content of modern Marxism is complete without more than a passing reference to dialectics. Conversely, the critique of 'dialectical materialism' can be comprehensively formulated without being linked with the other non-rational aspects of Marxist-Leninist doctrine and practice. The fact that 'diamat' confirms the dogmatic nature of the doctrine in its contemporary form is mentioned in the text; and it does not deserve more than a mention. In view of all this I felt that the inclusion of the lengthy piece on dialectics in the study of Marxianity would have made the latter top-heavy, while, on the other hand, a separate treatment tends to make for greater coherence and cogency of argument.

I am aware that to present Marxist dialectics as a non-rational dogma means to incur the wrath and the contempt of the 'Marxologists', the committed adepts of Marxian philosophy. Some of them will probably accuse me of the vulgarization of the theory, or perhaps repeat the charge which Lukács levelled at the 'demolishers of Marx', in his preface to *History and Class Consciousness*, when he stressed 'their total inability to grasp even the ABC of the dialectical method'. The obstacle to a meaningful discussion with these orthodox adversaries stems from their question-begging insistence on conducting the debate in their own chosen arena – by assuming the validity of the dialectical method and vocabulary. But to accept such terms as a basis for discussion seems neither practicable nor necessary. The burden of the polemic in this inquiry into Marxist dialectics is directed against prominent practitioners who claimed to be orthodox Marxists – men like Lenin, Trotsky, Stalin and Mao Tse-tung. In their writings and speeches they tried to demonstrate the dialectical method and the significance of dialectics for framing and judging revolutionary policies on the level not of philosophical abstractions but of normal understanding and ordinary terminology, by putting forward concrete examples which they thought would illustrate the practical efficacy of dialectical criteria. The counter-argument must consist in bringing into focus the absurdity of some of their deductions and the irrelevance of their method. I think it can be shown that either their conclusions are fallacious or else that valid results could have been obtained without recourse to dialectical techniques. Lukács and his fellow Marxologists, who put so much emphasis upon the Marxian postulate of the 'unity of theory and practice', could not, without being inconsistent, challenge this form of argument which is directed primarily against the views and assertions of outstanding representatives of Marxism in action.

Finally, while these studies are concerned with fundamental problems of Marxism they are not meant to be Marxist analyses. In Marxist theory such happenings within the ideological 'super-structure' as the emergence of a new religion are ultimately determined by developments at the economic base, in the sphere of production and reproduction. Hence a Marxist who shared my view that Marxism was not originally but has now become a religious creed (and a true Marxist might well arrive at such a conclusion) would try to establish which socio-economic events accounted for the rise of a new religion in each case – twentieth-century Marxism, Buddhism, Christianity and Islam – in their respective periods of history. Marxist scholars have, in fact, under-taken to interpret religious phenomena in the light of the material-ist conception of history: examples that come to mind are Karl Kautsky's *Foundations of Christianity* and Engels's work concerning uprisings in the sixteenth-century German states, *German Peasants' Wars*. I do not, in these studies, dispute this conception, nor do I deny the existence of links between economic and ideological developments; in fact, I draw attention to such links in the essays on communist revisionism and on the Soviet Union's international policy. But an investigation of the nature of similar links in the context of dialectics or of Marxianity would be beyond the scope of these studies. It would not by itself resolve the question of the character of contemporary Marxism; nor would it even facilitate the search for an answer.

Marxism and Marxianity: *The Rise of a New World Religion*

Communism and Millennium

The essence of socialist philosophy, shorn of socio-economic intricacies and of the esoteric terminology peculiar to some theoretical systems, can be summed up in a few simple words: socialism[1] strives for a world of plenty, which guarantees a free, full and happy life to all people everywhere. As a German economist remarked about the turn of the century,[2] the socialist gospel of happiness has found poetic yet concise expression in some verses which Heinrich Heine wrote in 1844:

> A new song, ay, a sweeter song,
> My friends, I'll sing to you:
> The dream of heaven, we'll make sure,
> Shall here on earth come true.
>
> Men will be happy here on earth;
> To starve is not our fate.
> The idle rich no more shall feast
> On what the poor create.
>
> There's bread enough upon this earth,
> Enough for all – and more.
> There's beauty, roses, myrtles, joy,
> And sugar-peas galore![3]

This state of universal and lasting happiness, of heaven on earth, is the common aim of all truly socialist parties, groups and tendencies, of all those to whom socialism (or communism) does not only mean a programme of social reforms or social engineering but a complete transformation, in the direction of egalitarian collectivism, of existing society.

Marxism is one of these socialist systems – the most comprehensive and the most elaborate of all. It has had a more profound impact both upon human affairs and upon the social and economic sciences than any other socialist theory. Marxism is distinguished from rival doctrines, above all, by its determinism and by its emphasis on the role of the working class. It regards itself as a science – the science of social change – and claims to be able to predict history (i.e. the general lines, not the details) with scientific certainty.

The Age of Abundance, of universal prosperity and happiness, for which all socialists strive is, to a Marxist, more than just an aim. Marxists are convinced that it will actually happen in the not-too-distant future. Their concept of history and of the dynamics of capitalist society leads them to foresee the inevitable revolutionary collapse of the capitalist 'profit system' and its replacement by a socialist order, based on common ownership of the means of production and on economic planning for use. Socialism is thus regarded as the inevitable end-result of the interplay of social and economic forces which characterizes the mature stage of capitalism. According to the Marxists this future system of common ownership and socialist planning will in turn, with the same degree of inevitability, usher in the Millennium, the Golden Age of worldwide abundance, peace, brotherhood and prosperity. Capitalist production, in Karl Marx's words, leads to its own negation and to socialist revolution 'with the necessity of a natural process'.[4] The same necessity is seen at work in the subsequent transition from the socialist state, in which each worker will be paid according to his work, to the classless society where all citizens will contribute according to their ability and will receive according to their needs: once that stage is reached the state itself and all forms of coercion will gradually disappear.

Furthermore this inevitability, this irresistible trend towards capitalist collapse and socialist revolution, is, from the Marxist point of view, the principal *raison d'être* of the conscious struggle for socialism. Marxists, of course, regard the supersession of capitalism by socialism as desirable. At the same time they hold that it would be 'utopian' and futile to expect socialism or, for that matter, any new social and economic system, to prevail simply because it seems more just and reasonable than the existing order. In their opinion socialism will conquer because economic and political developments have placed it on the agenda of history; and they deem it to be their tasks as socialists not to try to change the course of history (which anyway they consider impossible) but to facilitate, and take a conscious part in, the inevitable process of world-wide social transformation which will culminate in the birth of the ideal society of the future.

Predictions and prophecies

To predict historic developments on the basis of an analysis of the contemporary period and its trends is certainly possible. Generally speaking historical predictions are often made, and are often accurate, as are forecasts in other fields of life and human knowledge. At a lower, non-scientific level they are purely empirical: expectations are based on observed recurrence. Men expected day and night or the warm and cold seasons to follow upon each other long before anything was known about the rotation of the earth or its orbit around the sun. If, according to observation, event B has invariably succeeded event A in the past, people are convinced that it will do so in the future, even if they do not understand the causal link between the two occurrences. Political events, too, are sometimes predicted on the strength of experienced repetition, although the sequence of events in this field is rarely as regular or as consistent as it is in nature. Thus the view is often expressed that an arms race *always* leads to war, or that anarchy *always* leads to tyranny. Those who make such forecasts do not normally go into details regarding the mechanics of cause and effect; they try to prove their point by induction – by showing that on numerous past occasions an arms race *was* followed by wars between the rival countries, and that a period of anarchy or near-anarchy in a nation's life very often *did* end with the establishment of tyranny.

As for the Marxist prediction that capitalism will be superseded by a socialist planned economy, the first phase of the predicted development – the revolutionary overthrow of the capitalist system – is to some extent based on empiricism, i.e. on an analogy with repeated historical precedent. From the history of past societies and of social transformations Marx claimed to have derived the general law of revolution: every society develops internal contradictions, products of the interaction of the mode and the material forces of production. At a certain stage in its evolution each socio-economic system develops traits which tend to frustrate the forces of production; in the case of capitalism this means that private ownership of the factories, the land etc., and the absence of overall planning, hamper creative expansion and economic growth.[5] This conflict between the productive forces and what Marx called the 'relations of production' is bound to lead to the downfall of the existing order and its obsolete economic and social institutions, to the emergence of a new mode of production which permits and furthers the expansion of the productive forces, and to the consequential revolutionary transformation of the ideological and political 'superstructure'. According to Marx this recurrent process of revolutionary transition from one order of society to another has been at work throughout history: during the period of 'bourgeois revolution', for example, when feudalism finally had to give way to modern capitalism.

Marx believed, and tried to demonstrate in his analysis of contemporary (i.e. mid-Victorian) capitalism, that the clash between the forces and the relations of production which always heralds the approach of revolution had led to the terminal crisis of the capitalist order, whose collapse was therefore at hand. Yet Marx was not content to argue that capitalism must succumb to its own inner contradictions because in analogous circumstances previous social systems had perished. He described what he considered to be the exact nature of the contradictions and set out to prove their lethal effect. In other words, he did not merely say that capitalism was doomed by the historic laws he had discovered; he went further and tried to lay bare the actual causal nexus between the capitalist contradictions and the revolution to which, in his opinion, they must lead: on the one hand, unavoidable recurrent crises of over-production of ever-increasing length and intensity; on the other, the polarization of society into an ever-diminishing minority of wealthy capitalists and the proletarian masses who have nothing to lose but their chains, and whose growing misery will inevitably engender revolt and revolution.[6]

All these forecasts stem from comprehensive economic analysis and cogent argument, and it must be said that they follow logically from Marx's two basic premises: his concept of the laws governing historic changes and his assessment of contemporary capitalism as afflicted with a mortal disease. If these premises are accepted, at least the prediction of impending capitalist collapse and an emerging new system is justified; the further assumption that the rule of the bourgeoisie would be brought to an end, and a new collectivist order initiated, by the revolutionary proletarian masses is a plausible though not absolutely compelling conclusion.

The premises themselves, whether or not they correspond to reality, were established by the rational appraisal of facts and by consistent reasoning: the forecasts which follow from these premises can therefore be characterized as scientific predictions – which is what Marxists claim they are. This claim is not invalidated by the fact that the developments foretold by Marx, Engels and their disciples have not occurred. The actual prediction failed to come true because both premises possibly, but certainly one of them, (concerning capitalism's inability to expand the forces of production) conflicted with reality. Yet the prediction was scientific, inasmuch as the events Marx forecast were the logical results of a situation which he – on rational though fallacious grounds – regarded as existing. If an astronomer, through either faulty observation or miscalculation, predicts an eclipse which does not in fact occur, his would still be a scientific prediction, albeit a mistaken one. The inaccurate forecast of an early downfall of capitalism was scientific in the same sense.

The Marxist predictions of what will happen *after* the revolutionary overthrow of capitalism – the character of the future society, etc. – are clearly not empirical in nature, since they do not stem from observation of recurrent sequences of events. For what Marx predicts is something that has never yet happened in history. Actually Marx himself never went into details regarding the shape of the future social order, but he and Engels took it for granted that the revolution would lead to the abolition of private property in production, that this would involve the disappearance of classes, and that in the resulting classless society the state would wither away. This means that the predicted revolution would create an unprecedented state of affairs. For as Marx and Engels themselves emphasized, ever since the dawn of civilization human society has been divided into classes. The communist classless society would be a completely new phenomenon in history. So would the other predicted features of the society of tomorrow: disappearance of the state and of all forms of coercion, lasting prosperity and peace, international brotherhood. Non-Marxist socialists hold such objectives to be desirable and, at least in part, capable of attainment. Marxists believe them all to be not only possible but, indeed, inevitable. There are a few other categories of people who declare themselves similarly convinced of the coming of the Golden Age. Confirmed Christians believe in the Second Coming of Christ and the Kingdom of God on earth. And some Christian sects even proclaim that the Millennium is imminent.[7]

It is not impossible to predict events the like of which have never happened before. Theoretically speaking, it would be possible for an astronomer to predict a cosmic catastrophe involving the destruction of our planet: it is within the scope of science to foretell both such a unique and unprecedented occurrence and the exact time of its happening.

Historical predictions, however, are in a different category. History is concerned with human beings and human activities, with human behaviour and human (individual and collective) reactions. Future happenings of this kind do not lend themselves to accurate forecasts such as those scientists are capable of making when computing the exact time of natural occurrences. A considerable element of unpredictability is inherent in any attempt to visualize the shape of historic things to come.

Yet Marxist philosophy teaches that history can be scientifically predicted, i.e. that it is possible – without fixing the exact days and hours of a future event – to foresee what men will do collectively, even in circumstances that have never yet arisen, and how they will react to a situation which is utterly different from anything experienced in recorded history. Some second-generation Marxists, as we shall see, have offered detailed descriptions of the features of the coming socialist society. Marx and Engels were more reticent in this respect, but they, too, claimed that the proletarian revolution, and certain of its short-term and long-term consequences, could be predicted with scientific accuracy.

Is there any rational basis for this claim? In other words, does the prediction follow from the Marxist premise (which, though mistaken, had been rationally expounded) that private capitalism is bound to give way to a system of collective ownership and economic planning? Or, since the disappearance of classes and of the state will be the result of human action or inaction, are the Marxists right in asserting that under a system of collective ownership and planning men would behave in such a way that first the division of society by class and then the coercive power of the state would vanish?

Let us consider the abolition of classes in the post-capitalist era. According to Engels's explanation, class division was made unavoidable in the past by the low productivity of human labour:

So long as the really working population were so much occupied with their necessary labour that they had no time left for looking after the common affairs of society – the direction of labour, affairs of state, legal matters, art, science, etc. – so long was it necessary that there should constantly exist a special class, freed from actual labour, to manage these affairs; and this class never failed, for its own advantage, to impose a greater and greater burden of labour on the working masses. Only the immense increase of the productive forces attained by modern industry has made it possible to distribute labour among all members of society without exception, and thereby to limit the labour-time of each individual member to such an extent that all have enough free time left to take part in the general . . . affairs of society. It is only now, therefore, that every ruling and exploiting class has become superfluous and indeed a hindrance to social development, and it is only now, too, that it will be inexorably abolished. . . .[8]

Neither Marx nor Engels nor, for that matter, the twentieth-century Marxists ever bothered to explain the actual mechanics of the transition from one phase to the next, from the socialist state the revolution would create (the dictatorship of the proletariat which, by definition, is still a form of class rule) to the classless, homogeneous society of the future. What Engels's reasoning amounts to is that there would be no apparent need for class divisions in the post-capitalist society; and it is somehow inherent in the Marxist conception of history that institutions which have no functions to fulfil in social production or in the 'superstructure' cannot survive. This view also plays a part in the theory of the disappearing state:

Society thus far, based upon class antagonisms, has need of the state, that is, of an organization of the particular class, which was *pro tempore* the exploiting class, for the maintenance of its external conditions of production, and . . . for the purpose of forcibly keeping the exploited classes in the condition of oppression corresponding with the given mode of production (slavery, serfdom, wage-labour) . . . As soon as there is no longer any social class to be held in subjection; as soon as class rule and the individual struggle for existence based upon our present anarchy in production…are removed, nothing more remains to be repressed, and a special repressive force, a state, is no longer necessary . . . State interference in social relations becomes, in one domain after another, superfluous, and then withers away of itself . . . The state is not 'abolished'. *It withers away.*[9] (Engels's italics.)

The assumption underlying these visions of the future is that socialization of the means of production plus economic planning would stimulate unprecedented growth resulting in material superabundance, which would also permit a drastic shortening of working hours: once modern technology was harnessed to a rationally planned economic system, which had eliminated exploitation and was producing for the benefit of all instead of for the profits of a minority, there would be enough, and more than enough, to satisfy all needs. This assumption may have sounded plausible in the days of Marx and Engels, although the belief in unlimited growth had already been challenged by Malthus and others. Today we know more than did Marx's contemporaries about the ecological limitations of growth which affect all countries and all societies, regardless of socio-economic systems. And what we now know about the dangers of pollution, about the possible exhaustion of mineral resources, about the population explosion and its effect on the adequacy of food supplies, etc., might tend to make us somewhat less sanguine about the prospects of superabundance and increased leisure. But even if, for the sake of the argument, we dismiss the warnings of the ecologists and assume that modern technology does remain a potential source of superabundance for all people on earth, we would still be behaving irrationally to expect socialization of the means of production to lead to the disappearance of classes and of the state; for unlike Marx and Engels we can and must take into account the experience of several decades of communist state power in action.

In terms of economic growth, material progress and higher living standards, the switch from capitalist free enterprise to state ownership and planning may have been beneficial in some of the countries concerned and harmful in others, but in none of the countries with totally planned economies has material plenty become a practical prospect; in fact, progress towards it has been faster in parts of the capitalist world. Left-wing Marxist fundamentalists in the West who are not committed to either Moscow, Peking, Belgrade or Tirana have advanced a variety of reasons why wholesale nationalization plus planning did not have the results predicted by Marx and Engels;[10] why, for example, a country like Russia, with its economic self-sufficiency and its wealth of resources, is still a totalitarian dictatorship and cannot, more than half a century after the 'socialist' revolution, offer its workers the standard of living enjoyed by their exploited class brothers in the advanced capitalist countries. We are told that the proletarian revolution broke out prematurely in Russia, or else that it was not a genuine *proletarian* revolution, or that, though genuine to start with, it has been betrayed by selfish and corrupt rulers bent on perpetuating their own economic and political privileges. Similar arguments are used to explain un-Marxist developments in the East European 'People's Democracies' or in China.[11] The gist of these explanations is that no really socialist societies have come into being, or have survived, in any of the countries concerned, and that therefore their modest economic performance has not disproved Marxist theories and predictions.

The fundamentalist critique of communism in power is certainly justified. Not one of the regimes that claim to be Marxist has been the product of a working-class revolution or exemplifies working-class rule. Hence these regimes are not socialist or communist in the Marxist sense, and their performance has no direct bearing on the question of whether socialism is superior to capitalism (as Marxists assert) or not. Yet however grossly the communist rulers may have violated Marxist principles, certain economic methods and policies adopted in the so-called socialist states would also have been adopted, with certain modifications, by a genuine Marxist leadership. Anarchy in production – allegedly the main source of recurrent capitalist crises – has been replaced by central economic planning. The purpose has been to achieve, not least in the interests of the ruling communist bureaucracy, maximum economic growth as speedily as possible: according to the theory, this would also have been the overriding objective of an authentic 'workers' state' – in the interests of the working class as a whole, not in the sectional interest of an upper stratum. Under a truly Marxist regime there would have been less inequality in the distribution of the social product; but more equality would not necessarily have meant greater efficiency and a higher rate of growth. In the sphere of planning the communist rulers have proceeded by trial and error, often responding to setbacks and crises by reorganizing the machinery of planning, and by alternating between rigid command economies and various forms of decentralization, with partial autonomy for the works managers and adjustment to market requirements. Seeing that Marxist theory is silent about the principles of post-revolutionary economic planning, a genuinely 'proletarian' administration would likewise, inevitably, have resorted to a good deal of experimentation, presumably with more or less the same effect on the tempo of material progress.

The record of communist economic achievements is, therefore, not irrelevant to the Marxist thesis of the superiority of wholesale socialization and planned production. This record does not prove economic socialism to be unworkable or inefficient; nor does it prove that socialist planning is *more* efficient and *more* conducive to economic growth than capitalist free enterprise. Communists in power usually proclaim the aim of 'catching up with and over-taking' advanced capitalist countries in regard to productivity and living standards, describing the success of this drive as a test of socialism's superiority. By this token they have never yet suc-ceeded in proving their point. What the experience of recent decades has shown is that a socialist economic system is, at best, a viable alternative to capitalism. The professed belief of present-day Marxists that the revolution will usher in the Golden Age of universal and lasting prosperity is not based on empirical fact and on reasoning, but solely – in so far as it is sincere – on apocalyptic faith.

Left-wing Marxists who feel entitled to ignore the experience of communism in power tend to overlook the fact that the departure from orthodox Marxism was highly probable, or even unavoid-able, from the start. Many Marxists now admit the theoretical possibility of a wholly collectivized and planned economy run on class lines, with a managerial class controlling and directing pro-duction and determining the distribution of the social product, while the bulk of the working population is engaged in industrial or agricultural labour. In this kind of society the 'managers' would, in effect, be the collective or corporate owners of the entire pro-duction apparatus; and they would, following the example of all ruling classes in history, use their dominant status and their power to obtain for themselves and their families a higher-than-average standard, i.e. to exploit the subject classes in much the same way as, according to the Marxists, they have always been exploited.

What has actually happened is that a new class society of this type has emerged from the colossal transformation which, under the leadership of Marxist parties, has occurred in parts of Europe in the course of this century. The 'socialist' regimes which were established in Russia after the First World War, and in most East European countries after the Second, are all 'managerial', in the sense that there is a sharp division, in terms both of power and of living standards, between the party and state bureaucracy on the one hand and the working masses on the other. And it has made no difference in this respect whether the abolition of private capitalism was the result of what Marxists call a 'proletarian revolution' – as in Russia – or of Soviet military occupation and of the political hegemony which the USSR has attained in Eastern Europe.

As class divisions persist, these regimes are not socialist by Marxist standards. In fact, class antagonisms – workers versus state, party and managerial bureaucracy – are acute in the East European 'People's Democracies', where proletarian resistance has repeatedly exploded into violent confrontation.[12] Needless to say, the state has not begun to wither away in any communist country: in view of the survival – or re-emergence – of class divisions it would indeed have been contrary to Marxist theory if it had. Significantly the coercive machinery of the state is far less forceful and pervasive in most of the capitalist world than it is in the regions where the state should, in theory, be dead or dying.

The truth is that there has always been an element of unreality in the Marx—Engels thesis of the classless society and the disappearance of the state. The experience of what has happened in Russia since 1917, and in Eastern Europe since the end of the Second World War, has merely confirmed what should have been apparent a priori: the nation-wide substitution of public for private ownership is more likely to lead to new class divisions than to a classless society. The high level of productivity which, in the Marxist vision, would permit a drastic shortening of working hours and thereby eliminate the need for a division of labour on class lines would, in any case, not be a fact of the immediate post-revolutionary phase. The revolutionary seizure of power by the working class, even if it were not followed by a prolonged civil war, could not but create chaos in the economy and the machinery of production. Strikes in industry and transport, factory occupations, etc. – the usual concomitants of revolution – must cause disruption and dislocation. Once things got back to normal, production would have to start from a low level. This means that in the first phase the industrial apparatus of the country concerned would have to be reorganized by groups of experts, technologists, professional administrators, under the guidance of political and trade union leaders, civil servants, etc. By the time socialist planning was moving towards superabundance (if indeed it ever did) a new bureaucracy would have been established, with control over the state, the police, the armed forces and the economy, and with a vested interest in the *status quo* which guaranteed its position and its privileges. And if its position should really be threatened by the approach of superabundance – an unlikely contingency in view of the record to date – an Orwellian 'Ministry of Plenty' could be relied upon to organize the requisite scarcity so as to save the ruling élite from redundancy. Hence it would take a new revolution to drive the communist rulers from power, and this second revolution would merely reproduce the situation existing after the first; the process of the emergence of a new ruling stratum would start all over again.[13]

There is, thus, a basic difference between the Marxist notion of capitalist doom and the Marxist forecast of the classless society. The former may have been refuted by actual developments, but it was a rational deduction from rational assumptions and, hence, a scientific prediction. The view that a society without classes, without conflict, without coercion was not merely possible or probable but absolutely certain has always lacked a rational foundation.[14] This was, and still is whenever it is repeated, a non-rational prophecy.

This charge of irrationality applies to an even greater extent to the detailed descriptions of the future Golden Age which abound in the works of the second-generation Marxists. I do not intend to ridicule these visions of the future, or even to assert that they are fantastic and unattainable. The point is that the perfection of the world of tomorrow is being presented by Marxist disciples not just as something desirable, something worth striving for, but as something that is quite certain to come about. There is no rational link between the scientific aspects of Marxist theory and this optimistic determinism of the latter-day disciples. Their conviction is tantamount to the belief in the truth of an avowedly religious prophecy: it is in keeping with the belief in the Kingdom of God on earth or in the Second Coming of Christ – beliefs which are proclaimed by those who hold them with the same emphatic assurance, although they are not accorded scientific status. This is the irrational, religious aspect of Marxist theory as developed by the *epigoni*. If the blessings of the ideal society of the future were put forward as the long-term targets of the political struggle one could argue about whether they are, in whole or in part, capable of achievement. But there is no point in arguing rationally against the view that this splendid world of tomorrow is sure to materialize, just as one cannot argue rationally against someone's firm belief in the imminence of the Second Coming.

One of the more specific Marxist prophets about the turn of the century was the German socialist leader August Bebel. He spelled out the practical implications, as he saw them, of the disappearance of classes and the state:

The disappearance of the state means the disappearance of its representatives: Ministers, Parliaments, standing armies, Courts of Law, lawyers, prosecutors, prison warders and officials, tax and customs inspectors – in one word, the entire political apparatus will go. Barracks and other military installations, judicial and administrative buildings, prisons, etc. will be put to some better use. Many thousand laws, decrees, ordinances will be so much pulp, of merely historical interest . . . All that will be left will be administrative commissions and other bodies whose task it will be to determine the best possible organization of production and distribution . . . the introduction and application of new forms and methods in the arts, in education, transport . . . industry and agriculture . . . Hundreds of thousands of former state officials and public servants will be free to engage in creative activities and will help . . . to increase the wealth and the amenities of society. There will be no criminal offences, neither political nor ordinary crimes. No more thieving, since private property will have disappeared, and since everybody will easily satisfy their wants by performing suitable work. No more tramps and vagabonds – they are the products of a society based on private property. Murder? Manslaughter? No one can profit by seizing that which belongs to another person; murder prompted by hatred and lust for revenge will also disappear, because such crimes, too, are linked, directly or indirectly, to the structure and character of society. Perjury, forgery, fraud, fraudulent bankruptcy? The abolition of private property will remove the basic motives to commit these crimes. Arson? Who could find pleasure or satisfaction in that, when there will be no scope for feelings of hatred? Blasphemy? Nonsense, it will be left to God Almighty to punish those who offend him, if indeed the argument about the existence of God should still go on.[15]

In Bebel's view the perfect society of the future will create a new, higher morality, a new, superior type of human being: 'perfect man'.[16] This notion of human perfection as the foreseeable result of the socialist transformation of society and of life is a frequent theme in Marxist writings of that period. Kautsky also thought a new type of man would evolve.

... superior to the highest types hitherto created by civilization ... A 'superman', if you like, but as a rule, not an exception; man will be superior to his ancestors, but not to his contemporaries ... he will strive to be, not a giant among stunted dwarfs, but a giant among other giants, happy in unison with his happy fellow-men ... A realm of strength and beauty will take shape, worthy of the ideals of the most lofty and profound thinkers.[17]

Leon Trotsky's idea of Communist Man was not much different; he went into more detail:

Man will strive for complete self-harmony ... He will control the semi-conscious and eventually the unconscious processes of his own organism – breathing, circulation of the blood, digestion, conception. ... Life, including purely physiological life, will be subject to collective experimentation. The human race will enter a phase of radical transformation and will be the object of sophisticated methods of artificial selection and psycho-physical training ... Humanity will not have ceased to prostrate itself before God, before monarchic rulers and before capital in order meekly to accept the rules of the obscure laws of heredity and of the blind forces of sexual selection ... Man will aim at ... creating a higher social-biological type – 'superman', if you like. Man will be incomparably stronger, more intelligent and more versatile. His body will be more harmonious, his movements more rhythmical, his voice more musical; his life will be marked by dynamic beauty. Average man will attain the heights of men like Aristotle, Goethe or Marx; and above that high ridge new peaks will rise.[18]

In a more general way, the following quotation from a privately printed work by William Z. Foster, erstwhile leader of the American Communist Party, reflects the unbounded enthusiasm with which many communists looked into the post-revolutionary future:

The proletarian revolution . . . initiates changes more rapid and far-reaching than in the whole experience of mankind. The hundreds of millions of workers and peasants . . . will construct a society of liberty and prosperity and intelligence. Communism . . . will bring about the immediate or eventual solution of many great social problems – war, religious superstition, prostitution, famine, pestilence, crime, poverty, alcoholism, unemployment, illiteracy, race and national chauvinism, the suppression of women, and every form of slavery and exploitation . . . We may be sure that the revolution will carry humanity to heights of happiness and achievement far beyond the dreams of even the most hopeful utopians.[19]

These detailed features of Marxist, or rather post-Marxist eschatology – Foster's state of universal happiness, Bebel's crime-less society, Kautsky's and Trotsky's superman – must again be evaluated in the context of historical determinism. Unlike the Nietzschean superman, they are regarded not at poetic visions or flights of fancy but as realistic anticipations. The Marxist thinkers do not speculate on what *might* happen under socialism but describe what, in their view, inevitably *will* happen after the revolution. And there is again no discernible link between the analysis of capitalist economy, leading to the prediction of its downfall, and the perfect – economically, morally and intellectually – communist society. No serious, consistent attempt has been made to demonstrate a causal nexus between the two. Marx's appraisal of nineteenth-century capitalist economy tended to show that anarchic production must, in the foreseeable future, give way to collectivization and economic planning: that sounded convincing at the time and, to a limited extent, it has even come true. The change, in Marx's view, would be the result of a revolutionary seizure of power by the working class: that seemed a reasonable expectation, though its inevitability had not been proved. The further prediction of the disappearance of classes and the state was conjecture: the attempted proof is a *non sequitur*. That communist society will be harmonious, free from conflict, conducive to a maximum of human happiness, and that it will engender a superior type of human being, infinitely wise and noble: that is not a prediction based on experience and deduction, but a prophecy born of pious hopes. This does not mean that it cannot come true: prophecies sometimes do; some Marxist prophecies have, though most of them have not.[20] But since it does not follow rationally from the theorists' own premises it has nothing to do with science.

The rationality of a prediction in relation to the premises from which it is deduced is not the only possible criterion for distinguishing scientific forecasts from religious or, at any rate, unscientific prophecies. According to Karl Popper, 'a theory which is not refutable by any conceivable event is non-scientific'.[21] This, as Popper himself pointed out, is eminently applicable to Marxism:[22] in fact, the case of Marxism exemplifies the value of Popper's 'test of falsifiability'. Original Marxism, and in particular Karl Marx's theory of the early revolutionary overthrow of capitalism, would be refuted, and has in fact been refuted, by the failure of the predicted event to occur within the time-range envisaged in the formulation of the theory. When Marx said[23] that the German 'bourgeois revolution' of 1848 would be the immediate prelude to a proletarian revolution he made a prediction, based on his concept of history and on his assessment of the situation in the 'class struggle' in Germany, which was falsified forthwith by events. His further assertion, made in the same context but with reference to the bourgeois world as a whole, that 'society can no longer live under this bourgeoisie – in other words, its existence is no longer compatible with society', was seen to be definitely incorrect within a few decades.[24] Early refutation overtook many other Marxian (and Engelsian) predictions, including the one about the steadily increasing misery of the working classes.[25] Yet to some extent Marx and Engels themselves, and to a far greater extent their disciples, either ignored the factual refutation or advanced elaborate arguments explaining that what had happened, or had failed to happen, did not affect the correctness of the theory. As Popper puts it, they 're-interpreted both the theory and the evidence in order to make them agree; in this way they rescued the theory from refutation; but they did so at the price of adopting a device which made it irrefutable ... By this stratagem they destroyed its much advertised claim to scientific status.'[26]

The criteria of rationality and falsifiability can sometimes, but do not always, lead to the same result. A theory may be non-scientific even though it leads to refutable predictions. A devout Christian who holds that all biblical prophecies must come true and who predicts, on the strength of his interpretation of an Old or New Testament passage, that the world will come to an end on 31 December 1999, could not – and probably would not want to – claim scientific status for his theory about Bible prophecies. Astrology has been proved to be non-scientific – as Popper has stressed – by the astrologers' methods of explaining away contradictory evidence. Yet an astrologer could not now re-establish the scientific character of his theories by making a falsifiable prediction.[27]

Some theories which aspire to scientific status are in fact non-scientific, both by the standard of rationality and by that of falsifiability. The Marxist theory of violent proletarian revolution in the advanced capitalist countries is a case in point. The view that bourgeois society would perish in a mass revolt of the working class was rationally tenable when Marx developed his theory over a hundred years ago; it was still a rational assumption between the two world wars. But for some decades past it has been remote from reality. If and when the capitalist system comes to an end – as one day it must, either by gradual erosion or by a violent upheaval – history will not have confirmed the Marxian diagnosis. In an era of universal interference by official bodies in the capitalist economies[28] the system's demise is hardly likely to be the result of chaotic overproduction. Less credible still is the notion of a revolt by starving, desperate proletarians. The working classes, whose living standards have risen steadily in the course of this century and especially since the last war, are not now – and perhaps never have been – vehicles of violent revolution. It is significant that working-class participation was minimal or entirely absent wherever, in the aftermath of the Second World War, communist parties seized power.

The prospect of rebellious workers mounting the barricades in any of the advanced capitalist countries now seems so improbable that the more realistic Marxist-Leninists no longer pretend to believe in it. Thus most of the Moscow-oriented communist parties have, since the 1960s, abandoned the so-called 'catastrophic vision' of the end of capitalism and have replaced it with a theory of gradual and mainly peaceful transition from 'state-monopoly capitalism' to socialism; according to some communist theorists the transition has already begun. This new concept has occasionally met with restrained criticism from the Kremlin ideologues, but not with outright condemnation.[29] Far more outspoken and forceful have been the attacks by the Soviet media on the 'Euro-communist' line of some West European communist parties, a line which combines the abandonment of certain orthodox shibboleths, such as the dictatorship of the proletariat, with a stance of independence from Moscow and even with strictures on the internal policies of the USSR and other communist states – particularly in respect of the treatment of 'dissidents' in these countries.

The concept of peaceful and gradual transition to which the Euro-communists and other moderates are committed may or may not prove to be a correct appraisal of the contemporary scene. But it is a realistic and rational proposition, devoid of religious content. On the other hand, those left-wing Marxists who still proclaim the inevitability of a violent proletarian revolution – Maoists, Trotskyists, and other hard-liners – adhere to a theory which, at this stage, is non-scientific on two counts: it is non-rational and it is not falsifiable by any conceivable future event.[30] Its irrefutability stems from the absence of the time factor in the predicted revolutionary overthrow of capitalism. Unlike the earlier exponents of Marxist doctrine who asserted the imminence of revolution, the modern prophets of capitalist collapse do not commit themselves even to an approximate time-range:[31] the workers will resort to revolution some time – this year, next year, next decade, next century. At no point in the future will anybody be able to say that the non-occurrence of revolution has falsified the theory.

The Party and the Church

The postponement of the socialist revolution to a more or less indefinite future is a fairly recent development. The original Marxist prediction of the revolutionary overthrow of capitalism had a short-term character: the revolution was declared to be imminent. The nineteenth-century phenomenon of economic depressions of ever-increasing frequency and intensity had convinced Marx and Engels that the system had entered its moribund phase. The next severe crisis, they felt, might spell the end.

Indeed Marx's expectation of an early proletarian revolution preceded his critique of the capitalist system in *Das Kapital*. The *Manifesto of the Communist Party*, which was composed jointly by Marx and Engels in 1847-8, asserts the progressive pauperization of the industrial worker and deduces:

It becomes evident that the bourgeoisie is unfit any longer to be the ruling class in society, and to impose its conditions of existence upon society as an overriding law. It is unfit to rule because it is incompetent to assure an existence to its slave within his slavery . . . Society can no longer live under this bourgeoisie – in other words, its existence is no longer compatible with society.

The *Communist Manifesto* was even more specific in forecasting an imminent proletarian revolution in Germany, the authors' own country. It stated, correctly, that Germany was on the eve of a 'bourgeois' revolution (which actually broke out within weeks of the publication of the Manifesto) and added: 'The bourgeois revolution in Germany will be but the prelude to an immediately following proletarian revolution.'

The inaccuracy of this prediction did not deter Marx from hazarding further forecasts. In 1857 he thought the severe economic crisis would lead to revolution in Great Britain. In 1862 he detected signs of an approaching revolution in Germany, and the following year he expressed the view that the Polish insurrection against tsarist rule would spark off a revolution throughout Europe. None of these forecasts came true. The only event that could be described as a working-class rising of sorts – the Paris 'Commune' in 1871 – had not been foreseen by Marx.[32]

When Marx and Engels were dead (and capitalism was still very much alive) their disciples continued to affirm the correctness of Marx's theories and predictions. They also continued in the tradition of prophesying an early end to capitalism. When the Bolsheviks had seized power in backward agricultural Russia – an event no orthodox Marxist would have predicted or approved[33] – many Marxists, as well as some non-Marxists, felt sure that the triumph of world socialism could not be long delayed. At the time of the big slump in the early 1930s few Marxists had doubts about an early victory of the cause. When, at the end of the decade, not the proletarian revolution but the second 'imperialist' world war had broken out, one of the foremost Marxists of our century expressed his faith in the imminent disappearance of the capitalist order in terms reminiscent of the formulae used by Marx and Engels nearly a hundred years before. In September 1939, when the Second World War was but a few weeks old, Leon Trotsky wrote: 'The disintegration of capitalism has reached extreme limits; so has the disintegration of the old ruling class. *The further existence of this system is impossible.*'[34] (My italics.)

In Trotsky's view the outbreak of the war furnished 'incontrovertible proof that society can no longer live on the basis of capitalism'. He mentioned the failure of the international working class to take advantage of the recurring revolutionary opportunities during the preceding quarter of a century, but went on to declare his 'firm belief' that the war would end in a proletarian revolution. The alternative, to his mind, was that power would pass to a new class of 'commissars', i.e. to a fascist or, at any rate, totalitarian bureaucracy whose task it would be – since *laissez-faire* capitalism had patently failed – to organise the productive forces on the basis of a planned but non-socialist economy: this would mean the further fusion of monopoly capitalism with the state, the displacement of democracy, where it remained, by a totalitarian regime, and the growth of a new exploiting class from the fascist bureaucracy. According to all indications, Trotsky added, this kind of regime would 'signalize the eclipse of civilization'. He felt, furthermore, that the Second World War was the world proletariat's last chance to establish its own rule. As he put it:

It is absolutely self-evident that if the international proletariat, as the result of the experience of our entire epoch and the current new war, proves incapable of becoming the master of society, this would signify the foundering of all hope for the socialist revolution, for *it is impossible to expect any other more favourable conditions for it.*[35] (My italics.)

Trotsky had few followers in the last years of his life. Yet at that point in history socialists of all shades shared the view that the moment of decision was at hand. Most Marxists were also inclined to agree with the pessimistic alternative advanced in Trotsky's appraisal of the situation in September 1939: the emergence of a totalitarian bureaucracy as a ruling class. It seemed obvious that there would be no return, at least on the continent of Europe, to old-style capitalism, with parliamentary democracy, the rule of law, working-class rights, free trade unions and individual liberties. The pluralist society, with its open contest between classes and parties, had shown signs of obsolescence in the twenties and thirties; clearly the future would belong either to proletarian socialism or to anti-socialist totalitarianism.

This was another prediction which seemed warranted by the facts then known, not a prophecy unconnected with rational deduction. Yet history again refused to bear it out. In fact things developed very much in the opposite direction. The Second World War produced neither socialist revolution nor world-wide Fascism. After a few unruly years the capitalist countries of Western Europe completely recovered from the war and post-war disruption. In the 1950s the industrialized capitalist countries achieved an extremely high standard of prosperity and economic growth. More startling still were the political developments after 1945. 'Bourgeois democracy cannot be saved,' Trotsky had written in May 1940, when he told the French and British working classes that by helping their bourgeoisie against Hitler they would merely 'accelerate the victory of fascism in their own country'.[36] Ten years later, what Marxists call 'bourgeois democracy' was firmly re-established in Italy and Western-occupied Germany, as well as in the countries where it had been destroyed during the war – not by 'class co-operation' but by fascist occupation. Contrary to Marxist predictions, totalitarian dictatorship succumbed in all advanced capitalist countries, but it spread to the territories which the Soviet Union had brought under her sway in the name of Marxism and of the proletarian revolution. In effect, since 1945, totalitarianism has become the corollary not of bourgeois capitalism but of Marxist-Leninist 'socialism'.[37]

There is something remarkable about the way in which history has disproved the predictions of Marx, Engels and their twentieth-century disciples. If an ordinary, intelligent person, with a sound judgement and a fair knowledge of world affairs, but without the support of a comprehensive theory of the 'laws of history', tries to predict the general character of the period ahead, the odds are that he will make some correct and some erroneous forecasts. Marx and the Marxists, who claim to have discovered the law of motion of the contemporary world and to be able to foresee its immediate history, have almost invariably been wrong. And the leading theorists, men like Marx, Engels, Lenin and Trotsky, were not just highly intelligent: they were, indubitably, intellectual giants. The conclusion seems unavoidable that it was their comprehensive philosophy which caused them to err more often and more decisively than ordinary human beings.[38]

In these circumstances one would have thought that the enemies of the existing order would evolve a different theoretical system to serve as a guide to revolutionary action. Yet for some reason

Marxism achieved the rank of the leading anti-capitalist philosophy even before the October Revolution in Russia; and the fact that the revolution was led by people who claimed to be Marxists helped to strengthen the prestige of the Marxist interpretation of history and to spread belief in its infallibility.

Marxism has retained this supreme position, despite its refutation by the events of the post-Second World War period. 'Marxist' ideas are, in fact, very influential at present, both in backward countries, where they lack relevance, and among young Western intellectuals. And Marxism-Leninism is, of course, the established creed in all communist countries, however much the various national leaders may differ in their interpretation of the doctrine: it is unchallengeable dogma in the USSR and in China, in Yugoslavia and Albania, in the East European 'People's Democracies', as well as in North Korea, Indo-China and certain African countries.

Obviously active Marxists in the capitalist West could not all have remained unaware of the widening gap between theoretical expectations and reality. The party hierarchies have usually reacted by reinterpreting the theory and/or the facts so as to eliminate the discrepancy: in Popper's words, they have made Marxism non-scientific. But there have been exceptions – leading party members, sometimes representing substantial rank-and-file minorities, who have openly declared that Marx made mistakes in his analysis, that some of his predictions were therefore wrong and that policies derived from his faulty analysis should be abandoned. This critique of Marxist orthodoxy from inside the socialist movement was one of the factors leading to the great schism in the world socialist movement between communists and moderate or democratic socialists.[39]

One of the most articulate early critics of the orthodox stance was the German Social Democrat, Eduard Bernstein (1850–1932), father of the so-called 'revisionist' school, who in the 1890s began to challenge accepted views and strategies. The remarkable thing about Bernstein and his revisionist followers was not that they advocated un-Marxist policies. In the course of the present century many, if not most, Marxist parties and politicians have pursued policies which were inconsistent with Marxist principles.[40] But the protagonists of these policies have always claimed to act as true Marxists; they have never stated that Marxist theses were out of date, let alone that Marx erred in his appraisals and predictions. Eduard Bernstein did precisely this: he made no attempt to reinterpret Marxist theory in order to make it fit reality. In his book *The Pre-conditions of Socialism and the Tasks of the Social Democratic Party*, which appeared in 1899,[41] he asserted bluntly that Marx had underestimated the resilience of the capitalist system; that the Marxist thesis of class polarization – the disappearance in bourgeois society of the intermediate sections between capitalists and proletarians – had been disproved by the actual growth and increasing prosperity of these middle layers; that the theory of the pauperization of the working classes had likewise been disproved by the events of the preceding decades. Bernstein rejected the concept of the dictatorship of the proletariat; he made it clear that he had no use for Hegelian or Marxian dialectics and did not share the millenary outlook of the orthodox: 'What is commonly called the "final aim" of socialism is nothing to me,' he declared, 'but I strongly believe in the socialist movement, in the march forward of the working classes, who step by step must work out their emancipation by changing society from the domain of a commercial land-holding oligarchy to real democracy which . . . is guided by the interests of those who work and create.'[42]

Whether Bernstein's criticisms of Marxist doctrine were valid in every detail is debatable. What matters in the present context is that Bernstein and his fellow revisionists – or 'reformists', as they were often called by their orthodox opponents, since they preferred reform to revolution – did not treat the works of Marx and Engels as sacred texts and that they professed indifference to the non-rational aspects of the creed: dialectics and the notions of the perfect society and the everlasting Age of Plenty.[43] The revisionists were pragmatic politicians, not religious visionaries.

In his introduction to the American edition of *Evolutionary Socialism* the American philosopher Sidney Hook speaks of the vehement hostility of the Marxist orthodox establishment to

Bernstein's ideas: 'In Marxist circles to pin the label of "revisionist" on the ideas of a socialist thinker is comparable to exposing a Christian writer as a "heretic" or "atheist" during the heyday of Western religious faith.'[44] 'Atheist' is more apt than 'heretic' in this case. Revisionism was not a heresy, that is to say, an interpretation of a common doctrine which differed from the accepted one: it was the rejection of the religious elements in Marxist and post-Marxist philosophy, coupled with an attempt to replace the prevailing creed by a secular political ideology. The real issue in the fierce debate provoked by the publication of Bernstein's views was whether organized socialism should develop as a pragmatic political movement, a party, or become a spiritual community, a church.

The issue was eventually resolved by the split in international socialism which began at the turn of the century and finally took shape after the Bolshevik revolution in Russia. The Bolsheviks followed up the success of their coup by taking the initiative for the creation of a new International, the Third: the Communist International ('Comintern' for short) was founded at a congress in Moscow in the spring of 1919. Stringent conditions were laid down for socialist parties and groups wishing to adhere to the new body; they included the rejection of revisionism and the expulsion of 'reformist' leaders. In practice the International quickly developed in such a way that the principal conditions for affiliation were wholehearted acceptance of Marxist-Leninist doctrine and recognition of the authority of the Executive Committee of the Comintern in Moscow. As the years went by the Third International became a mere tool of the Soviet government and the Bolshevik leadership. Membership of the Comintern soon came to mean unconditional obedience to the Soviet rulers.[45]

The split in the world socialist movement was not clear-cut. Apart from the two main blocks, social democrats and communists, it produced a crop of smaller parties and fringe groupings.[46] Various communist groups sprang up, mostly to the left of the Moscow-controlled parties, which consisted of orthodox Marxists who believed in violent revolution and the final aim of a classless society, but refused to approve the Comintern's and the USSR's policies or to bow to Moscow's dictates. Structurally and ideologically these groups – like the 'official' communist parties – were religious communities rather than political parties. Acceptance of Marxist doctrine, including the belief in proletarian revolution, in the classless society and the so-called philosophy of 'dialectical materialism' was obligatory. A modicum of free speech and free debate (non-existent, since about 1927, in the parties of the Communist International) survived but did not encompass the right to question doctrinal principles. Decisions taken by a conference majority or an elected executive were binding on all members. Expulsion was the penalty both for heretical denials of fundamental beliefs and for failure to obey instructions. Re-admission usually presupposed an act of 'self-critical' repentance.

Plurality of groups and tendencies was – and is – also a feature of the social democratic camp, on the other side of the great divide; and some of the left-wing break-away factions were indistinguishable, in terms of mentality and organizational principles, from communist groups. But the social democratic mass parties – such as the British Labour Party – are altogether different. There is no supreme authority, no iron discipline, no enforcement of sacred principles. A wide measure of dissent is usually tolerated, and the membership normally comprises a broad range of political opinion. Expulsions are rare and hardly ever decreed on grounds of ideological deviation; they mainly occur when a member is felt to be an infiltrator from a hostile camp.

Many members of social democratic parties are Marxists who reject the communists' interpretation of the theory, and some social democrats believe in, or hope for, the ideal classless society. But the chiliastic vision does not impinge upon the parties' day-to-day struggle. The professed aims are greater equality, full employment, social security, higher living standards for the working people and similar short-term objectives. Party activities and campaigns are not concerned with prophecies of superabundance. Individually the militant members are political partisans, not believers; collectively they form a party, not a church.

'The kernel of the scientific outlook,' Bertrand Russell once wrote, 'is the refusal to regard our own desires, tastes and interests as affording a key to the understanding of the world.'[47] This is not meant to furnish a criterion; it does not imply that a theory, a view, an expectation cannot be scientific if those who share it want it to be true. The fact that we want the sun to rise tomorrow does not mean that we are adopting an unscientific attitude if we believe that it *will* rise tomorrow. But it would be true to say that where a comprehensive theory leads to highly optimistic predictions (optimistic from the point of view of the theorist and his followers) there are grounds for suspecting the presence of bias and the lack of scientific detachment. The more optimistic the expectation, the greater the suspicion. A man who believes that his physical death is but the beginning of an eternal life of boundless bliss does not normally claim that his hopes stem from a scientific outlook, although he might maintain that his faith gives him absolute certainty. A theory which states that the whole world will, in the not-too-distant future, change into some kind of earthly paradise would have to pass a very stringent test if we were to be convinced of its scientific basis. Marxist communism has failed this test: on the strength of its own reasoning the predicted development does not appear likely, let alone certain. Present-day Marxists who still assert the inevitability of world communism (meaning, *inter alia*, superabundance) do not display a scientific outlook: their interpretation of the world situation is based on their own wishes and not on empirical phenomena and rational deduction.

A scientific approach to the world of today and its problems may, of course, lead the observer to expect profound and far-reaching socio-economic changes in the next few decades, comparable with those which have taken place since Marx analysed the contemporary economy and formulated his predictions. The failure of Marxist prognosis is not that it foretold great changes but that society changed in a different way and a different direction from those predicted. To be more precise (at the risk of being repetitious for the sake of greater clarity), two crucial predictions have turned out to be erroneous: (1) in none of the industrialized countries has capitalism been overthrown by a proletarian revoluion; (2) where private ownership of the means of production has been replaced by collective ownership and economic planning (with or without a preceding revolutionary upheaval) the result has never been a classless society, or even a trend towards the classless society, but always the emergence of a new class society with a totalitarian superstructure. Experience has also shown that some planned, non-market economies are rather less efficient than capitalist ones, in terms of the rate of growth and of high living standards, and that – witness the Sino-Soviet rift – the spread of 'socialism' across state boundaries is by no means a guarantee of harmony and peace between the countries concerned.

Evidently the Marxist's belief in the revolution which will bring the Millennium is no more rational or 'scientific' than the Christian's belief in the return of Christ and in life after death.

The World revolution and the Parousia

Apocalyptic hopes and secular realities

It is a paradoxical fact that Marxism has achieved the status of a world-wide creed *after* its refutation by events. There is a precedent in history, another case of a doctrine's becoming a world religion, and the fundamental ideology of a world Church, after its principal expectations had been seen to be fallacious: I am referring to Christianity in the first centuries of the Christian era. There are remarkable similarities between the eschatological expectations of the early Christians and the 'final aim' – the future ideal society – of the Marxists.

The early Christian communities did not form an organized Church. They did not feel the need for one. Their chief task was to prepare for the *Parousia*, Christ's triumphant return, which they believed would happen in the near future. Like the Marxists, the early Christians were determinists: they were convinced that a certain predicted development would take place. Like the Marxists, they felt sure that history had reached a turning point, that the era ahead would be something quite new and unprecedented, and that the future of man and of human society would differ radically from the past and the present. Like the early Marxists, the early Christians had a short perspective: they were certain that Christ would return very soon to usher in the New Age.[48] Like the Marxists, the early Christians, too, were eager to spread their gospel, though from a different kind of motive. They wished to ensure the salvation of the greatest possible number of people. (Unlike the Marxists, they did not believe that the propagation of their faith would hasten the day of the hoped-for event; nor did they ever think of this event in terms of a scientific prognosis. Their certainty about the *Parousia* was, in their own consciousness, an act of faith: they believed in the truth of the prophecies made by Christ, whom they considered to be divine. In other words, they believed in the Second Coming because God had promised it.) Like the Marxists, the early Christians had the disappointment of waiting in vain for the fulfilment of the prophecy that was central to their creed. And their reaction was not dissimilar: they abandoned the hope of an immediate *Parousia* and resigned themselves to a lengthy period of 'peaceful coexistence' with the pagan state. This inevitably went hand in hand with the organization of an authoritative Church, whose function it was to lay down the law on doctrine and ritual, and to devise a strategy which would ensure the survival of the faith and of the Christian communities.

The Marxist movement, too, dispensed at first with a formal organization. In the *Communist Manifesto* Marx and Engels proclaimed:

The Communists do not form a separate party opposed to other working class parties.

They have no interests separate and apart from the interests of the proletariat as a whole.

They do not set up any sectarian principles of their own, by which to shape and mould the proletarian movement.

The founders of 'scientific socialism' did not attach any particular importance to party organization. Marx, as we have seen, believed a proletarian revolution to be imminent at several junctures from 1848 onwards, when no Marxist revolutionary party existed anywhere. Marxist parties gradually emerged and evolved as a matter of course in all states possessing a party-political system and some form of parliamentary life. The first Marxist group to insist early this century on the necessity of a tightly knit, disciplined, centrally controlled party organization as the 'vanguard' of the proletariat was the Bolshevik faction within the Russian Social Democratic Workers Party. The Bolsheviks did not then foresee an early seizure of power by themselves. In their view the Russian revolution had still a long way to go before reaching the proletarian stage: socialism would come to Russia after it had triumphed in Germany, Britain, France and other Western countries.[49] Lenin and his friends felt that the long uphill struggle they foresaw against tsarist semi-feudalism and incipient bourgeois capitalism could only be won if the proletarian masses were led by a well organized party of professional, full-time revolutionaries. Like the Christian Church from the second century onwards, the revolutionary party, too, was to act as an authority to safeguard the purity of what the leaders held to be orthodox doctrine.[50]

The Bolsheviks' view that some considerable time would elapse before Russia was ripe for socialism did not imply readiness to coexist peacefully with the tsarist establishment, or with the capitalist establishment which they expected would take over after the impending 'bourgeois revolution'. Yet when it became clear in the 1920s that the Bolshevik seizure of power had not been the prelude to a European socialist revolution, and that none of the industrialized countries would have a proletarian regime in the immediate future, the Bolshevik rulers and the Moscow-oriented communists throughout the world adjusted their policies to the new situation. Communist Russia, unable to rely on the solidarity of fraternal regimes in Central or Western Europe, had to come to terms with the capitalist world. The exigencies of industrialization at home and of security from foreign aggression forced the Kremlin to establish normal commercial and diplomatic relations, and sometimes to conclude military alliances, with foreign 'bourgeois' governments: at the Soviet rulers' behest, or at any rate under their influence, the communist parties in a number of capitalist countries softened their militant hostility towards the bourgeois state, especially where trade or military ties with Soviet Russia formed an important aspect of the capitalist government's policy.

This tendency towards acceptance of prolonged coexistence with the bourgeois world became more pronounced some years after the Second World War, when the prospects of revolution (revived during the final stage of the war and during the immediate post-war period) appeared to recede again. In the 1950s and 1960s – the decades marked by stability and prosperity throughout world capitalism – the larger communist parties in the West curbed their militancy and exercised moderation in the 'class struggle'.[51] This did not harm them in the eyes of the workers: moderate policies were in keeping with the mood then prevailing among the working masses; full employment and rising standards of living seemed to leave little scope for revolutionary *élan*. Some Marxist theorists went so far as to declare that the working class had become part of the establishment of the bourgeois state and had lost therefore, once and for all, the ability to play the role which history, according to Marx, had assigned to it.[52] The communist parties' restraint was not primarily, at this stage, motivated by the interests of the Kremlin's international policy; in fact, in the 1960s certain communist parties, both inside and outside the 'Soviet bloc', began to display a measure of independence from Moscow. What had happened was simply that the communist leaders had lost their belief in revolution and were attempting to evolve a new philosophy of gradual and peaceful transition to socialism – a concept which dictated a modicum of compromise and even 'class collaboration'.

It is instructive to compare the communists' reaction to the non-advent of revolution a hundred years after Marx with the Christian reaction, a hundred years after Christ, to the non-advent of the *Parousia*. When in the second century AD the bulk of Christianity, including the hierarchy, had come to the conclusion that the Kingdom of God would not materialize for quite some time yet, it formed itself into a political movement with secular objectives. Whilst retaining its fundamental faith and its religious dogmas, the Church set out to exert political influence and to Christianize the Roman state. Its efforts finally succeeded towards the end of the fourth century, when the Emperor Theodosius the Great made Catholic Christianity the state religion and pronounced an anathema upon paganism and all Christian heresies (especially Arianism). When, on the other hand, the various parties, groups and sects of international Marxism realized that the proletarian revolution would not break out in the near future, they remained political organizations pursuing political objectives, but at the same time they allowed their chiliastic ideology to wax still more religious in content.[53] Under the impact of history's refusal to fulfil the basic prophecy of their creeds, both the world Marxist movement in our days and world Christianity eighteen centuries ago became hybrid religious-political bodies, their religious philosophies and political strategies designed partly to win more power and partly to propagate the creed.

Deviations and heresies

Similarities between Christianity and communism in their early phases are not confined to the eschatological field. There are parallels, too, in the composition and mentality of early Christian and communist groups, their relations with society as a whole and the emergence of ideological conflict. These parallels are too striking to be ignored by the Marxists themselves. Without implying that communism was a new religion, Frederick Engels drew attention in 1894 to some of the features which the early Christians shared with the nineteenth-century socialists:

The history of primitive Christianity shows remarkable points of contact with the modern workers' movement. Like the latter, Christianity was originally a movement of the oppressed: it appeared at first as the religion of the slaves and the freedmen, of the poor and the outlaws ... Both Christianity and working-class socialism proclaim the imminent delivery from servitude and misery ... Both are persecuted and hunted, their followers are outlawed and subjected to special legislation – the

Christians as enemies of the human race, the socialists as enemies of the state, of religion, of the family, of the social order. Yet despite all persecution, or perhaps even because of it, they both advance victoriously and irresistibly. Within three hundred years from its inception Christianity became the established state religion of the Roman Empire, while in barely sixty years socialism has secured a position which makes its triumph an absolute certainty.[54]

What Engels calls the 'victory' of Christianity was very much a *pis aller* from the point of view of the early Christians, who had hoped for the speedy advent of the Kingdom of God and would have viewed the prospect of a Christian state Church with comparative indifference. Writing in 1894, Engels could not foresee that the doctrine formulated by Karl Marx and himself would achieve a similarly dubious triumph. Within sixty years 'Marxism' had attained the status of an established creed for one-third of mankind – but not the way the founders had imagined it, and not where they thought it would conquer. If St Peter and St Paul had lived to see the days of Constantine and Theodosius they would have been bitterly disappointed at the non-occurrence of the *Parousia* and at the shape of fourth-century Christianity. Marx and Engels, were they alive today, would be no less dismayed at the survival of capitalism in the industrial countries and at the Soviet and Chinese reality of 'Marxism'.

The schismatic tendencies in the early stages of both movements did not escape Engels's notice. He states:

The struggle against an initially overwhelming secular power, and the simultaneous struggle of the revolutionaries among themselves, are features the early Christians and the socialists have in common. Neither of these two great movements was created by leaders and prophets – although there was no lack of prophets in either movement; they are mass movements, and mass movements are necessarily confused to begin with ... This confusion is reflected in the emergence of numerous sects which have fought each other with at least the vehemence they have displayed in the fight against the common external enemy. This is what happened in primitive Christianity, and what happened again in the first phases of the socialist movement – to the chagrin of the well-intentioned folks who preached unity where no unity was possible.[55]

Confusion there may have been, but this is not the whole story where the proliferation of sects and factions is concerned. An important source of internecine struggles, at least in the later stages of both Christianity and socialism, has been the collision between accepted prophecy and ensuing reality.

When adjusting themselves to a world situation in which they have had to accept the fact of the non-arrival of the promised New Age, both Christianity and Marxism have suffered denunciation and defection on the part of some of their adherents. In both cases groups of fundamentalists and fanatics have persisted in disregarding factual evidence and the dictates of common sense and in clinging to the pristine belief in the inevitability and the imminence of the predicted event of unique, world-historic importance: the *Parousia* and the proletarian world revolution.

The Christians of the second century AD who, with the passing of time, had ceased to expect the early return of Christ but had not lost their faith, felt that the longer perspective made it necessary for them to accept an organized Church possessing doctrinal and administrative authority. Under the Church's guidance the Christian communities gave up their separateness from the pagan environment and largely adopted the customs and the way of life of the world which, they now believed, would for a long time go on as before, unaffected by the events surrounding Christ's ministry, death and resurrection.

This gradual secularization of the Church was not accepted by all the faithful. In the late second century the movement known as Montanism or the 'New Prophecy' made its appearance. It was essentially a revolt against the compromise the Church was now ready to make with the established powers and a campaign for the return to original, non-secular Christianity. The Montanists revived the belief in the imminence of the Second Coming. In practical matters they embraced the puritanical attitude of the age of the Apostles. They preached moral rigorism, prescribed fasts, forbade flight from martyrdom and discouraged marriage.

Montanism started in Asia Minor as a primitive set of beliefs, which included the expectation that the heavenly Jerusalem would shortly descend on a plain near Pepuza in Phrygia; the movement grew more sophisticated as it spread westwards. The great Christian writer and theologian Tertullian, who lived in Carthage, was its most important Western protagonist. He rallied to it at the beginning of the third century; in 212–3 he broke with the official Church, whose cause he had consistently defended against pagans and earlier heretics. Tertullian had no quarrel with Catholic doctrine; he held that the New Testament was the supreme rule of Christian life, and that the bishops were the successors of the Apostles. But he had become convinced that by adopting secular modes of life the Church had entered upon a path that must lead to destruction. He did not share the naive belief of the Eastern Montanists in the descent of the new Jerusalem on Pepuza, but he accepted the movement's chiliastic faith in an early *Parousia*. He supported its rigorous moral tenets and rejected what he regarded as the shamefully lax tolerance of the Catholic bishops. He condemned all Christians who co-operated with pagans in secular affairs such as education, military matters, commerce or public administration; he proscribed second marriage and flight from persecution and called for a return to apostolic simplicity.

The Montanist movement failed. In so doing it hastened the consummation of the development against which it had risen in revolt. In the fight against Montanism and other heresies such as Gnosticism, the Catholic Church completed her hierarchical organization and formulated her new theology. The essence of this new Christian philosophy was that the Church was no longer just a society of religious believers but that she was ready to undertake a comprehensive, long-term world mission with the aim of making Christianity the religion of the Roman Empire and its people. Some traditionalists continued to make a stand, in the name of the Gospel, against these secular trends; but their protests proved unavailing.

Conflicts comparable with the struggle between Catholicism and Montanism broke out within the world Marxist movement in the 1920s, when the Russian Bolshevik government had to come to terms with the fact that it was likely to remain, for the time being, an isolated 'proletarian' regime in a hostile capitalist world.

At the end of the Russian civil war in 1921 the Bolshevik regime broadly commanded the allegiance of the Left of the international labour movement. Most social democratic or labour parties had split during or immediately after the First World War, and the left wing had rallied to the banner of the Comintern between 1919 and 1921. In its life-and-death struggle the young Soviet Republic even received assistance from moderate or right-wing socialists, as for instance when the British Labour leaders opposed their Government's anti-Bolshevik intervention in the Russian civil war. The Left was committed to all-out support for Soviet communism, but its loyalty was not uncritical. Rosa Luxemburg, who denounced the dictatorial methods of Lenin, Trotsky and the other Bolshevik leaders from her prison cell in Germany in 1918, was not their only critic among left-wing socialists. In fact the emergence of the Comintern between 1919, when the new International was founded, and 1921 was a painful process, punctuated with acrimonious debates, recriminations, expulsions and reunions.

Opposition from within the communist ranks led to embittered factional struggles and splits when the Soviet Government, faced with the threat of economic collapse after the end of the civil war, adopted the so-called New Economic Policy (NEP). It involved the reintroduction of free-enterprise methods in agriculture, trade and industry, including competition and the return of small and medium factories to private control and management. At the same time Soviet Russia resumed trade with the capitalist world, concluding commercial treaties first with Britain (March 1921) and then with most other European countries. The Bolshevik Government also solicited foreign capitalist investments in Soviet territory; this met with a limited response.

This change in economic policy coincided with an official modification of the party line regarding the prospects of world revolution. The Third World Congress of the Comintern, which met in Moscow in the early summer of 1921, decided that armed risings, such as had been staged by communist parties in Central Europe in preceding years, were not now on the agenda: a longer period of preparation was deemed necessary. This decision marked, of course, merely the approval by the International of the conclusions reached earlier by the Kremlin leaders: their correct deduction that the revolution was not about to engulf Europe had been the basis of the new approach to the economic problems facing the Soviet state.

The new policy of concessions to capitalism in Russia and abroad and postponement of the day of reckoning naturally caused alarm among dedicated communists everywhere. Some of these feared a wholesale reversion to capitalism in Russia, and the tacit abandonment of the world-wide revolutionary campaign.

Dissension increased a few years later when, after the death of Lenin in 1924, Stalin proclaimed that the building of socialism could be successfully completed in Russia even if the proletarian revolution did not spread to any of the advanced industrial societies. Left-wing critics of this concept of 'socialism in one country' soon imputed a sinister meaning to the new Kremlin course; they alleged that Stalin and his henchmen had lost interest in the progress of international revolution and were ready to restrain the militancy of the foreign communist parties whenever this seemed to be in the interests of the Moscow power clique. Towards the end of the twenties, when Stalin had vanquished the various 'right'- and 'left'-wing opposition factions in the Russian party (Trotsky, Zinovyev, Bukharin, etc.), break-away groups had proliferated in nearly all sections of the Comintern.

The dissidents, defectors and expellees, especially the 'Left Opposition' militants, who included the supporters of Trotsky, castigated Stalin and his Politbureau in terms redolent of the criticisms which Tertullian and the other Montanists had levelled at the bishops of their day. The Kremlin leaders were accused of betraying the principles of the founders and of being over-eager to compromise and co-operate with the enemies of the cause.[56] The critics called for a return to doctrinal rectitude, and strove for the revival of the chiliastic idealism of the early days of the revolution.

The anti-Stalin opposition was no more effective than the Montanist rebels had been. And just as the Catholic Church had grown into a fully organized, hierarchical institution in the fight against Montanists and Gnostics, Stalinist communism was consolidated by its successful struggle against the Trotskyist and other 'deviations'. In both cases the revolt had the effect of speeding up the process it was trying to arrest. Trotsky's critique was directed, in part at least, against the erosion of inner-Party democracy and the growing power of the Party and state bureaucracy. There was not, in fact, much democracy in Russia, in either the Party or the state, when Lenin and Trotsky were the leading exponents of the regime. Theirs was a dictatorship, but not a totalitarian one; a measure of free speech and open dissent was tolerated, especially within the leading cadres. But all freedom died once Stalin had defeated his internal opponents. By 1930 the Soviet Union was a fully-fledged totalitarian state, ruled by a self-perpetuating bureaucracy, and the Comintern was a dogmatic monolith. In Russia as well as in the communist parties abroad all political life and all discussion were stifled; decisions were taken at top level and had to be carried out without demur. The Soviets and the Party congresses and conferences merely exercised rubber-stamp functions. In liquidating the heresies Stalinist communism, like the Church in bygone days, assumed the right of authentic inter- pretation of the creed:[57] Marxist-Leninist philosophy was re- formulated to suit the requirements of the policy which the victors in the inner-Party conflict intended to pursue.[58]

The apparent right-wing course which the Soviet Government and the Comintern steered in the 1920s did not, in fact, signify the final abandonment of revolutionary expectations and policies. The phraseology of the Comintern and the affiliated parties remained radical and revolutionary throughout the decade, and some parties staged armed coups when they believed the situation to be ripe for such ventures; for example, the German communists prepared for a rising in the autumn of 1923 but then lost their nerve and called it off; and there was an abortive communist coup in Estonia the following year.

A period of moderate Comintern policies from 1925 to 1928 was followed by a sharp swerve to the left, and from 1929 to 1934 – the years of the great recession and of Hitler's rise to power – most communist parties pursued what could be called an 'ultra- left' policy, rejecting, for example, all forms of united action with the social democratic parties against the menace of Nazism or other dictatorial right-wing movements. At that time Trotsky and other left-wing critics attacked the communist leadership for their doctrinaire intransigence and their stubborn extremism. In 1934–5 the Comintern executed another turn to the right: its 'Popular Front' policy in France and in other countries involved far-reaching co-operation not only with the social democrats but also with parties of the centre.

The communists' left turn in 1928–9 coincided with the withdrawal in Russia of the concessions made at the beginning of the decade to capitalist free-enterprise methods and to foreign investors. Stalin now embarked upon a policy of forced industrialization and centralized economic planning. This was linked with a rigorous drive towards collectivization in agriculture; in the process the section of the peasantry which had grown more prosperous under the dispensation of the New Economic Policy was liquidated.

The heretical reaction which every new departure, every change in dogma or policy is apt to provoke both in the world communist movement and in the Christian (and some other) Churches leads sometimes, though not always, to a split or schism, to the emergence of organized 'deviation'. Over a hundred years ago the proclamation of the doctrine of papal infallibility brought about the formation of Catholic break-away communities which renounced allegiance to Rome. In recent times changes in Roman Catholic liturgy following the Second Vatican Council (Mass in the vernacular, etc.) have been harshly criticized by some Catholic clerics and laymen, although they have not so far resulted in excommunications or schismatic developments. As for international communism, the USSR's intervention in Hungary in 1956 and in Czechoslovakia in 1968 caused many militants to leave the Party and join one of the existing 'ultra-left' groups, but there was no split in the shape of new rival communist organizations formed by Party members opposing the Soviet move. The Stalin—Hitler pact on the eve of the Second World War had similar effects. On the other hand, the Sino-Soviet rift did lead to the foundation, by dissident communists, of Maoist parties and sects in a number of capitalist and Third World countries.[59]

The attitude of the Churches to individual or collective heresy is bound to differ, in one important respect, from the attitude of an 'orthodox' Marxist party (e.g. the pro-Soviet Communist Parties in France or Britain) to deviationist groupings (such as Maoists or Trotskyists). The struggles of a Marxist party are thought to have a direct bearing on the achievement of the millennial objective; no comparable relationship exists between Christian activities and the advent of the Messianic Age. In the communist view a 'correct' Marxist policy promotes the cause and may even advance the day of the victorious socialist revolution; hence, those who propagate and pursue 'incorrect' policies are enemies who harm or even ('objectively') betray the cause. Christians do not believe (unless they ascribe extraordinary efficacy to prayer) that acts of worship or good deeds will make for an earlier establishment of God's Kingdom on earth. Their objection to heresy is chiefly that the heretic might bar the road to salvation to himself and others. He is not an enemy whose actions might prevent or delay the Second Coming but an erring child of the Church. The Christian is enjoined to hate the heresy but to love the heretic. There is no love lost, either in theory or in practice, between Marxists of different persuasions.

Leaving aside the question of the apocalyptic expectation, the policies of the Christian Churches, the pronouncements of dignitaries and the actions of the faithful do, of course, influence day-to-day happenings, but not on anything like the scale of Marxist policies in their impact on world events. For this reason disputes between Marxist factions possess a dimension of intensity which has long ceased to be present in intra-Christian controversy. Marxists argue about doctrinal interpretation: so do the various Christian Churches and sects. But members of different Christian denominations no longer accuse each other of being in the service of Satan, whereas in Marxist eyes a rival Marxist group or party often acts in the interests, if not actually at the behest, of the 'class enemy'. In Stalin's days the official theory had it that any 'left' or 'right' opposition to the Party's general line was bound to lead to counter-revolutionary and anti-socialist activity. Thus in the Moscow show trials in the late thirties Bolsheviks who at one time had belonged to an opposition group were accused, tried and convicted, on the strength of their own 'confessions', of having deliberately sabotaged the Soviet economy in order to discredit the (truly Marxist) Party leadership and to restore capitalism on the territory of the USSR. The expatriate Marxist critics of the Stalinist leadership were less absurd but hardly less scathing in formulating their strictures. They maintained that Stalin and his henchmen had betrayed the revolution in Russia and were persistently striving to frustrate the struggle of the revolutionary workers in the capitalist countries because they feared the repercussions inside the USSR of the forward march of the proletarian world revolution.

The reaction, in a given situation, by the orthodox to the Christian heretic or the deviating communist depends partly on the general climate and partly on the scope for imposing sanctions. When the Christian religion was still an all-pervasive element in society, as in medieval Europe, anti-heretical measures ranged from excommunication to physical destruction. This has completely changed. Excommunication is rarely practised in any of the Christian Churches, and execution, even if Church authorities had the power to order it, would be utterly incompatible with the climate of opinion within the Church. But punitive sanctions of this kind, including death for active heresy, have been applied in the lifetime of the present generation by Marxists wielding state power. Where such powers are in use submission and repentance on the offender's part do not guarantee remission or even alleviation of punishment. This goes both for twentieth-century communism and for Christianity in times past. Cranmer did not save his life by recanting; neither did Zinoviev.

Earlier in this section we dealt with the schismatic tendencies in the early Christian Churches and with similar tendencies in the corresponding stage of the modern socialist or communist movement. In a different context the present phase of the international Marxist movement is similar to the situation arising from the Reformation. That revolutionary event partly reproduced the situation existing in the West before the consolidation of the

Roman Catholic Church; it put an end to the monocentric and universal dominance of the Church of Rome and substituted a plurality of Churches, sects, denominations, each of whom proclaimed its own beliefs to be truly Christian.

Moscow used to be for world communism what Rome was for medieval Western Christianity. The Roman Church lost its position in the sixteenth century: for Moscow the dissolution began in 1948 with the Yugoslav defection from the Soviet bloc. It is a moot point whether the Kremlin could have halted the fissiparous trends then appearing by taking resolute action against the Titoite revolt. It probably could not. Intervention might have forestalled other attempted defections or near-defections in Eastern Europe; it could hardly have prevented the fateful historic event which spelled the end of Moscow's dominance – the Sino-Soviet rift.

The position of world communism is now that two giant states confront one another, mutually hostile on both the ideological and the power-political level.[60] Both communist powers protest loyalty to Marxism-Leninism, while each denies the claim of the other and looks upon its rulers as renegades and traitors. Of the other communist states, some are still fully-fledged satellites of one or other of the giants; some could be described as semi-satellites, while others are uncommitted and even neutral as regards East—West relations.

As for the Marxist parties in the capitalist countries and the Third World, the strongest single block is still that of the Moscow-oriented communist parties (just as the Roman Catholic Church is still numerically the strongest of all Christian Churches). But there exist now a multitude of Marxist or Marxist-Leninist parties, groupings and factions, some within the confines of a single state, others linked with 'fraternal' groups or parties in other countries. Many shades are represented (some barely distinguishable from others) and all groups are fiercely hostile towards almost all others.

The overall picture, to repeat, is not unlike the physiognomy of sixteenth-century Christianity. But after more than four hundred years the intra-Christian antagonisms have lessened; the various Christian denominations now coexist and tolerate each other. In the world of Marxism, as we have seen, the schisms are much more recent and more acute; debates are more acrimonious, enmities sharper. This poses the following questions: will these differences lead to violent clashes, as those between Protestant and Catholic states in the sixteenth and seventeenth centuries? Will there be intra-Marxist religious wars?

We have already witnessed armed confrontations. The Soviet interventions in Hungary in 1956 and in Czechoslovakia in 1968 have their historic parallels in such events as the thirteenth-century Catholic 'crusade' against the Albigenses in southern France. The conflicts among communists have so far been localized; there has as yet been nothing on the scale, say, of the Thirty Years' War. But the dispute between the two great communist powers – both of them possessing a nuclear arsenal – and their respective satellites shows no sign of abating. So long as this tension continues, and inasmuch as the doctrinal differences reflect a conflict of interests, the possibility of an intra-communist war of continental dimensions cannot be excluded.

Ideology and faith

There are, then, numerous parallels between Marxism and Christianity: the chiliastic vision (based at least partly on non-rational faith), the genesis of organization, internal conflicts and schismatic tendencies, and the transformation of the movements in their adoption of a long-term strategy after their initial expectations failed to materialize. There are other common features: both Christianity and communism began as ideologies for the under-dog, for the poor and oppressed, to whom the prospect of boundless future happiness was held out. Opposed to the established order, or at least outside it and refusing to integrate, both creeds have at times invited persecution and oppression; yet where the coercive power of the state has been placed at the disposal of a Marxist party or a Christian Church, they themselves have often used this power to persecute unbelievers, dissidents and heretics.

These similarities pose the question of the relationship between Marxism and religion: is Marxism just a phenomenon very much like religion, or could it, in fact, be classified as a religion in the full sense of the word?

What, first of all, do we mean by religion? Nearly every author who has dealt with this subject has tried to provide a definition of some kind. Most of these definitions are either selective, omitting certain essential aspects, or, conversely, they are too wide and include characteristics shared by some but not all religions existing now or in the past. Some of the formulae convey no clear meaning;[61] others imply the truth of definite beliefs, such as belief in the existence of one God.

A. C. Bouquet begins his own investigation into the meaning of religion with a whole catalogue of definitions by previous writers – eighteen in all, not counting his own.[62] Only one of them, that of Max Müller, contains the criterion of non-rational faith.[63] Most of the definitions quoted by Bouquet speak of religion in the abstract and ignore the collective element, i.e. they regard religion purely as the personal attitude of the individual concerned, and not also as the creed of a community, a Church.[64] Others again confine themselves to religious feelings and beliefs, ignoring the important aspects of ritual and other religious practices.

When comparing Marxism with such mass religions as Buddhism, Christianity and Islam we naturally place the emphasis on the religious *movement*, on the words and deeds of the parties, groups and communities which are united in accepting the basic creed, however much they may disagree on its interpretation and on the activities and policies to be derived from their joint beliefs. From this point of view the following definition would seem to cover all essential aspects: 'Religion is a unified system of beliefs, precepts and practices based, at least in part, on faith rather than on experience and reason, and relating to revered entities or powers – beliefs, precepts and practices which unite into a community all those who adhere to them.'[65]

This formula is wholly applicable to modern Marxism and to Marxist parties and organizations. Present-day Marxism is a unified system of beliefs, precepts and practices.[66] Some of its beliefs and tenets stem from faith rather than reason, and the people sharing a certain interpretation of the theory belong to the same community, the same party, group or sect.[67] An equivalent of the 'revered entities or powers' is contained in the Marxists' concept of the dialectical process of history – of the irresistible forward march to socialist revolution – and in their veneration for the revolutionary proletariat as a dynamic instrument of history.[68] All essential features of religion (if the definition offered above is accepted) are thus present in Marxist theory and the Marxist movement.

It is not, however, sufficient to show that Marxism is a religion within the terms of the above definition. This study is concerned with Marxism not as a static ideology but as an active element in contemporary political life. The question to be answered is whether Marxism is a world religion comparable with, say, Christianity or Islam in their initial stages. For this to be the case Marxism must display the features and tendencies which, *mutatis mutandis*, the older religions possessed in a given period of their development. In other words, the issue is not merely whether Marxism is a religion in the strictly logical sense, but whether the genesis of Marxism and its history to date have followed a pattern that can be shown to be peculiar to the old world religions. We have already encountered similarities between Marxism and Christianity in regard to eschatology and to the interaction of orthodoxy and heresy. It remains to be shown that Marxism fits comprehensively into the pattern of world religion.

If Marxism *is* a religion, it is not just a world religion but the most widespread known religion to history. The total number of people who must be described as either 'practising' or at least nominal Marxists – and these include the bulk of the populations of the Soviet Union and China, as well as all other communist countries – far exceeds 1,000 million: a figure representing about one-third of humanity, more than the total number of Christians, Buddhists and Moslems (all sects and denominations, and both the practising and nominal variety) added together. Furthermore while the old creeds grow more tolerant and their influence wanes, Marxism is on the ascendant and Marxist rulers are increasingly intolerant and totalitarian.[69] Hence ideological indoctrination is more intense, more comprehensive and probably more efficacious in the Marxist-Leninist part of the world, and Marxism-Leninism is an integral part of the accepted way of life in communist countries. Christianity no longer plays a comparable role in the Western world, except possibly in some staunchly Roman Catholic countries like Spain or the Irish Republic.

Similarities between Marxist philosophy and practice on the one hand, and religion and Church practice on the other, have been discerned and described by many writers, but not all of these make it clear whether or not they consider Marxism a genuine new religion. Some writers draw parallels between communism and religion, but also point to one characteristic of religion which communism appears to lack: belief in the supernatural. Thus Glenn M. Vernon speaks of 'cultural phenomena' in communism 'which would meet our definition of religion except that they lack this supernatural element'; on the other hand, the communists have 'shared beliefs and practices which identify for their followers what is good and what is bad ... They have their own rituals and a specialized leadership, a kind of "priesthood".'[70]

Crane Brinton does not shrink from asserting that Marxism, at least as it is practised in the USSR, is a religion in the full sense of the word.[71] In *Ideas and Men* he argues:

Marxism, especially as it has been worked out in Russia, is one of the most active forms of religion in the world today ...

The Marxist God is the omnipotent if impersonal force of dialectical materialism ... The Marxists themselves do not hesitate to use the word determinism with all its overtones of St Augustine and Calvin ... The Marxist heaven ... is the classless society ... which has in common with the eschatologies of other advanced religions the concept of a state of things where no human desires will be frustrated ... As in most religious bodies, the awareness of belonging, of *knowing the truth* ... is balanced by the performance of certain symbolic acts that bind the believer to the whole body of the faithful ... The Marxist has his works as well as his faith: he reads his ... holy books, he goes to meetings, he has ... his party duties. He has a clue to everything, an answer to all his questions. ... [72]

The religious character of modern Marxism is, of course, disputed by Marxists, but it is frequently stressed by Christian thinkers and some of these especially mention the parallels with Christianity. Thus an article headed 'Stalinist Scripture' in *The Christian Century* lists the similarities 'between the development of the Christian institution and apparatus and the communist institution and apparatus', and says:

Think of almost any element supposedly distinctive in the Christian Church – its inspired revelators, its inerrant dogma, its heresy trials and excommunications, its saints, its martyrs, its hagiology, its demonology, its pope, its hierarchy, its consecrated priesthood, its missionaries, its initiatory vows, its sacred shrines and ikons, its reliance on an apocalyptic future to compensate for a grim present – and communism, less than seventy years after the death of Karl Marx, already shows a counterpart.[73]

The French Catholic writer Jacques Maritain, like Crane Brinton, actually considered communism to be a religion:

Communism . . . above all the communism of the Soviet Republics, . . . is a religion, and one of the most imperious quality; certain that it is called to replace all other religions; a religion of atheism for which dialectical materialism supplies the dogma, and of which communism as a rule of life is the social and ethical expression.[74]

In an essay published in 1935 the American Protestant theologian Reinhold Niebuhr discusses the political relevance of the contest between Christianity and communism: 'The political failure of Christianity has encouraged the emergence of a new religion . . . Though communism is avowedly irreligious, its significant attitudes are religious . . . Its interpretations of life and history are dogmatic rather than scientific. Like all vital religion it engages the entire human psyche. . . .'[75]

The Russian Christian thinker Nicholas Berdyaev also viewed communism as a religion engaged in a struggle with Christianity:

Communism, both as theory and as practice, is not only a social phenomenon, but also a spiritual and religious phenomenon. And it is formidable precisely as a *religion*. It is as a religion that it opposes

Christianity and aims at ousting it; it gives in to the temptations Christ refused, the changing of stones into bread and the kingdom of this world.[76]

There are other features, not emphasized by these authors, which communist day-to-day practice – as distinct from Marxist theory – shares with certain religions. There is the deification of leaders, past and present, and the uncritical reverence shown to their writings and pronouncements.[77] One could mention such things as the confession of errors, acts of contrition and penance to re-enter a state of grace, and the unquestioning acceptance of supreme authority and even infallibility ('You cannot be right against the Party') – practices and attitudes that are alien to normal non-totalitarian parties, movements and regimes.

Ritual is another essential characteristic of religion. The writers who, as we saw, regard communism as a form of religion hardly mention this aspect. Yet if contemporary communism (or Marxism-Leninism) is, indeed, a religion, it must have evolved at least an *element* of ritual.

Ritual is a phenomenon which does not pertain exclusively to religion. It is to be found in a variety of customary or obligatory human activities: handshakes, table manners, military salutes, birthday greetings, speeches at prize givings and the like are rituals of a sort. There also exists what can be described as para-religious ritual: masonic rites, oaths of allegiance and the kindling of the flame on the tomb of the Unknown Soldier are examples that spring to mind. Thus there can be ritual without religion; but inasmuch as religion is not just a set of beliefs but a *practised* creed there can be no religion without ritual, without some kind of pre-scribed and organized worship or other forms of solemn conduct and action.[78]

Religious ritual can be defined as the habitual performance of actions, or sequences of actions, which have no inherent purpose in terms of benefit or enjoyment and which are carried out by a body of believers and/or the individual believer in a manner ordained or sanctioned by religious authority.[79]

The rise of a new religion is usually linked with the partial or total rejection of the ritual evolved by the cult from which the new faith has sprung; this rejection is normally followed by the gradual emergence of new ritual forms and institutions. Thus while Christianity retained the fundamentals of the monotheistic faith of Judaism, it abandoned, during the apostolic period, the Jewish system of worship and religious observance, including the rite of circumcision and the dietary laws, without substituting an elaborate new system of rules and rites. There was not, at that stage, much Christian ritual besides a simple new prayer (the Lord's Prayer), baptism, the laying on of hands in ordination and the Eucharist. As time passed many complicated rites were added while little or nothing was dropped, until the age of Reformation brought massive reinterpretations and ritual changes. And in the seventeenth century the Quakers, one of the radical sects which emerged in the wake of the English Reformation, did to traditional Christianity what the Christians of the first century had done to Judaism: they made a clean sweep of the entire ritual, including such fundamental rites as baptism and the Lord's Supper, and only rudimentary forms of Quaker ritual have developed since.

A similar process of all but total rejection of ritual occurred when Muhammad combined elements of Jewish and Christian doctrine. And in the more recent past, Marxism, a product of the thought of a basically Christian Western civilization, has completely rejected the metaphysical doctrines, the eschatology and the rites, but not altogether the ethics, of Christianity.

As a fairly young religious ideology, Marxism could not be expected to have evolved an elaborate ritual of its own. Yet the beginnings of ritual can certainly be discerned in the customary behaviour, on specific occasions, of the leading cadres and the adherents (including the nominal members) of the Marxist movement, especially in the countries where some variant of Marxism has become the official creed. As in other religious communities, the rites to be performed affect the lives and the work of the 'priesthood' – in this case the state and party hierarchy – far more than the lives and daily routine of rank-and-file members.

Some of the writers who list the religious features of contemporary Marxism mention the compulsory attendance of party meetings or the existence of sacred shrines and ikons as elements of Marxist ritual. Examples of this kind abound, indeed. There is the Lenin Mausoleum in Moscow's Red Square, where the embalmed body of the Soviet Union's founder lies, an object of adoration and a symbol of spiritual immortality. Some communist countries in Eastern Europe have introduced rites for certain groups of people, such as youth-initiation ceremonies, in conscious or subconscious rivalry with Christian confirmation. In all communist countries there are, on the walls and hoardings, giant portraits of admired leaders, past and present; somewhat smaller (but still over-life-size) portraits are carried in processions.[80]

There are, furthermore, certain usages which, while common in many non-communist countries, have assumed the character of ritual in the communist states.

According to A. N. Whitehead, ritual 'exemplifies the tendency of living bodies to repeat their own actions';[81] for instance, 'the actions necessary in hunting for food, or in other useful pursuits, are repeated for their own sakes.'[82] It is debatable whether hunting for pleasure could properly be described as a ritual.[83] But it is quite true that purposeful actions are sometimes repeated as pure rites, after they have lost their purpose and practical usefulness. Thus in and long after the Middle Ages the paying of homage to a sovereign was meant to strengthen his power and to ensure the protection of the vassal. In modern West European monarchies homage is still paid, and oaths of loyalty are still sworn, to a sovereign who has no political power, who issues no commands and expects no obedience. What was once a meaningful act, both in legal and in practical terms, has been reduced to a purely ceremonial rite.

The same applies, in actual fact though not in theory, to procedures and usages developed in democratic regimes and copied, in outward form, by totalitarian dictatorships. The most striking examples are parliamentary elections, parliamentary debates, party congresses, conferences and the like in all or nearly all communist states. These institutions have a practical purpose in pluralist regimes which permit open dissent. In the USSR and the East European satellites (the pleonastically styled 'People's

Democracies'), parliamentary elections and proceedings are pure ritual.[84] Some of these countries – e.g. Poland and East Germany – even sport a multi-party system, but the parties do not criticize or fight each other, and in elections they present a joint single list for which all vote as a matter of course. The issues debated in Parliament have invariably been decided beforehand by a small group of top hierarchs, sometimes even by a single dictator. The debate usually consists of set speeches containing stereotype formulae of unstinted praise for the government and its policies. The government's (or ruling party's) proposals are carried unanimously, which is no less a ritual action than the congregation's 'Amen' in church.

The ritual element is still more pronounced at party congresses and conferences and at political rallies where speeches (like sermons in church) may vary in accordance with the problems at issue while the perorations are stereotyped and so repetitious that comparisons with readings from the Prayer Book suggest themselves. Here again a practice that once had a function to fulfil has been emptied of substance and turned into a ritual.

While the performance of the ritual has no ostensible practical end, the adoption or imposition of rituals usually serves to strengthen the hold of the faith on the faithful, who are constantly reminded of the creed and the deities and compelled to devote time and energy to their religion. Collective rites, such as worship in church and singing of hymns (attendance at meetings and singing of fighting songs, in the case of a political movement) tend to weld the membership into a homogeneous whole; they strengthen the feeling of belonging, of emotional solidarity with the co-religionists – they 'bind the believer to the whole body of the faithful', as Crane Brinton put it.[85]

Such are the normal effects of ritual, whether it has developed spontaneously and organically or in accordance with a deliberate plan, like the democratic-parliamentary ritual under a communist dictatorship. In this connection it should be mentioned that some of the communist ritual is spontaneous in origin: the mass rallies and demonstrations (militant practices that are common to nearly all political mass movements) are symbolic repetitions, in keeping with Whitehead's explanation of ritual, of such warlike preparations as the mustering of troops and the march into battle. But the introduction of the trappings of parliamentary democracy in the Soviet Union and the East European 'People's Democracies' was decreed from above for the obvious purpose of blurring the dictatorial character of these regimes.[86] It is, nevertheless, a genuine ritual: the actions involved have no practical effect but are performed, routine-fashion, by those entrusted with them, viz. by the whole adult population in the case of elections, by the 'cadres' in parliamentary and Party meetings.

The possession of sacred scriptures as sources of unchallengeable authority is not an essential characteristic of religion and does not figure in the definition given above,[87] but it is a feature which Marxism shares with all the great world religions. The Marxist Holy Writ – the works of Marx, Engels and Lenin for nearly all sections of the movement, the writings and speeches of Stalin and Mao Tse-tung for some and those of Trotsky for other communist groups – is as fundamental to this creed as is the New Testament for Christianity or the Koran for Islam.[88]

Marxist-Leninists, of course, claim that theirs is a purely secular, indeed 'scientific', ideology, devoid of dogmas (i.e. of maxims proclaimed as true by superior authority and accepted by followers as articles of faith, regardless of rational demonstrability). But it can easily be shown that Marxist teachings are so regarded by orthodox disciples. A case in point is Lenin's way of clinching an argument with other Marxists whose interpretation differed from his own. For example, in one of his philosophical essays he tried to refute the theses of his fellow Bolshevik A. A. Bogdanov, who shared the epistemological views of the Austrian physicist and philosopher Ernst Mach;[89] Lenin's typically theological approach to the debate is aptly described by Bertram D. Wolfe: '[Lenin's] proofs are all proofs of authority – the authority of Marx and Engels ... When Lenin has succeeded in confronting some quotation from Bogdanov ... with some quotation from Engels, and has shown some divergence between them, his task is finished.'[90] Lenin's own sayings and teachings have been similarly treated as gospel truth by many of his followers and admirers. The editing of his writings in the communist countries reveals truly religious veneration. Thus in the official Soviet edition of his *Collected Works* not only are his rough notes faithfully reproduced, but even his doodles.

Like the Bible, the Koran or the Pali Canon, the communist scriptures contain much profound wisdom, much that is the work of genius, as well as some mystical dogmas. The Marxist-Leninist equivalent of the doctrine of the Trinity or the concept of *nirvana* is dialectical materialism or, to be more precise, the three so-called laws of dialectics which Marx and Engels – with some modification and reinterpretation – borrowed from Hegel. But it must be emphasized that what Marxists nowadays call the 'science' of dialectical materialism is essentially a post-Marxian development. Marx and Engels never evolved a comprehensive theory, let alone a 'science', of dialectical materialism: the very phrase is absent from their writings. Engels, in the course of a polemic he felt obliged to conduct against a critic of Marxism, did write a great deal about dialectics, but in a context which is not relevant to the basic tenets of the Marxist concept of history or to Marxist economic teachings; in fact, the main point Engels makes in his polemic is that dialectics, contrary to his adversary's assumption, had played no part in Marx's deductions. Dialectical materialism was elaborated, after the death of Marx and Engels, by the Russian Menshevik Plekhanov (who actually coined the phrase) and other twentieth-century *epigoni*, including Lenin and Trotsky: it is they who introduced into the system a number of non-rational assumptions, thereby helping to convert Marxism, a scientific theory, into 'Marxianity' – which is what one might call, by way of analogy, an ideology combining substantial elements of religious faith with many of the rational tenets of the original doctrine.[91]

It would appear, then, that a catalogue of the main characteristics of Christianity, or religion in general, would hardly include a single feature that is not also a feature of Marxism-Leninism – ignoring for the moment the notion of the 'supernatural'. On the other hand, most of the authors whose statements on communism as a religion were quoted above omit what should be considered a criterion for distinguishing religion from scientific systems: belief in the truth of a non-rational assumption.

The other characteristics which, in the view of those authors, Marxist communism and religion have in common can be described as distinctive features of all 'closed systems', of all creeds, ideologies and philosophical systems which purport to answer all relevant questions about the world, the meaning of life and human society.[92] Yet a closed system can be rational and scientific (which does not imply its veracity), so long as its conclusions do not depend on non-rational assumptions.

The creeds of most religions include the non-rational belief in unverifiable facts. In the case of Christianity these are, *inter alia*, Christ's divinity, his resurrection, his influence on men's actions, life after death, the *Parousia*, the Kingdom of God. As for socialism, the vaguely socialistic ideas expressed in Heine's verses are not religious:[93] they offer a programme of action, setting out desirable aims to be pursued; there is no protestation of certainty that these aims will be attained. For similar reasons the position of the men Engels called 'the three great Utopians' (Saint-Simon, Fourier and Owen) cannot be described as religious. Their object was to persuade mankind to adopt a more rational and more just form of social organization, a socio-economic system that would produce maximum happiness for the greatest number of people.[94] The Utopians were not determinists: they did not think of their respective theories in terms of 'science', nor did they profess certainty that the desired perfect society would necessarily materialize; in other words, they did not hold non-rational beliefs in certain future developments. · The same goes for the social philosophy of modern pragmatic socialism, like that of the British Labour Party or of continental social democracy: their ideas and programmes have no religious content.

Ironically it is 'scientific' rather than 'Utopian' socialism which tends to assume the character of religious faith. Socialists who are 'Utopian' enough to believe that the Millennium is not the inevitable outcome of the class struggle, but that a more just and sensible order *can* be attained if those who want it try hard enough, display a strictly rational approach: they are political partisans, not religious believers. Their view that a better society is possible may be mistaken but it is not irrational. Marxists who are convinced that the perfect society is the necessary end-result of an inexorable historic process believe in something very much like a miracle. To quote Karl Popper: 'If things cannot be improved by the use of reason, then it would be indeed an historical or political miracle if the irrational powers of history by themselves were to produce a better and more rational world.'[95] Strictly speaking this is an understatement. What the irrational powers of history are said to be producing is not just 'a better and more rational world' but the best of all possible worlds.

What these Marxist determinists are saying in effect is this: men cannot achieve a better, let alone an ideal, society by dint of reason and determined endeavour if the course of history does not happen to run in the desired direction. But by a fortunate coincidence history has, in our time, reached the stage where it is moving towards a Golden Age of permanent superabundance, peace, harmony, when all that men desire will be available to all. This will happen: we can speed up or delay the process but not prevent its consummation.

Religion is often defined as a set of beliefs which include faith in a supernatural deity, in a being (or beings) outside and above nature, all-knowing and all-powerful.[96] The classification of Marxism or communism as religions has been questioned on the grounds that they are avowedly atheist and reject all notions of the supernatural.

These doubts are unwarranted. In the first place belief in God is not an essential characteristic of religion. For example, the notion of a supreme being is alien to Buddhism and to Jainism in most of their manifestations. Nor has Buddhism a religious mythology, except for some miraculous events in the life of the founder, events which are not essential to the creed. This absence of myth and of a belief in God has not prevented Buddhism from becoming a world religion.[97]

Furthermore religious belief in God cannot be equated with acceptance of the supernatural.[98] For primitive man the idea of a superhuman agency is, at a rudimentary level, a kind of scientific hypothesis. The existence of such an agency seems the most plausible explanation of certain natural phenomena or events which are redolent of the effects of human action yet possess a vehemence beyond human power. Man can shout and trumpet but not thunder. He can cause fire and illumination but not lightning; he can shift earth but not produce an earthquake or a landslide. So these occurrences are attributed to some powerful agency which is superhuman but not supernatural: it is thought to be part of nature, a conscious and personified force of nature as yet invisible to man. The idea of a superhuman agency as the author of a thunderstorm is on a par with the theory held by the ancient Romans that thunder and lightning resulted from the collision of clouds. Both assumptions are fallacies, but neither of them implies belief in the supernatural.

It may, of course, be argued that the primitive notion of super-human agencies behind the forces of nature – like the Romans' belief in cloud collision – does not contain any non-rational elements and is, therefore, no basis for religion. This is indeed so. So long as man merely ascribed natural phenomena to invisible supermen (or superwomen) he was not yet a religious believer. That stage was only reached when he began to act and think irrationally; when he believed that these beings could be moved by worship, prayer and sacrifice; when he treated things belonging or pertaining to them as sacred or untouchable; and when he attributed to them powers which he had no empirical reason to think they could possess, such as the ability to assume human or animal shape, turn men into beasts or vice versa, to move mountains, etc. Such things had not been observed by anyone; hence, belief that they could or were likely to happen is non-rational.

It is non-rational assumptions of this kind, together with non-rational attempts to influence the behaviour of the personified forces of nature, which turns the superman into a god, the sum total of beliefs into a religion and the plurality of people sharing the beliefs and participating in ritual and worship into a church.

To ascribe supernatural qualities to God (or *a* god) means to assume that he acts, whenever he chooses, in disregard of the laws of nature. This is implied, for instance, in the belief that he sometimes performs miracles. It is *not* implied in the assertion that God created the world. On the contrary, this statement is meant to explain the origin of the universe within the terms of the laws of logic and of nature: the world, like everything that exists *in* the world, must have had a beginning in time (so the argument would run). The birth of the universe, like everything that happens *within* the universe, must have had a cause, i.e. it must have been brought about by something that preceded it. It may be faulty logic (it almost certainly is) and it may also amount to a misinterpretation of the laws of nature; but it certainly purports to explain the world in accordance with these laws by postulating the existence of a prenatural, but not supernatural, agency.

The element of the supernatural does not figure in the philosophy of the pantheists or of the deists of the seventeenth and eighteenth centuries who rejected revealed religion but derived a 'natural religion' from human reason and the principles of rational morality. Nor were the manifold attempts of medieval and post-medieval thinkers to *prove* the existence of a supreme and perfect being based on acceptance of the supernatural – although many of these thinkers did accept other supernatural aspects of Christianity. The gist of all these 'proofs' is that the existence of God is postulated by logic and the natural laws: in other words, without God there would be no logical or natural explanation for certain phenomena which would then have to be classified as 'supernatural' in origin. This goes both for the 'ontological' and for the 'cosmological' proofs which derive the knowledge of God's existence primarily from logical reasoning; it goes above all for the teleological or (to use Kant's phrase) 'physico-theological' proof, which argues that the harmony and order in nature, the aptness and perfection of all the earth's creatures, are evidence of purpose, of design on the part of a thinking creator. This is the oldest and most familiar argument for the existence of God, and although eighteenth-century philosophers like Hume and Kant had already shown it to be flawed, it retained much force and plausibility until the theory of evolution was formulated. Yet the crux of this argument is again that any explanation other than divine creation would be incompatible with logic and with what we know about the workings of nature.

It is interesting in this context that the existence of a demiurge is put forward as a scientific hypothesis in modern physics. While Darwinism appears to have disposed of the 'physico-theological' proof, an act of creation is still held by some to be the only explanation of certain phenomena. Thus Sir James Jeans deduced the fact of conscious creation from the irreversible process of the increase of entropy established by the Second Law of Thermodynamics. Since, owing to the constant diffusion of energy, 'the universe is like a clock which is running down ... [it] must at some time in the past have been wound up in a manner unknown to us'.[99] 'There must have been what we may describe as a "creation" at a time not infinitely remote.'[100] And since (in Jeans's opinion) the universe is a universe of thought, '. . . its creation must have been an act of thought . . . Modern scientific theory compels us to think of the creator as working outside time and space, which are part of his creation, just as the artist is outside his canvas.'[101]

This vision of a prenatural creator is clearly a scientific concept; true or false, it excludes the idea of a supernatural agency.

It seems pertinent at this stage to spell out the exact relationship between the non-rational elements of an ideology or religion and belief in the supernatural. While belief in the supernatural is, by definition, non-rational, a person can hold non-rational beliefs without accepting the supernatural. The Marxists' conviction about the impending Millennium is non-rational, inasmuch as its inevitability is affirmed without the support of rational argument, but the theory does not expect the Millennium to result from supernatural intervention. Revealed religion always comprises non-rational but not invariably supernatural elements. Belief in a God who acknowledges prayer and who interferes at will in the course of nature is not only non-rational but also bound up with belief in the supernatural. On the other hand, religion within the limits defined by Kant – the existence of God being a matter not of knowledge but of faith – is non-rational but dispenses with the supernatural.

Yet it is possible for belief in a divine creator to be free not only from supernatural and mystical but also from non-rational elements. The primitive man who believes in divine power manifesting itself in vehement natural phenomena concludes rationally though erroneously, within the narrow limits of his knowledge and experience, that superhuman intervention is the most plausible explanation for the events observed. The scholar who uses Aristotelian logic to prove the existence of a supreme being, or philosophers like Descartes or Leibnitz who uphold the ontological or 'physico-theological' proofs, may arrive at their conclusions through faulty reasoning or through ignorance of such facts as evolution: but their belief in God as such (i.e. as distinct from their acceptance of certain mystical aspects of Christianity) cannot be described as non-rational. The deist who accepts God as the creative 'first cause' but denies his power to influence worldly events holds non-rational beliefs. Again, Jeans's concept of creation as an act of thought may be – and has, in fact, been – disputed by fellow scientists and logicians, but it is put forward as a serious hypothesis and not as the product of an irrational act of faith.

If the holding of non-rational beliefs is one of the criteria of religious faith, then certain philosophies embodying the view that God exists might be devoid of religious content, while an emphatically atheistic ideology like Marxism-Leninism has to be classified as a religion. This seems absurd at first glance but is, in fact, quite logical. Pantheism, or the theories of Sir James Jeans or the deists can hardly form a basis for religion. A *deus otiosus* who wields no influence on human affairs, who does not listen to prayers and would anyway be incapable of fulfilling them, who does not punish sin or reward obedience to his laws: such a god cannot with sincerity be loved and worshipped. Nor could belief in that kind of god arouse the fanaticism which most true religions (as well as Marxism) are able to engender. And no form of religious piety or practice has ever emanated from such austere concepts of the divine. As for primitive man's notion of divine action producing natural phenomena, this normally developed into a sophisticated religion when the original assumption of what could be called 'natural divinity' had been embroidered and supplemented with a plethora of non-rational ideas, beliefs and rituals, of miracles, taboos, myths and esoteric and mysterious practices, mostly products of folkloristic collective imagination.

World communism and universal religion

In its development to date Marxism bears a resemblance to the early phases not only of Christianity but also of the other great world religions, Buddhism and Islam, and certain characteristics are shared by all four universal creeds.

We are not here concerned with similarities regarding points of doctrine, or with religious concepts the four creeds may have in common, or with the way they influence, or borrow from, each other. This is not a study of comparative religion. What matters in the present context is how Marxism fits into the historic pattern of universal religion, and this calls for an examination of common features, of characteristics shared by Marxism and the other three world religions in their genesis and their initial stages. This investigation might also provide some material for forming an opinion (though not for making predictions with any degree of certainty) on the likely future course of Marxism as a movement and as a practical creed.

One of the classifications of human religion that has been attempted by some writers is linked with the difference between religions which can be said to have grown gradually and naturally and those established by a prophetic founder and his contemporary, or near-contemporary, disciples or apostles.[102] The three older world religions, as well as Marxism, belong to the latter category. This is by no means astonishing. A religion which has developed gradually over the centuries in a tribal or national setting is normally bound up with the climatic and evolving economic conditions of the region concerned, and with the temperament and ethnic or racial characteristics of the community in which it arose. Such a religion will tend not to spread beyond the tribal or national boundaries; nor will the believers be

inclined to display proselytizing fervour. Animistic and poly-
theistic religions based on ancestor worship and/or deification of
the forces of nature – like those of ancient Greece and Rome, and
of the Germanic tribes before the advent of Christianity – will
generally remain endemic: their adherents are unlikely to send
missionaries to foreign parts to propagate the creed. Certain ideas,
rites, symbols, mystical beliefs and practices of this kind of
regional religion may spread from the home ground to neighbouring territories and beyond,[103] just as certain elements of
national civilization may reappear, in the original or a modified
form, in other countries. This is not a case of religious conversion
but of cultural interaction and diffusion.

Thus the adoption by the Romans of the Greek deities and
religious ideas, and their adaption to, and partial fusion with, the
autochthonous Italian religion, was not the result of missionary
propaganda: it happened in the context of the comprehensive
influence which Greek culture, literature, mythology, etc.,
exerted upon the inhabitants of Italy and especially the Romans.

Even a naturally grown monotheism, whose god is more than a
personification of the forces of nature, will not spread if it is
essentially – like Judaism – the religion of a regionally and ethnically restricted community. A close relationship such as exists
between the God of the Old Testament and his chosen people
would tend to make the faithful indifferent towards the prospects
of converting large numbers of foreign infidels.[104] To attain
universality a creed must be potentially all-embracing, free from
all notions of racial and national inequality. This requirement is
met in the creeds propounded by Gautama Buddha, Jesus Christ,
Muhammad and Karl Marx, though none of these four started
with the deliberate plan of founding a new world religion.[105]

The Buddha's mission was to point the way to individual salvation by impressing on people what they must do to achieve
ultimate tranquillity and to avoid rebirth and the suffering that
flows from it; his was primarily a system of ethics that had to be
modified profoundly before it could become the religion of the
masses in a secular society.[106] Jesus at first meant to preach to his
own people; the feebleness of their response, coupled with the

stronger faith shown by some Gentiles, led him and the Apostles to the concept of a supra-national religious community. Muhammad's original idea was to convert the idolatrous tribes of Arabia to what he declared to be the monotheistic faith of their biblical ancestors, Abraham and Ishmael. At the height of his campaign to convert his fellow Arabs – by a mixture of persuasion and military force – his conception altered and he began to think of Islam as a potential world religion. Even before he had captured his native Mecca and made himself the ruler of virtually the whole of the Arabian peninsula, he sent messages to the potentates of the civilized world, including the East Roman Emperor and the King of Persia, enjoining them to adopt Islam as the national religion and to submit to his rule. As for Marx, while he was primarily concerned with an analysis of contemporary capitalism, he considered his materialist conception of history and his prediction of proletarian revolution to be of world-wide application. But he certainly did not think of his system as a possible foundation for a new world religion. He was no dogmatist and he would have been appalled by what twentieth-century 'orthodox Marxists' have done to his teachings. Most probably he would have roundly condemned the primacy of non-rational faith, the deification of the 'Party' as an unerring instrument of history, the (unwritten) dogma of his own and his followers' doctrinal infallibility – not to speak of heresy trials and excommunications, or the induced confessions and 'self-critical' self-abasement of alleged renegades.

The birth of Buddhism, of Christianity and of Marxism occurred in times of religious-ideological ferment, when people were longing for a new spiritual and social departure and when large numbers of teachers and preachers competed for mass response to their doctrines. The triumph of those three religious systems over the rival creeds was, in each case, due to the efforts of the prophet and his foremost apostles. In India it was the Buddha himself who expounded the creed and laid the foundations for the growth of the spiritual community. On the other hand, a trait which Christianity and Marxism have in common is the dichotomy between the prophetic founder of the creed and the founder, or founders, of the Church, the ideological community. When Jesus died on the cross, the global expansion of Christianity seemed by no means assured; Christ's followers formed only a small sect within a small theocratic nation. Nor could Marx and Engels, during their lifetime, be certain of the ascendancy of their particular brand of socialism. Both Christianity and Marxism achieved universality thanks to the teachings and the dedication of apostles of the following generation.

Christianity would probably not have become a world religion – it might, in fact, have disappeared like so many contemporary sects – if St Paul had not performed three vital tasks: the massive propagation of the new faith; the organization of Christian communities in important parts of the Roman empire; and the freeing of the creed from the stifling rigidity of the Mosaic law. Without St Paul's missionary and organizing zeal, and his rejection of much of the Jewish ritual restrictions, Christianity would not have conquered the Roman empire, and had it not become the religion of that empire it might not have spread to other parts of the civilized world.

Which Marxist apostles played a role similar to that of St Paul? There is no exact parallel. In an era of much faster and easier communications there was no need for the painstaking, laborious efforts by which St Paul secured the survival and the spread of his faith. Marxist mass parties sprang up quickly, in Marx's own time, in several industrial countries. Yet the world-wide propagation of the beliefs and of the programme of Marxism was the result of the work of disciples who supplemented its founders' achievements.

Comparisons between individuals who contributed to the respective successes of Christianity and of Marxism can only be tentative and approximate. If Lenin's part in the creation of the Marxist world movement corresponds vaguely to the part which Constantine and Theodosius played in the rise of Christianity, the Marxist equivalent of St Paul was a man who lived to see the victory of a Marxist party in his native country – and who then accused the victorious leaders of a betrayal of Marxist principles. He was Georgy Plekhanov (1856–1918), pioneer in Russia of

Marxist theory and Social Democratic Party leader, the man who converted Lenin and hundreds of members of the Russian intelligentsia to Marxism.[107] Without Plekhanov Lenin might still have become the leader of a revolutionary party and might have seized power in Russia, but his party and the post-revolutionary regime would perhaps not have been 'Marxist'. And had it not been based on state power Marxism might not have attained global universality.

It is a fact that all four systems became world-wide creeds with the help of a powerful state which embraced and institutionalized the new religion and sought to spread it. One method of propagation was used by Buddhism and Christianity, an entirely different one by Islam and Marxism as state religions. The touchstone in this respect was not the belief in a divine power – where the two monotheistic religions, Christianity and Islam, differed substantially from the two non-theistic or atheistic creeds – but the adoption of revolutionary violence as against peaceful penetration.

In the case of Marxism and Islam there has never been any inconsistency in the fusion of religion and political (or state) authority. In Marxist theory the seizure of state power by the proletariat is a necessary step on the road to socialism, and the use of insurrectionary force is deemed essential in nearly all cases where objective conditions are ripe for the transition from capitalism to socialism. Extreme violence was, in fact, used when a party that claimed to be Marxist made itself master of Russia, half a century after the comprehensive formulation of Marx's theory. In the initial phase of Islam the proclamation and propagation of the new creed went hand in hand with the creation, by force, of an Arab nation-state. When Muhammad had his first religious visions (about AD 610) the Arabs were still but a set of tribes – some of them nomadic, others settled in towns – without central administration or government. The prophet died some twenty years later, the undisputed ruler of an all-Arab state with Islam as its established religion, and this new nation was poised to launch aggressive wars against neighbouring countries for the dual purpose of conquering territory and of spreading the new faith:

nothing in the doctrine of Islam conflicted with the waging of murderous, all-out wars of conquest.

The notion of active co-operation with the secular state, and of attaining religious ends by wars of conquest or by violent revolution, must have been very far from the minds of the founders of Buddhism and Christianity and of their early disciples and converts. Both creeds are, originally and fundamentally, 'not of this world'. They are both religions of peace, of compassion, of self-abnegation. Buddhism preaches renunciation and mortification of desire, as well as non-violence and gentleness to all beings (*ahimsa*). Christianity preaches forgiveness and love, even of one's enemy. Both Buddhism and Christianity became institutional universal religions after a process of secularization which their founders and early apostles would not have countenanced.

Buddhism was, from the start, a missionary doctrine. The breakthrough in its establishment as a world religion occurred in the third century BC[108] (some 250 years after Buddha's 'Enlightenment') when India's Emperor Asoka Maurya became a convert to Buddhism and repented of the wars of territorial expansion which he had previously waged with considerable success. He made Buddhism the state religion of India and sent missions to all parts of the sub-continent, as well as to north-east Africa and to south-eastern Europe. The most important of these missions – the one crowned with lasting success – was the mission that led to the conversion of Ceylon.

Asoka was a benevolent dictator. He set his people an example of high moral standards and used his absolute power in the interests of general welfare. Thanks to him Buddhism was transformed from a school of thought popular in north-east India into a world religion. But in the process the creed itself underwent a fundamental change.

The essence of Buddhism is to teach the way to achieve salvation by attaining the blissful state of *nirvana*. The life of holiness which is essential for the attainment of the ideal is clearly not apt to be embraced by the people at large. If all or most members of a community were to strive for *nirvana*, social life would come to a standstill and the community would become extinct. A compromise which took account of the needs of society and of the wish to ensure a normal and prosperous life for the community and its members was, therefore, an important aspect of institutional (as distinct from original) Buddhism. Hence Buddhism, as a very tolerant doctrine, has evolved a set of less stringent moral precepts for its lay followers – mainly negative commandments like those of the Decalogue: not to kill humans or animals, not to steal or rob, not to commit adultery, not to lie, not to imbibe intoxicating liquors. Members of the *sangha*, the Buddhist monastic order, are bound by further, much stricter rules, which include poverty, frugality, complete sexual abstinence and fasting after midday: only those who obey these rules can hope for enlightenment and *nirvana*.[109]

The secularization which overtook Christianity in the second century, when the hope for an early *Parousia* began to fade, was described in a previous chapter.[110] Here, too, the need for coexistence with the non-Christian state, and the wish to influence the state and to make it an instrument for defending and spreading the faith, led to practical policies and tactical manoeuvres which its founder would have rejected. For Christianity the turning point came in the fourth century. All persecution of Christians ceased in the Roman Empire under Constantine the Great (306–37), who became a Christian himself and recommended conversion to his subjects. In 380 Theodosius the Great made Christianity the official religion of the Empire.[111] This enabled the new creed gradually to establish itself among the nations of the Empire and beyond. And Christianity also adopted the two-tier system which Buddhism had developed on its way to universality: two sets of rules for the two categories of the faithful – stringent precepts, including poverty and celibacy for the monastic orders, and a laxer moral code for the laity, the worldly masses.[112]

A two-tier system of sorts also arose in the Marxist movement. Lenin and the Bolsheviks insisted that the Party must be an élite organization of professional revolutionaries who were supposed to show more devotion and readiness for sacrifice than would be expected of ordinary followers and sympathizers. The militants did not have to embrace an ascetic or austere life-style but they had to be willing to subordinate their private life and their private ambitions to the cause and to obey party instructions unflinchingly. This climate of absolute discipline, and the mentality that went with it, may well be among the factors accounting for the willingness of many old Bolsheviks, in the show trials of the late 1930s, to suffer death and dishonour for what they thought were the interests of the cause. Communist parties outside Russia largely adopted the tenets of Bolshevik party structure: the results were seen in the purge trials in communist Eastern Europe which followed the Yugoslav defection from the Soviet bloc in 1948.

Buddhism and Christianity, then, became world religions with the help of secular state power, after revoking the renunciation of worldly affairs which, in both cases, was a characteristic of the founder's original message. Islam and Marxism achieved similar results much faster, without any revocation of original doctrine and by recourse to violence which was in keeping with the founders' own concepts. Muhammad was not only a prophet and a statesman but also a successful army commander in battle. Marx and Engels were at least theoreticians of violent revolution. The discrepancy between primordial other-worldliness and the subsequent fusion with secular state power which marked the progress of the two non-violent religions was not a feature of the rapid expansion of Islam and of Marxism. Their founders themselves regarded the seizure of state power as a basic condition for the triumph of the cause.[113]

Universality through fusion with state power is thus a characteristic which Marxism has shared with the three metaphysical world religions. With Islam it also shares the thesis that both propagandistic conversion and military action are justifiable as means of spreading the faith. Christianity and Buddhism are doctrinally committed to non-violent missionary activity. In practice, of course, Christianity too has often relied on forcible conversion. It can be called a non-violent religion only as far as the first three and the most recent centuries of its 1,900-year existence are concerned. The Christian Roman emperors from the fourth century onwards exerted pressure to ensure conversion and Athanasian orthodoxy. And in the later Middle Ages the Church as well as Christian princes frequently imposed Christianity of the established denomination upon pagans and heretics by brute force. Charlemagne's campaigns against the Saxons were just as much holy wars – *jihads* in Moslem terminology – as the Arabs' conquests of Persia, North Africa and Spain. Internal 'crusades' against heretical communities and the operations of the Inquisition, especially in Spain where Moslems and Jews were compelled to embrace Christianity, bear witness to the readiness of the Church or the Christian state to resort to violence for the purpose of making proselytes. The attempts by sixteenth- and seventeenth-century English rulers to foist Protestantism upon Ireland reflect the same willingness to try conversion by compulsion.

In our age Marxist communism is the only religious ideology which still practises expansion by force. Christian, Moslem and Buddhist missions are working peacefully, with varying success, to gain new adherents. 'Christian' countries and governments may wage war from a variety of motives: religion would not be one of these. Arab governments or organizations may proclaim a *jihad* for the recovery of lost territories or for other economic or political aims, but not for the propagation of Islam. Communists, too, indulge in a great deal of spoken and written propaganda, but their 'missionary' efforts have not, in recent decades, been nearly as successful as their campaigns of conquest or their military interventions. The very substantial growth of the area under communist rule in Eastern Europe and east Asia since the Second World War has been due almost entirely to military action. Communist regimes have been imposed in nearly all territories under Soviet military occupation, and the establishment of communist Party rule has invariably been followed by massive, totalitarian indoctrination. Soviet intervention in Hungary in 1956, where dissident communists and defectors had co-operated with non-communists, was no different in character or motivation from medieval or post-medieval wars of religion.[114] The invasion of Czechoslovakia by the USSR and other East European communist countries in 1968 was something very much like the 'internal crusade' against the Cathars in southern France in the early thirteenth century.

Splits and schisms occur frequently in all religions, as well as in many political movements. The ideological and organizational fragmentation of twentieth-century Marxism has parallels in the corresponding phases of the three older universal religions. Sectarian developments are not uncommon in political parties and groupings, as well as in non-religious schools of thought (e.g. in psycho-analysis); but there is something distinctive in the type of internal conflict that has erupted in the Marxist movement and in the other three religions which originated in the pronouncements and actions of a prophetic founder. This is the clash (already mentioned in this essay) between the pure, original doctrine and the concessions and compromises which have come to be seen as unavoidable as soon as the new movement has become a factor in a wider community. Leading members of the new creeds have felt constrained to accept such compromises and to make the necessary tactical adjustments when the faithful still formed a minority within the pagan or, at any rate, dissident society. This is what happened to the Christian Church in the first three centuries AD, when its inevitable practical arrangements and partial co-operation with the authorities of the Roman Empire seemed sinful and unacceptable to the fundamentalists, who insisted on upholding the untarnished faith and the precepts of the Gospels and the Apostles.[115] It happened, against a completely different background, when at the beginning of this century moderate socialists – who still proclaimed themselves Marxists – made pacts with 'bourgeois' parties and even entered 'bourgeois' governments, only to be anathematized instantly by the rigidly orthodox. This clash between fundamentalist fanaticism and realistic flexibility has also occurred at a later stage, when the creed has become institutionalized, and it has then, again, produced purist indignation and sectarian breakaways, or even major schisms. Examples, in the sphere of communism in power, are the Russian NEP in the 1920s and the frequent pacts and instances of co-operation between communist and capitalist powers.[116]

The reactions of the fundamentalist die-hards to the policies of compromise are frequently branded as 'heretical' by the establishment, which is itself guilty of heresies against the original doctrine. The NEP provoked the emergence of the 'Workers'

Opposition' in Russia and of similar non-conformist factions in the European communist movement: the leading members of these opposition groups were disciplined or expelled as deviationists and disrupters. The puritanical critics of the papacy in the fifteenth and sixteenth centuries fared no better: Savonarola was put to death for glorifying apostolic austerity and for preaching against the corruption and the sybaritism of the Roman Curia.

A split between the orthodox and the compromisers occurred in Buddhism during Asoka's reign, in the third century BC. The Mahayana, or Northern School, rejected what they felt to be the sterile, anti-mundane doctrine of the orthodox Theravadins and proclaimed a creed that seemed more secular and, hence, more conducive to universality. The Theravada, or Southern School,[117] was indeed too puritanical and too austere for the masses. As one writer on Buddhism puts it: 'When Buddhism became universal in spirit and embraced large masses, the Hinayana could no longer serve. A religion more catholic, a less ascetic idea, was required.'[118]

The Mahayana abandoned the orthodox Theravada doctrine of salvation by self-abnegation and preached instead salvation by faith, which meant that the desired blissful state could be achieved by all mankind and not only the members of the monastic orders. Elements of the Brahmin religion and of Hindu polytheism gradually filtered back into the faith of the Mahayana and other heretical sects, and in the end these went so far as to promise the virtuous not *nirvana* but rebirth in Heaven instead.

The early Buddhist schism differed in an important respect from the conflicts that occurred in the Christian Church in the second century and in communism in the 1920s. The Montanist 'heretics' and the left-wing critics of the Bolshevik Government's policy of compromise with capitalism vanished from the scene after a brief sectarian existence; the Theravadins, who opposed the watering-down of the creed and looked upon Mahayana as a corruption of Buddha's teachings, did not fade away: they continued as one of the major branches of the Buddhist community. But in the course of the centuries the Theravada, too, arrived at a *modus vivendi* with secular activities and aspirations. Original, non-worldly Buddhism had as little chance of survival and of becoming a world religion as the Christian Church would have had if it had taken the Sermon on the Mount literally and had tried to impose strict observance of all of Christ's instructions on all the faithful.

The early history of Islam was not marked by a major crisis resulting from a conflict between orthodox purists and pragmatic compromisers. The split which occurred within a few decades of the Prophet's death, and which persists to this day, hinges on a different issue – on whether or not the Caliphate should be limited to the descendants of Ali, the fourth Caliph and Muhammad's nephew and son-in-law. In spite of Islam's supernatural eschatology, the teachings of the prophet reflect a firmly positive attitude towards life on earth and towards human society, however organized. There is no dichotomy here regarding that which is God's and that which is Caesar's: Muhammad himself was both Allah's prophet *and* Caesar; his kingdom was both of this *and* the other world. Muhammad did not, like Jesus, feel indifferent about the state: it was he who created the state and the army, and he and his successors used both as instruments of religious expansion.[119]

In Islam, recognition of the realities of life and practical accommodation with society as it was did not emerge gradually, as happened in the Christian Church and the Buddhist community: it was there from the start. Muhammad's own actions did not display doctrinal inflexibility. He was, throughout his ministry, a man of pragmatism and he gained his ends by a combination of military force and subtle diplomacy. Yet there seems to be an element in most religions that generates fanatical loyalty and an insistence upon ethical standards which were not demanded or expected by their founders. The Montanists, and later the Puritans and Calvinists, preached a moral strictness not suggested in the Gospels. Loftier still was the morality which Savonarola strove to impose upon the citizens of Florence. And in our century Marxists have, individually or collectively, displayed a fanatical intransigence and ruthlessness in the service of the cause which were not prescribed in the writings of Marx and Engels. A case in point, as far as intransigence is concerned, is the position of a small, staunchly Marxist organization in this country: the Socialist Party of Great Britain proclaims in its Declaration of Principles that it is 'determined to wage war against all other political parties, whether alleged labour or avowed capitalist' – a sectarian attitude which Marx implicitly rejected over a hundred years ago in his *Critique of the Gotha Programme*.

Islam, too, experienced this clash between die-hards and moderates, although the ensuing split was not as deep and far-reaching as in the other religions. In the seventh century there arose a fanatical sect of Moslems whose interpretation of the Koran was more rigid and narrow than the practice of the man to whom the Holy Book had been revealed. The occasion was the acceptance by Caliph Ali of arbitration after his victory over a rival in 648. A group of Shi'ites (i.e. Ali's followers) objected to this submission to human arbitration on the grounds that Ali had thereby acted against the will of God, 'the sole judge and arbiter'. These *Khawarij* or Kharijites ('Seceders') then formed a sect based on a no-compromise doctrine. It laid great stress on purity of life and asserted that anyone guilty of grave sin was an unbeliever and an apostate. The sect branded those who refused to fight unjust rulers as infidels and anathematized all forms of dissimulation in word or deed. They thus set up standards of moral behaviour far above those established and practised by the Prophet himself.[120]

The four religious systems scrutinized in this chapter have, among other things, this in common: that they hold out the prospect of salvation to all mankind. But their eschatological concepts differ. Buddhist eschatology is strictly individual. Each human being is capable of working out his or her salvation, and the Buddha has taught his fellow men how to achieve this end. There is no Golden Age, no Millennium for all.

The Christian vision is primarily that of universal salvation. The Second Coming of the Saviour will usher in the Kingdom of God; eternal life and eternal bliss for all the just, for all those who have earned and found forgiveness. Christians are divided about the circumstances and the timing of individual salvation. Some theologians hold that judgement will be passed on each person immediately after death; the damned will go to Hell forthwith, while those who are saved will either enter Paradise or, according to Roman Catholic doctrine, go to Purgatory for a time, if their imperfections are too great, and to Heaven eventually. Another view is that those who die in a state of grace ('die in Christ') will await Judgement Day in their graves or in some intermediate state between earthly life and blissful eternity.[121]

The eschatology of Islam is similar to that of some Christian authorities: immediate punishment in Hell for the sinful and for infidels; immediate rewards in Heaven for just believers; a Day of Judgement for all beings.

Lastly, communism professes a general and secular eschatology: Heaven on earth for all those who live to see the Day, but no salvation for the individual outside the communist community – and, of course, no individual immortality. In the communist Millennium men will probably live longer, due to the expected immense progress in all branches of human knowledge and power, but they will not live for ever.

This examination of the eschatological concepts of the four universal religious ideologies shows that Buddhism, rather than Marxism, is the 'odd man out' as far as the world's future is concerned: the individual man or woman can achieve enlightenment and *nirvana*, but humanity at large will go on much as before. For Christians, Moslems and Marxists human history[122] will come to an end on the Day of Judgement or the attainment of world communism.[123] Christianity, Islam and Marxism have a common root and share important characteristics. They all stem from the Judaeo-Christian messianic vision. This is natural in regard to Islam, which deliberately adopted – and modified – the essential theology of the Old and New Testaments. The Moslem Paradise is more primitive, more earthy and more sensual than the Christian one; but the basic idea of infernal punishment for the wicked and eternal bliss for the just is common to both religions. And Marxism, for all its atheism and its rejection of the supernatural, is patently the child of Western (i.e. Christian) civilization, whose ideals of justice and peace for all men of good will Marxism has made its own.

Many writers have commented on the obvious resemblance

between the Marxists' perfect society and the messianic vision of the people of the Old Testament. As a Christian thinker has pointed out: 'In both [the Old Testament and the Marxist visions] the oppressions and struggles of the time were to be succeeded by a period of righteousness, by a kingdom of plenty and of peace.'[124] The Old Testament messianic expectation has helped to shape the eschatological doctrines of the various Christian Churches and sects; and Christian eschatology, in turn, is mirrored in the Utopian visions which, from the sixteenth century onwards, have influenced the thoughts and the imagination of the Western world and which have culminated in the concept of a communist class-less society.

Thus Christianity, Islam and Marxism – particularly post-Marxist 'Marxianity' rather than the original variety – have a common Judaeo-Christian root. Buddhism has grown and developed in a different environment and intellectual atmosphere. While it shares many of the ethical values of Christianity (and of many other religions), it has an eschatology all of its own: it lacks the common eschatological feature of the other three world religions, the promise, to the faithful and militant, of an apocalyptic future that will make suffering and sacrifice appear worth while.

An aspect peculiar to Marxism is that it arose and began to spread at a time when it was bound to collide with the long-established world religions. This means that, in addition to the enmity which Marxism inevitably encountered from the ruling classes everywhere, it had to face the antagonism resulting from its incompatibility with the other creeds.

This problem did not exist to the same extent at the corresponding stage in development of the older world religions. Christianity had a fertile field in the Roman Empire, whose official anthropomorphic polytheism had little to offer to those educated Romans who were casting about for a more spiritual set of beliefs, and still less to the great mass of the underprivileged, the slaves, the throw-outs, the poor, who now found comfort and hope in the Christian message which proclaimed the equality before God of all men, and promised salvation to the faithful of all nations and all classes. No comparable and potentially universal religion existed in the territories where St Paul and the early Christian missionaries went to work for their faith. Nor did Buddhism in its initial phase have to compete with another world religion; it spread, thanks to its superiority as an ethical and egalitarian philosophy, over a complex polytheism which sanctified the existing caste system. Islam, on the other hand, did clash with one – only one – world religion from the start. Conflict with Christianity broke out at first at the national level, since many Arabs, individuals as well as entire tribes, had received baptism during the preceding five centuries (with Monophysite and Nestorian communities in fierce, and sometimes deadly, rivalry); it then spread, in step with the two-pronged Arab-Moslem expansion – westwards in North Africa and Spain, and northwards in the direction of Byzantium. The hostility between Islam and Christianity, later aggravated by the crusades, lasted for many centuries. At a later stage Islam also clashed with Buddhism, when India was invaded and partly subdued by Moslem conquerors: the virtual disappearance of Buddhism from its country of origin was due, at least in part, to the intolerance of Moslem rulers.[125]

Marxism, ever since its inception, has found itself in confrontation with not just one but three older world religions. The latter, having divested themselves of their proselytizing dynamism, now coexist peacefully.[126] Could a similar, conflict-free relationship develop between them and the new creed, which has not shed its missionary fervour?

Marxists officially regard religion as a private matter for the individual – for all except Party members: Marxist militants are expected to conform with the official atheistic materialism and to sever all ties with whatever Church they may have belonged to from the cradle. In communist countries the Churches enjoy a degree of toleration but are not allowed to propagate their faith. The extent of toleration is sometimes linked with reciprocal services rendered by the Church. During the Second World War the Russian Orthodox Church was given wider scope by Stalin's Government than it had enjoyed previously; in return, it exhorted the faithful to give unstinted support to the communist Government in its war effort.

Since all communist countries are totalitarian dictatorships and must strive for universal acceptance of their ideology, the present precarious coexistence with the Churches cannot last indefinitely. The communist state refrains from massive persecution because the rulers feel that they can rely on the state's monopoly in education to eliminate the rival creeds within a few generations. On the other hand, so long as the state has not completely asserted its totalitarian grip on the minds of the people, the Church can become the catalyst of political resistance not only by the faithful but by all opponents of the regime: in a rudimentary form this began to happen in Hitler's Germany before and during the Second World War.

In non-communist, pluralist societies communism is likely to remain a tolerated religion, in mainly peaceful rivalry with other creeds and other secular ideologies. Like all religions, communism will continue to change and develop and to experience fission and fusion, splits, reunion, renewed splits.

There is no reason why the communist religion should not also persist for centuries, even if communist rule does not spread to new territories and even if it is overthrown where it now holds sway. Buddhism, Christianity and Islam attained universality after being institutionalized in powerful empires; those empires fell long ago, but the three creeds are still alive – and still world religions. In some modified form the various communist Churches would probably survive the downfall of one or both of the great empires which have made Marxism-Leninism, as they interpret it, the state religion.

Conclusion: Marxist theory and Marxian reality

The view that communism or, to be more precise, Marxism-Leninism is a dogmatic religion is shared by a number of prominent Christians, both theologians and representative laymen. We have seen that men like Reinhold Niebuhr, Nicholas Berdyaev and Jacques Maritain not only endorsed this interpretation of the new universal creed but also discerned similarities between the institutions and concepts of communism and those of Christianity. But it cannot be said that this view has found general acceptance in the Christian Church. When in 1974 an education authority in the English Midlands decided to include the study of Marxism-Leninism in the syllabus of a school course on the world's religions, some spokesmen of the Church of England protested both against the inclusion of what they regarded as an anti-religious theory[127] and against the way Marxism-Leninism was to be presented.

While Christians are divided about the classification of communism as a religion, Marxist-Leninists are not: they insist that Marxism is a science and that there is no affinity between their philosophy and religion or their institutions and those of a Church.[128] Marxism is thus unique as a religion, in that its followers deny that any of their beliefs are religious in character. No Christian would deny that the divinity of Jesus, the Second Coming or eternal life are articles of faith; no Christian would claim that the articles of the Nicene Creed are based on reason and empirical evidence.[129] But this is what Marxists claim in respect of their doctrines. However much they may differ, and fight each other, on issues of strategy and tactics or on the evaluation of events and socio-economic phenomena, Marxist-Leninist as well as non-Leninist Marxists are unanimous in affirming that Marxism has been from the start a strictly scientific ideology. Each of these groups and parties also claims that its particular brand of Marxism has retained the character of a science: 'Scientific socialism,' all Marxists assert, differs fundamentally from all other systems which try to interpret the world and propose to change it. This includes not only religions but also the attempts of the so-called 'Utopian' socialists, Saint-Simon, Fourier and Robert Owen, to evolve a design for a perfect, egalitarian society which mankind could be persuaded, by propaganda and model experiments, to substitute for the existing imperfect pattern of human organization.

To many Marxist-Leninists the suggestion that theirs is a religious philosophy, and that their movement is not essentially different from a Church, is not just a falsehood but an insult. In the symposium *Christianity and the Social Revolution* which has been mentioned before,[130] a communist contributor has this to say about the relationship between Marxism-Leninism and religion:

It is sometimes declared that communism itself is a religion . . . Religion involves belief in and dependence upon a supernatural order. Communism . . . believes rigidly that there is nothing but the universe in time and space . . . that there is no power but the power exercised by men who understand the laws of nature and of the development of society.

It is sometimes foolishly asserted that the body of Lenin has become a kind of mummified saint or god. This is grotesquely untrue, because for even the humblest Russian worker or child it is the ideas, the historical understanding of Lenin, that matter. Leninism is a working guide to daily action; not even a body of doctrines, but rather a map of the very ground over which men are walking. No Russian is ever asked to venerate Lenin for himself alone. . . .[131]

Apart from the blatant untruth of the assertion that Leninism is not, *inter alia*, a body of doctrines, much the same could be said by a Moslem about the Prophet, or by a Buddhist about the Buddha. But our communist author is more outspoken in his condemnation of religion:

Lenin looked upon religion as something obscene, as the vilest form of subjection of the human spirit. The gods are the symbol of man's subjection to man . . .

There was a time when helpless humanity, impotent in its struggle on earth, sought comfort and reward in Heaven . . . But as the social and political relationships of men lose their obscurity and the relations between man and nature become intelligible, religion becomes unnecessary.[132]

Yet not all Marxists treat religion and religious feelings with the same scathing contempt. In the same volume another communist contributor compares the situation in the Roman Empire in the first century AD with the contemporary situation (i.e. the 1930s) and the historical role of Jesus with that of the modern socialist revolutionary. His peroration is couched in terms which show no trace of Marxist-Leninist jargon:

We cannot expect any recovery of the Jesus of history in those who are reconciled to the social order and its moral values, or who flinch from class and party strife.

The apocalyptic crisis has descended upon our age, not prematurely as in the time of Jesus, but in the fullness of time. Opportunity as it confronts us is also the final sifting of chaff from wheat, the day of judgement. The Church may try, but it cannot succeed in crucifying the Christ. The new Christ is an insurgent Proletariat, the uprisen people of God, and the Church which fails to do Him reverence must be cast forth into the outer darkness.

The Day of the Lord is at hand.[133]

Whatever Christians and communists may think about the incompatibility of their respective creeds, it would seem that revolutionary socialist aspirations are fully compatible with genuine religious sentiment.

Notes

Marxism and Marxianity: The Rise of a New World Religion

1 Marx and Engels used the terms 'socialism' and 'communism' as synonyms; the later distinction between socialism as the first and communism as the ultimate stage in the post-revolutionary transformation of society was first made by Lenin and is now accepted by all Marxist-Leninists. In this essay the two terms are treated as interchangeable, except where the Leninist distinction is relevant to the argument.

2 Werner Sombart, in *Socialism and the Social Movement*, English edition (London 1909), p. 24.

3 In the first canto of *Deutschland, ein Wintermärchen* [Germany A Winter's Tale].

4 Yet in original Marxist theory only the collapse of capitalism and the proletarian revolution are seen as absolutely inevitable; the Millennium is not. Marx considered a catastrophic alternative to be possible (albeit improbable): the breakdown of civilization and mankind's relapse into barbarism. This pessimistic alternative has largely disappeared from present-day Marxist theory. Most Marxists now predict the communist classless society with a profession of certainty which was absent from Marx's own thought.

5 Cf. the famous passage in the preface to *A Contribution to the Critique of Political Economy*, quoted in C. Wright Mills, *The Marxists* (Harmondsworth 1963), p. 43.

6 Marx and Engels admitted the possibility of peaceful trans-

ition from capitalism to socialism in some countries, such as Britain and the USA. Lenin and his disciples later held that the conditions for peaceful transition no longer applied in any capitalist country. Many present-day communists, on the other hand, regard the peaceful, parliamentary road as practicable nearly everywhere.

7 The sect of Jehovah's Witnesses is one of these.

8 *Anti-Duehring* (London 1969), pp. 217–18.

9 *Anti-Duehring*, pp. 332–3.

10 Besides those foretold by Bebel or Trotsky; cf. pp. 18ff. below.

11 Chinese communism is most certainly not the outcome of a 'proletarian revolution': the contribution of the industrial working class to the emergence of Communist China was negligible.

12 E.g. East Germany in 1953, Poland and Hungary in 1956, Czechoslovakia in 1968, Poland again in 1970; the 'class struggle' in the industrial countries of the West has been fairly peaceful by comparison during the same period.

13 Things would perhaps work out differently under a Western-style parliamentary system with competing parties and an alternative government – a system rejected by Marxist-Leninists who have, in practice, invariably established rule by a self-perpetuating élite. That a managerial ruling class would not become superfluous in a wholly collectivized and planned economy is one of the central theses in James Burnham's book, *The Managerial Revolution* (London 1943). Burnham's conception of a world-wide managerial revolution has been overtaken by events, but he argued convincingly that whole-sale state ownership and planning were not in the least likely to lead to superabundance and the abolition of classes: cf. *The Managerial Revolution*, pp. 115ff.

14 Apart from the near-certainty of the emergence of a managerial ruling class there is also the probability of divisions within the victorious working class to which K. R. Popper has drawn attention: 'There is no earthly reason why the individuals who form the proletariat should retain their class

unity once the pressure of the struggle against the common class enemy has ceased. Any latent conflict of interests is now likely to divide the formerly united proletariat into new classes, and to develop into a new class struggle' (*The Open Society*, London 1969, II, p. 138). 'It was romantic, irrational, and even mystical wishful thinking that led Marx to assume that the collective class unity and class solidarity of the workers would last after a change in the class situation. It is thus wishful thinking ... which leads Marx to prophesy the necessary advent of socialism' (*The Open Society*, p. 333).

15 *Die Frau und der Sozialismus*, first published in Zurich, 1883; quoted in I. Fetscher, *Der Marxismus: Seine Geschichte in Dokumenten* (Munich 1967), p. 40.

16 *Die Frau und der Sozialismus*, quoted in I. Fetscher, *Der Marxismus*, p. 398. William Morris did not take quite so lofty a view of human nature; in his Utopia crime has not been eradicated.

17 *Die Soziale Revolution* (Berlin 1907); quoted in I. Fetscher, *Der Marxismus: Seine Geschichte in Dokumenten*, p. 48.

18 *Literature and Revolution* (Moscow 1923), pp. 187ff.; quoted in I. Fetscher, *Der Marxismus: Seine Geschichte in Dokumenten*, pp. 792–3.

19 William Z. Foster, *Towards Soviet America* (New York 1932); quoted in Charles Lowry, *Communism and Christ* (London 1954), p. 54.

20 It stands to reason that in the course of evolution man will indeed attain a higher standard of intelligence, though not necessarily of morality, and there are no grounds for believing that this will be the consequence of mankind's adopting a specific socio-economic order. It would make more sense to see things the other way round and assume that the wiser men of the future will organize society more wisely: but such an hypothesis would be rejected as 'Utopian' by orthodox Marxists.

21 *Conjectures and Refutations*, 3rd edition (London 1969), p. 36.

22 *Conjectures and Refutations*, p. 37.

23 In the *Communist Manifesto*.

24 Cf. p. 24 above.

25 Cf. p. 29 above.

26 *Conjectures and Refutations*, p. 37. A typical example of how a falsified theory is made irrefutable in retrospect is the method by which modern Marxists have 'rescued' the theory of 'increasing misery' (*Verelendung* in German). Faced with steadily rising working-class standards of living throughout most of the twentieth century, neo-Marxist theorists have explained that 'increasing misery' is a relative term and has acquired a new meaning in a technological era and in relation to the raised requirements of technical know-how in a modern industrial society. Failure to give working-class children a scientific education and training to qualify them for sophisticated employment, or the inability to own modern educational devices such as television sets, are contemporary versions of 'increasing misery', of sinking below subsistence level. Cf. André Gorz, *Stratégie Ouvrière et Néo-Capitalisme* (Paris 1964), pp. 24ff., on the attitude of the French communists regarding 'increasing misery' as a contemporary problem.

27 After the outbreak of the Second World War in September 1939 some British astrologers read in the stars that Germany would suffer a crushing defeat by 1940 or, at the latest, by 1941: the refutability – and factual refutation – of such predictions did not turn astrology into a science.

28 At government or, as in the case of the EEC, at supra-national level.

29 The Chinese communists, who have stuck to their revolutionary guns, were quick to denounce the Soviet and pro-Soviet communists as 'revisionists' and 'social democrats'.

30 Ironically the ultra-left, for whom the Soviet leaders are 'renegades', are closer to them in Marxist orthodoxy than are some of the Euro-communists who are still, in principle, Moscow-oriented and in favour of co-operation with the Kremlin.

31 Experience has taught them caution. For several years after the last war they were still in the business of predicting: not

generally an immediate revolution but an immediate, or almost immediate, world-wide slump of more than pre-war magnitude. When instead of the crisis an unprecedented boom developed, the Marxist prophets grew less and less definite and confident in their forecasts. The recession which did materialize in the 1970s had *not* been widely predicted in Marxist publications.

32 After the outbreak of the Franco-Prussian war in July 1870, in a letter to Engels, Marx stresses the backwardness of the French workers' movement as compared with the German one.

33 The same goes for the Chinese Revolution after the Second World War.

34 'The USSR in War', in *In Defence of Marxism* (London 1966), p. 9. This is a collection of essays, articles and letters by Leon Trotsky, written in 1939 and 1940, plus an Appendix of pieces by James Burnham.

35 'The USSR in War', p. 18.

36 'Manifesto of the Fourth International on the Imperialist War and the Proletarian World Revolution', in G. Breitman and E. Reed (eds), *Writings of Leon Trotsky (1939–40)* (New York 1969), p. 46. This position of 'revolutionary defeatism' was also adopted, from September 1939 to June 1941, by the Moscow-oriented communist parties of Britain and France. The advice, then proffered by both Stalinists and Trotskyists, to withhold support from the war against Nazi Germany was prudently ignored by the bulk of the British labour movement but followed by some sections of the French working class: the results in both cases failed to bear out the predictions made by the exponents of 'revolutionary defeatism'.

37 The mid-1970s saw the collapse of the remaining non-communist dictatorships on the continent of Europe – in Portugal, Greece and Spain. The division became clear-cut: *all* major capitalist countries were parliamentary democracies and *all* communist countries (*de facto*) one-party dictatorships.

38 To mention other errors of judgement and prediction: in 1866 Engels expected the Austrians to win the war against

Prussia. In 1878 Engels wrote that the weapons of war had reached such a state of technological perfection that further progress in this field was inconceivable. Trotsky asserted in the summer of 1936 that the proletarian revolution had begun in France, where the workers had staged a number of sit-down strikes. In 1940 he predicted that Stalin and the Soviet bureaucracy would fall from power within a few years, if not months. John Strachey wrote in the 1930s, when he was a confirmed Marxist, that there would never be more than one communist state in the world, implying that the spread of communism would lead to a union at state level of all communist countries. Marx made a number of erroneous short-term forecasts regarding socio-economic develop-ments within capitalism: cf. Bernstein's criticisms, pp. 29ff.

39 'Social democrats' became the accepted term after the October Revolution: until 1917 nearly all Marxists, including the Bolsheviks, called themselves 'social democrats'.

40 For example, the totalitarian, one-party state which prevails in Russia, China and their respective satellites and which entails the disfranchisement of the bulk of the population, including the workers, is a gross violation of Marxist tenets: the same goes for the imperialist policies of the USSR and the Chinese People's Republic.

41 First published in English in 1909 under the title *Evolutionary Socialism, A Criticism and Affirmation*.

42 *Evolutionary Socialism* (New York 1963), p. xxii.

43 About the non-scientific, semi-religious character of Marxian dialectics, *see* the essay 'Diamat and Dogma' in this volume.

44 *Evolutionary Socialism*, p. vii.

45 This, by and large, remained the position for many years after the dissolution of the Comintern in 1943. The situation is less rigid now; the Moscow-oriented communist parties in the West still maintain close ties with the Soviet party but do not always follow its lead (*see* the essay 'Farewell to Revolu-tion' in this volume, pp. 209ff.).

46 Ironically two of Bernstein's most outspoken critics, the German Karl Kautsky and the Russian Georgy Plekhanov,

found themselves in the social democratic camp after the split: they castigated the communist regime in Russia more fiercely than they had attacked revisionism twenty years previously.

47 *The Scientific Outlook* (London 1931).

48 In the light of what actually happened – or, rather, of what did *not* happen – some Catholic and conservative Protestant scholars deny that the New Testament regarded the *Parousia* as imminent. The prevailing Protestant view is that Jesus himself taught his early and essentially apocalyptic return. This interpretation is in keeping with such New Testament passages as *Matthew* 24:30 ff., especially 34; *Mark* 9:1; 13:24ff., especially 30; *Revelation* 1:1. It is also clear from 1 *Thessalonians* 4:15–18 that St Paul expected the *Parousia* to occur in the lifetime of his generation. Cf. also Gibbon, *The Decline and Fall of the Roman Empire*, (London 1909), II, pp. 24–5 and n. 62.

49 Until 1917 nearly all Russian Marxists believed socialism to be a remote prospect for Russia. It is one of the paradoxes of history that the Bolsheviks, who originally shared this long-term view, were the first party to proclaim, at the end of 1917, that a proletarian revolution had actually taken place in Russia under their leadership.

50 Which, of course, conflicts with the assertion, in the *Communist Manifesto*, that the communists 'do not set up any sectarian principles of their own, by which to shape and mould the proletarian movement. . . .'

51 But not the smaller extremist groups (Maoists, Trotskyists, etc.).

52 E.g. Herbert Marcuse in the USA.

53 It is worth re-emphasizing that the Moscow-oriented communist parties, in modifying their concept of 'proletarian revolution', have taken up a more realistic and less 'religious' position than their radical rivals on the extreme left.

54 'Zur Geschichte des Urchristentums', in *Werke* (Berlin 1963), pp. xxii, 449.

55 'Zur Geschichte des Urchristentums', p. 460.

56 Trotsky himself never criticized the conclusion of trade or military agreements as such, but he accused Stalin of inducing the communist parties in the partner countries to give tacit or open support to their capitalist governments.

57 Heresies from the point of view of the ruling stratum, not necessarily from that of orthodox doctrine.

58 In *Ideas and Men – The Story of Western Thought* (London 1951) Crane Brinton, late Professor of Ancient and Modern History at Harvard University, drew a parallel – during Stalin's lifetime – between early Christianity and post-October communism, with the emphasis on inner-Russian developments. '. . . Stalin has been in some ways in a position analogous to that of the early Christian organizers when it had become fairly clear that Jesus was not going to return to earth immediately, that the whole elaborate Christian eschatology had to be fitted to a different time-scale and, indeed, to a different world. In Stalin's Russia the classless society has had to be postponed; there is frustration, unhappiness, competition and great economic inequality in Russia today. Stalin has had to try to temper the basic optimism of Marx to the facts of life on this earth. . . .' (p. 448).

59 Usually styled 'Communist Party (Marxist-Leninist)'.

60 The Sino-Soviet rift recalls the East—West Schism of 1054, when the issue was predominance (of Rome) rather than doctrinal differences.

61 E.g. Hegel's: 'Religion is "the knowledge possessed by the finite mind of its nature as absolute mind".'

62 *Man and Deity* (Cambridge 1933), pp. 30ff.

63 It reads: 'Religion is a mental faculty which independent of, nay, in spite of sense and reason, enables man to apprehend the infinite under different names and under varying disguises.' *Introduction to the Science of Religion* (London 1873).

64 One of the exceptions is E. Durkheim, *The Elementary Forms of Religious Life*, first published 1912, trans. J. Swain, 1961: 'A religion is a unified system of beliefs and practices relative to sacred things, that is to say, things set apart and forbidden – beliefs and practices which unite into one single moral

community, called a Church, all those who adhere to them.'
65 Based partly on Durkheim's and Max Müller's definitions.
66 Cf. pp. 53ff. above on Marxist ritual.
67 As in all mass religions, each denomination has its own Church, and most groups and sects have supra-national links.
68 One communist writer speaks of the proletariat as 'the new Christ ... the uprisen people of God'; cf. p. 84 above.
69 I.e. the dictators who claim to be Marxists; basically and originally both Christianity and Marxism – but not Islam – are anti-authoritarian.
70 *Sociology of Religion* (Provo, Utah 1962), pp. 56–7.
71 *See* n. 58 above.
72 *See* pp. 478ff.
73 Vol. 69 (22 October 1952), p. 1215; also quoted in Glenn M. Vernon, *Sociology of Religion*, p. 57.
74 *New York Times*, 7 October 1944; also quoted in Glenn M. Vernon, *Sociology of Religion*, p. 56.
75 'Christian Politics and Communist Religion', in *Christianity and the Social Revolution*, eds John Lewis *et al* (London 1935), a symposium comprising contributions by both communist and Christian spokesmen.
76 *The Russian Revolution* (London 1932), pp. 59–60.
77 The following 'Hymn to Stalin' appeared in the Soviet Communist Party's official newspaper *Pravda* in August 1936:

> O great Stalin, O leader of the peoples,
> Thou who broughtest man to birth,
> Thou who purifiest the earth,
> Thou who restorest the centuries,
> Thou who makest bloom the Spring,
> Thou who makest vibrate the musical chords ...
> Thou, splendour of my Spring, O Thou
> Sun reflected in millions of hearts.

Quotation from Charles W. Lowry, *Communism and Christ* (London 1954), pp. 49–50.
78 Or omission, as in the case of religious taboos.
79 Enjoyment can be the by-product but not the motive of the rite.

80 Similar rituals were established by other totalitarian movements, e.g. Fascism and Nazism, which might have become religions had they survived.

81 *Religion in the Making*: Lowell Lectures, 1926 (Cambridge 1927).

82 *Ibid*, p. 10.

83 Whitehead's very wide definition of ritual would also cover play, the visual arts, music, etc.

84 Often very elaborate: cf. B. D. Wolfe, *An Ideology in Power* (London 1969), pp. 261ff., on the ritual of Soviet parliamentary elections.

85 *See* p. 51 above.

86 In breach, incidentally, of the tenets of both Marxism and Leninism. Marx spoke contemptuously of the 'parliamentary cretinism' that marked the policies of some 'petty-bourgeois' socialists, and Lenin rejected the parliamentary 'talking shop' in favour of 'soviets', i.e. workers' councils which would not only deliberate but also carry out their own decisions. The 'Supreme Soviet' of the USSR is neither what it pretends to be, viz. a genuine parliament, nor a soviet of the Leninist type.

87 *See* p. 49.

88 Some groups, as, for example, the tiny Socialist Party of Great Britain, accept Marx and Engels but reject Lenin and all later communist authorities.

89 *Materialism and Empirio-Criticism* (London 1908).

90 *Three Who Made a Revolution* (Harmondsworth 1966), p. 571.

91 For a detailed exposition of the lack of rational deductions in dialectical materialism, see the essay 'Diamat and Dogma' in this volume, pp. 100ff.

92 Arthur Koestler, in this sense, brackets Marxism with 'the Freudian and Catholic Churches'; cf. *Arrow in the Blue* (London 1952), p. 251.

93 *See* p. 5 above.

94 This is basically the philosophy of most pre-Marxian and non-Marxian socialists, except that the 'Utopians' went into very great detail in describing their ideal systems.

95 *The Open Society* (London 1969), II, p. 143.

96 E.g. in the Soviet *Dictionary of Philosophy* compiled by M. Rosenthal and P. Yudin (Moscow 1967).

97 There are no theist or deist elements in the original and orthodox Theravada Buddhism, which is essentially a system of ethics. Several centuries after Buddha the Mahayana school of Buddhism (which the Theravada Buddhists regard as a heretical corruption of the original creed) developed teachings and ideas which got intermingled with elements of Hindu polytheism.

98 Cf. E. Durkheim, *Les Formes Elémentaires de la Vie Religieuse* (Paris 1912), p. 36. Durkheim points out convincingly that the distinction between natural and supernatural forces or happenings could not have occurred to the primitive mind.

99 *Eos* (London 1930), p. 52.

100 *The Mysterious Universe* (Harmondsworth 1937), p. 182.

101 *The Mysterious Universe*, pp. 182–3.

102 Cf. A. C. Bouquet, *Man and Deity* (Cambridge 1933), p. 88.

103 As Frazer amply demonstrated in *The Golden Bough*.

104 As Gibbon put it in *Decline and Fall* (II, p. 5), the Jewish religion is 'admirably fitted for defence, but it was never designed for conquest'.

The one example in history of large-scale conversion to Judaism is the medieval empire of the Khazars in the south-eastern corner of what is now European Russia. Many Khazars, including the dynasty, adopted the Jewish religion in the eighth century AD, but no pressure was brought to bear on Christian and Moslem citizens of the empire to follow suit.

105 The three older religions are not free from sex discrimination. Marxism is – in theory; in practice women play no greater part in the power apparatus of Russia, China and other communist states than elsewhere. There are many women in the 'Supreme Soviet', the (rubber-stamp) parliament of the USSR, but very few, if any, women are members of the Government or the 'Politburo' of the Communist Party.

106 The religious character of Buddhism has been questioned by

some writers. Yet the belief that rebirth is the normal destiny of all beings, although it can be avoided by 'enlightenment', is undoubtedly non-rational and religious.

107 Cf. Z. A. Jordan, *The Evolution of Dialectical Materialism* (New York 1967), p. 183, on the tribute which his Bolshevik opponents paid to Plekhanov; for example, Trotsky described him as 'the profound teacher and brilliant commentator of Marx, the teacher of entire generations, the theorist, the politician, publicist and creator of European fame and European connections.'

108 Comparable with Constantine the Great's reign in Byzantium.

109 After the schism which probably occurred under Asoka the Mahayana or Northern School went further in relaxing orthodoxy and turning Buddhism into a religion for the masses; cf. p. 75 above.

110 *See* pp. 39ff. above.

111 Some historians consider Christianity to have become the state religion in 325, when Constantine the Great called the Council of Nicaea. But, in fact, the position remained fluid during much of the fourth century. Constantine's successor, Constantius II, was pro-Arian, i.e. opposed to the Nicaean dogmas, and later Julian the Apostate (361-3) even strove to stem the Christian tide and to restore paganism. Only Theodosius's edict of 380 settled all doubts and disputes in favour of Catholic Christianity.

112 Sir James Frazer draws an interesting parallel between Buddhism and Christianity in this respect: 'The austere ideals which [both systems] inculcated were too deeply opposed . . . to the natural instincts of humanity ever to be carried out in practice by more than a small number of disciples, who consistently renounced the ties of family and the state . . . If such faiths were to be nominally accepted by whole nations or even by the world, it was essential that they should first be modified or transformed . . . This process of accommodation was carried out in after ages by followers who [were] made of less ethereal stuff than their masters . . . By their glorifica-

tion of poverty and celibacy both these religions struck straight at the root not merely of civil society but of human existence. The blow was parried by the wisdom or the folly of the vast majority of mankind, who refused a chance of saving their souls with the certainty of extinguishing the species.' *The Golden Bough*, one-volume edition (London 1950), pp. 361–2.

Islam and Marxism, too, underwent many changes during their initial phases. But since they did not preach asceticism to start with, the need for this particular transformation did not arise.

113 A religion can, of course, attain fusion with the state power without aspiring to universality: biblical theocracy is a case in point.

114 The Soviet-Finnish war of 1939–40 was started by the Russians for primarily strategic reasons, not for purposes of ideological expansion, but the Sovietization of Finland would probably have been a by-product of immediate and total victory which was foiled by the Finns' initial resistance.

115 Cf. p. 39f above.

116 Cf. pp. 41ff. above.

117 Or 'Hinayana', as the Mahayanists called it.

118 Christmas Humphrey, *Buddhism* (Harmondsworth 1952), p. 48.

119 Nor did he preach poverty, frugality and sexual abstinence; he himself had nine wives, not counting concubines.

120 Kharijites are still to be found in Moslem North Africa. Another fanatical and intolerant Moslem school was that of the Hanbalites, which originated in the ninth century; it later declined but was revived more recently in the shape of the Puritan *Wahhabi* movement, which has achieved dominance in the Saudi Arabian kingdom.

121 The New Testament is not consistent in this matter. Every eschatological school can quote one or several Bible passages in support of its own interpretation – except for the doctrine of Purgatory, for which no explicit scriptural authority exists at all. There is also, in John's Apocalypse, a curious reference

to two distinct resurrections, the first for martyrs and other saints, the second – after a millenial reign of Christ, followed by a spell of Satanic recrudescence – for all other mortals; cf. *Revelation* 20:4–15. Some Christian theologians reject the notion of eternal punishment altogether.

122 In Marxian parlance, 'pre-history'.

123 In William Morris's *News from Nowhere* the absence of politics is mentioned as a signal feature of the future society.

124 Martin D'Arcy, SJ, *Communism and Christianity* (Harmondsworth 1956), p. 51. Father D'Arcy is one of the writers who have tried to construct a connection between Karl Marx's alleged Jewish background and his adoption, *mutatis mutandis*, of the Old Testament promise of a perfect society. He writes (in *Communism and Christianity*): 'Marx from all the evidence we have knew very little at first hand of Christian theology. What is more likely is that the undying hopes of Jewry in the advent of a Messiah and the Kingdom of Israel influenced consciously or unconsciously his mind.' Nicholas Berdyaev, in *The Russian Revolution* (London 1932), p. 73ff., is more explicit still: 'Marx was a Jew; he had abandoned the faith of his fathers, but the messianic expectation of Israel remained in his subconscious ... His proletarian communism is a secularized form of the ancient Jewish chiliasm ...' Last, Arnold Toynbee (*A Study of History* (Oxford 1948), V, p. 178) speaks of 'the distinctly Jewish ... inspiration of Marxism' and enlarges upon the parallels between the messianic prophecy and the communist vision of the classless society. Such parallels exist, as we have seen: Marxist communism has adapted and absorbed certain aspects of the Judaeo-Christian eschatology. But speculations about the influence which Marx's Jewish antecedents may have exerted – consciously or unconsciously – upon his thoughts and theories are wide of the mark. Marx was born a Jew but was received into the Protestant Church at the age of six in 1824, when his father had the whole family baptized. Jewish tradition cannot have played a part in Karl Marx's parental home. Furthermore there is hardly a reference to the Jews or to Judaism in Marx's

writings or correspondence which does not express contempt for the people and their religion. Besides, Marx's writings do not contain any detailed description of the future ideal society. The Utopian elements are much more pronounced in the works of Engels, Lenin, August Bebel and William Morris, none of whom had any Jewish background whatsoever.

125 Islam has usually accorded a measure of tolerance to Jews and Christians – the people who worship the same God as Islam, but Moslem administrators regarded the temples, the symbols and rituals of Buddhism as wholly pagan and treated them accordingly.

126 The same goes for the various denominations and sects within the three main creeds. Sectarian clashes in Northern Ireland, communal riots in India and Pakistan and fighting between Christians and Moslems in the Lebanon reflect socio-economic rather than theological antagonism; they certainly do not stem from a desire to effect conversions.

127 Forgetting, perhaps, that nearly every new creed is 'anti-religious', in the sense that it rejects all other existing religions.

128 A possible exception was the Bolshevik A. V. Lunacharsky, who called Marxism 'a natural, earthly, anti-metaphysical, scientific and human religion' in *Socialism and Religion*, published in 1908. Lunacharsky was attacked by Lenin at the time, but he later served as People's Commissar for Education in Lenin's post-October Government. (Cf. B. D. Wolfe, *Three Who Made a Revolution*, p. 564.)

129 With the possible exception of Christ's Resurrection; some Christians accept the historicity of the evangelists' accounts.

130 *See* n. 75.

131 Ivan Levisky, 'Communism and Religion', p. 278.

132 'Communism and Religion', p. 279.

133 John Lewis, 'The Jesus of History' in *Christianity and the Social Revolution*, p. 102.

Diamat and Dogma: *A Study in Marxist Dialectics*

Communists regard Marxism as the science of social change. They claim that the materialist conception of history, together with the methodology developed by Marx, Engels and Lenin, enable them to assess correctly the character of a given society, as well as the general trend of social and economic changes. Inasmuch as their own revolutionary policies flow from this assessment Marxist theory is, in their view, a guide to revolutionary action.

Further, Marxists believe that the laws of motion of any society, including the capitalist society they strive to transform, are governed by what they call the scientific concept of 'dialectical materialism'. Since revolutionary action to abolish capitalism must be based on the knowledge of social dynamics, dialectical materialism plays, according to the theory, a vital part in determining and formulating revolutionary policy. Consequently, modern Marxists of all persuasions claim to attach axiomatic importance to dialectical materialism as the corner-stone of their philosophy.[1] Actually Marx, while adapting certain formulae of Hegelian dialectics for his own theoretical purposes, never produced a theory of dialectical materialism. The phrase itself was coined by neither but by the Russian Menshevik leader Georgy Plekhanov. Lenin subsequently adopted the term which he, erroneously, attributed to Marx and Engels and which is now generally accepted as characterizing the Marxist-Leninist philosophical system.

Although the significance of the concept of dialectical materialism for modern militant communism derives from the fact that it is supposed to contain the key to the understanding of the laws of motion of society, the concept itself transcends the field of historical and socio-economic analysis; it is said to apply to nature and to all branches of science, to the whole range of constantly evolving reality. The second part of the phrase, therefore, refers not only to historical but also to philosophical materialism as interpreted by the Marxists; in fact Marxists assert that there is a close connection between these two. The materialist conception of history – the view that production and reproduction ultimately determine historical developments – is seen to be linked, in the philosophical and epistemological sphere, to the thesis that our ideas are a reflection of a material reality which exists outside, and independently of, our consciousness. Orthodox Marxists often describe philosophical and historical materialism as two sides of the same coin.

The essence of dialectical materialism (sometimes called 'diamat' for short) is the application of the principles and the laws of 'dialectics' to the materialist view of the world and of history. The literal meaning of dialectics is 'discourse': it was a term current among the Greek philosophers and was chiefly used to denote the art of debate or dialogue, as a method of arriving at the truth and/ or winning an argument. The term acquired a variety of meanings in later philosophical systems. Marxist-Leninist textbooks usually define dialectics, following Engels, as the science of the general laws of motion, human society and thought.[2] The materialist aspect distinguishes Marxian dialectics from Hegel's idealistic philosophy, which regarded the 'dialectical' movement and development of ideas, the unfolding of the 'world spirit', as the determining element. Dialectical materialism has also been defined as 'the methodology of scientific thought', as the way in which phenomena have interacted and developed in the past and must be expected to act in the future:[3] this definition is not meant to conflict with the one given by Engels; it merely purports to stress a different aspect. The dialectical principle is said to apply to all fields of life and thought: inorganic matter, plants, animals, mathematics, empirical sciences, human ideas, historical sequences, scientific and political theories, social and political movements, religious beliefs, economics, etc.[4]

Dialectical materialism occupies a great deal of space in textbooks of Marxist and Leninist theory and is extensively taught in all communist countries, as well as in communist and other Marxist party schools, study circles, etc., in the West. The question naturally arises of the relevance to Marxist revolutionary doctrine of this diamat concept, which is not ostensibly concerned with issues of the 'class struggle'.

Historical and philosophical materialism

The materialist conception of history is undoubtedly an integral part of Marxist teachings. Whether or not it is a correct interpretation of what has happened throughout the ages, it is a cogently expounded theory which has a direct bearing on the determinist vision of social change. Thus the prediction of the inevitability of capitalist collapse – which is central to Marxism – follows logically from the materialist conception of history in conjunction with Marx's analysis of nineteenth-century capitalism.

The dialectical-materialist conception of reality was elaborated in great detail by Engels in his *Anti-Duehring*, and by some of his twentieth-century disciples, especially Lenin in his *Materialism and Empirio-Criticism* (1908). Marx himself, although he knew and approved Engels's work (to which he contributed a chapter), did not devote much attention to the philosophical aspects of materialist dialectics. To Lenin, on the other hand, this was a matter of supreme importance: he argued that any deviation from strictest materialism, any concession to an idealistic interpretation of the world, was a step along the road to what he called 'fideism', belief in some kind of supernatural deity.

Dialectics apart, the connection between philosophical materialism and the main body of Marxist thought is, in reality, extremely tenuous. Since this connection is declared to be in itself a 'dialectical' one, it would be pointless to argue about its existence with the orthodox, for no common debating ground could be established. From the point of view of ordinary common sense there is no reason why a person should not be able to accept in its entirety Marx's sociology, his materialist conception of history, his view of capitalism and of the inevitability of socialism and the classless society, and yet subscribe to some form of philosophical idealism and even religious faith. It could be argued, and has in fact been argued, that belief in God and in life after death is apt to have a debilitating effect on the class struggle: the prospect of a heavenly paradise for the meek and the peace-makers might diminish the workers' inclination to fight to end their present misery and to achieve a better life in this world, particularly as certain forms of this fight (e.g. violence and rebellion) could be said to be incompatible with the teachings of the Christian and other Churches. This may be so; but it does not mean that adherence to Marx's economic and political theories, and acceptance of his predictions, are logically inconsistent with philosophical idealism, or with belief, say, in God and Christianity. Many practising Christians have found no difficulty in espousing the cause of Marxian socialism and in endorsing the programmes of Marxist parties while retaining their religious faith.[5]

The meaning of Marxist dialectics

Whilst the link between Marx's social and political theories on the one hand, and a materialist world conception on the other, is at best very weak, the connection between those Marxist theories and the 'science' of dialectics is non-existent. The incorporation of dialectics in the Marxist theoretical system was largely an accident. It would not have occurred if, at the time Marx began to write, the German intelligentsia had not been under the spell of Hegelian philosophy.[6] No essential element would be lacking in Marx's economic, social and political doctrines if all mention of dialectics and of anything pertaining to it were excised from his writings.[7]

This statement, of course, requires proof, and I shall attempt to furnish proof when discussing the contents and the implications of dialectics and its 'laws'. But it should also be made clear that the term 'dialectic' is often used in Marxist literature in a sense which has little or nothing to do with these laws or with the so-called dialectic triad.[8] When students of Marxism are exhorted by the adepts to approach the subject under investigation 'dialectically', the meaning is that they should see and assess phenomena not as fixed and unchangeable objects, in rigid isolation from each other, but (as Engels put it) 'in their essential connection, concatenation, motion, origin and ending' – in other words, as parts of a continuous process of constantly changing reality.[9] This is undoubtedly sound advice, at least insofar as it refers to matters which are in a state of flux – which they invariably are in history and in social, economic and political life. The recommended method is one which has been applied, throughout the ages, by many (though not all) scientists, thinkers and ordinary, intelligent people who would see little use in the dialectical triad, and no use at all in such things as the 'interpenetration of opposites'.[10] What this really amounts to is that an understanding of non-stationary phenomena, of historic developments, of economic, social and political antagonisms and contests, etc., requires a flexible mind, one that is capable of taking everything into account which is related and relevant to the subject-matter, which influences it and is influenced by it.[11] It amounts to nothing else, and it does not presuppose acceptance of any aspect of the so-called science of dialectics as expounded by orthodox Marxist scholars.

This tendency of the dialectical materialists to subsume different things under the same category illustrates a terminological vagueness which has led to a good deal of confusion and incongruity. For example, we are told that dialectics is the science of the laws of motion not only of nature and history but also of human thought. The Marxists actually agree with Hegel's contention that dialectics is a form of logic; they maintain that it stands in the same relation to formal logic as higher mathematics does to Euclidean geometry. If this were so, then the laws of dialectics, like those of

formal logic, would simply be part of the science of valid infer-
ence: their successful application would not depend on the
conscious acquisition of knowledge regarding them. Just as one
does not have to study formal logic in order to reach the right
conclusion from given premises, one should be able to form
correct judgements on 'dialectical' problems without having
learned the rules of 'dialectic thought'.

This, however, is not how Marxist dialecticians see matters.
They insist, at least sometimes, that the ordinary person who is
unschooled in dialectics and simply relies on common sense will
tend to adopt the 'metaphysical' mode of seeing things in isolation, in rigid abstraction, and will therefore mostly reach the
wrong conclusions. At other times, curiously enough, Marxists do
not regard every scientist or writer who never mentions dialectics
and never uses dialectical terms as a 'metaphysician' – which is
what Engels, thanks to a misunderstanding of Hegelian semantics,
called the non-dialecticians. In the orthodox Marxist view there
are people who apply the rules of dialectics without knowing
them, just as Monsieur Jourdain, in Molière's play, does not realize,
until so informed by a 'philosopher', that he has been speaking
prose all his life.[12] According to Engels, Charles Darwin was one
of these 'unconscious dialecticians';[13] according to the more recent
editions of the *Great Soviet Encyclopaedia*, Albert Einstein was
another.[14]

In order to make sense of this ambiguous terminology one
might be inclined to explain the phenomenon of the 'unconscious
dialectician' by the natural propensity of all genuine scientists
spontaneously to absorb the dialectical laws which, the theory
maintains, are inherent in the subject-matter, and thus to develop
a 'dialectical' approach even without having studied dialectics. But
this is not necessarily so from the Marxist standpoint. Engels in
Dialectics of Nature and Lenin in *Materialism and Empirio-Criticism*
took eminent scientists (Helmholtz, Henri Poincaré, Ernst Mach)
to task for disregarding the laws of dialectics. Lenin wrote in 1908
that the bulk of contemporary scientists held 'correct' materialist
views, while a minority, owing to their ignorance in matters
dialectical, had adopted an 'incorrect' idealistic or semi-idealistic

position.[15] He also abused individual members of this idealist minority as 'reactionaries', 'stupid philistines', 'utter ignoramuses', and denounced their published opinions as 'unspeakable nonsense', 'idealistic rubbish', etc.[16]

Thus the problem of whether, in the view of the dialectical materialists, one has to absorb the science of dialectics in order to get the right answers remains unresolved. Scientists, philosophers, politicians, etc., who have studied and understood dialectics, will presumably always get things right. Of those who have not studied it, some are 'unconscious' or 'instinctive' dialecticians, while others, though endowed with the same intellectual powers and possessing the same educational background, never make the dialectical grade. How it is that the application of certain rules has to be learned by some while others apply them intuitively is not explained. Perhaps this is one of the 'contradictions' which figure so prominently in the descriptions of the dialectical process.

The question which concerns us here is not so much the truth content of diamat as the relations between this theory and the social, economic and political aspects of Marxist doctrine and practice. More specifically, if dialectics has no bearing on the fundamentals of Marxist teachings, why does it occupy so prominent a place in Marxist literature, and why do Marxist writers, whether they deal with theoretical subjects or with matters of strategy and tactics, profess to attach so much importance to it?

In assessing the relevance of dialectical materialism we shall concentrate on the first part of the phrase. There is no scope in this context for argument about 'materialism'. We have seen that the materialist conception of history is, indeed, an important part of Marxist doctrine; moreover it seems to contain a good deal of truth – it explains, at any rate, a certain type of historic development which might not be comprehensible on an idealistic interpretation. Philosophical materialism, though not strictly relevant to the essential teachings of Marxism, is likewise a serious theory: it can be argued about, but it cannot be dismissed *a limine* as illogical or unscientific.

So we shall deal here with what Marxists call 'the science of dialectics', with the dialectical laws which, as they claim, explain the interaction and the development of phenomena. How do phenomena interact and develop? Marxist dialectics finds the answer, primarily, in the Hegelian triad of thesis, antithesis and synthesis.[17] The initial stage of a given development, the thesis, is contradicted and eventually negated by an opposing movement or stage, the antithesis; the struggle between the thesis and the antithesis produces a third and higher stage, the synthesis, which in turn negates the antithesis but preserves and integrates the positive (or 'progressive') features of both the thesis and the antithesis. The synthesis may then become the first stage of a new triad, i.e. it will, in due course, produce its own contradiction or antithesis, and so on and so forth.

To illustrate this by an example from history, medieval feudalism is sometimes described in Marxist writings as a first stage, which is negated by the bourgeois revolution and the emergence of modern capitalism. The latter (the antithesis) is then negated by the proletarian revolution and socialism which, being the synthesis, preserves the cultural and certain material attainments of both the feudalist and the capitalist eras, as well as some of the potential for production and the advanced technology of capitalism.[18]

The dialectic triad furnishes one of the three main 'laws' of dialectics, the 'negation of the negation'. The other two are the 'transformation of quantity into quality and vice versa' and the 'interpenetration of opposites'.

Negation of the negation

As far as the triad is concerned, it could be said that this three-stage rhythm describes zigzag developments which *sometimes* occur in history, in such sequences as revolution, counter-revolution and the emerging new order, or thrust, counter-thrust and final decision in battle or war.[19] The progress of human thought and human knowledge can take the form of a similar zigzag movement: a theory (in natural science, economics or whatever) is formulated; it encounters criticism; the debate between the defenders and the critics of the new hypothesis clarifies the problems involved and produces, as the synthesis, a modified theory which takes the points made by both sides of the argument into account.[20]

Yet the fact that such sequences on the three-stage pattern are sometimes encountered does not establish a scientific law. The triad is not the invariable, and not even the usual, way in which historic events and natural processes occur or new theories emerge. A revolution can be victorious from the start, encountering no setback or serious counter-revolutionary attempt. In battle the attacker sometimes gains a crushing victory without meeting any real resistance, and sometimes the attack is a complete failure from the start. A new scientific hypothesis or economic theory might gain universal acceptance at once (which, admittedly, is rare); it could immediately be refuted, either by counter-argument or by empirical evidence; or, again, it might be modified by some of the criticisms but remain quite unaffected by others.[21] So the triad is very far from being the universal rule which some dialecticians make it out to be.

Even if it could be shown that the developments in nature, history, politics, economics, etc., generally follow the dialectical pattern, we could still not speak of a law or theory within the usual meaning of these terms. As Popper pointed out,[22] the dialectical triad would then be an empirical descriptive theory.[23] But a theory or law which merely states that developments or processes will provoke some kind of contradiction or negation, but does not specify what form this opposing movement will take and in what circumstances it will occur, would be of no theoretical or practical use.

A comparison with genuine empirical laws will make this clear. 'All men and all animals are mortal'; 'energy can be neither created nor destroyed': knowledge of these laws of general validity is obviously of signal importance. Even rules or generalizations which do not apply without exceptions can have great practical significance: 'the human life-span is less than a hundred years', 'the heart is on the left', or, to take examples relating to human behaviour, 'the bad money drives out the good', 'a glut of commodities leads to lower prices, a shortage to price increases'. These laws are not all valid without exception, but they all tell us what is at least likely to happen or to be encountered in given circumstances, and they enable those concerned – technologists, population experts, politicians, statesmen, etc. – to take the measures they deem appropriate. But what use is a 'law' which tells us that, for example, an initiative in the political arena will be countered by opposition of an unspecified kind, and that the resultant struggle is likely to lead to a constructive compromise or synthesis of an equally unspecified kind? Quite apart from the fact that things very often will not happen that way, this so-called law conveys no factual information; it does not help anyone to foresee what will happen and to prepare for it, to take any action to prevent a mishap or, alternatively, to ensure benefit from a potentially favourable development.

The assertion that not all that happens in history conforms with the pattern of the dialectical triad needs some kind of qualification: if one looks hard enough, without insisting on terminological exactitude, one can persuade oneself that history is full of, indeed seems to consist of, examples of the negation of the negation. Thanks to the lack of precision inherent in the dialectical formulae, almost any chain of events can be made to fit.[24] Changes are constantly taking place, and each change somehow embodies a negation of the position undergoing the change; furthermore, changes often restore some elements negated in a previous change – which is what the negation of the negation (the Hegelian 'higher unity') is supposed to do. Yet when we take a closer look at any such sequence we find invariably that no prediction could be based on the theory that an event which changes or negates the existing state of affairs will in its turn be subjected to a change or negation, and that the resultant synthesis will comprise elements both of the original and of the changed position.

The events surrounding the French Revolution are usually held by Marxists to exemplify the law of the dual negation. The

Revolution itself is said to have negated the regime it overthrew, the feudal society and its superstructure, of which the absolute monarchy formed an essential part. The Revolution was in its turn negated in 1799 by Napoleon's *coup d'état* and the establishment of Bonapartist dictatorship. This was a higher synthesis insofar as it accepted and confirmed the social and economic transformation wrought by the Revolution, while restoring some of the features of the system the Revolution had destroyed, viz. monarchy and aristocracy, but in a new and modernized form, adapted to the new social and economic order.[25]

Now it would no doubt have been possible for an intelligent and knowledgeable observer under the Directory in the late 1790s to foresee the second negation in the shape of a military or political coup designed to replace a corrupt and feeble regime by firm and stable government. Such a prediction could have been based on the evaluation of economic and political facts and trends, but definitely *not* on the law of the negation of the negation. If our observer were to have ignored the facts of the situation, and to have tried to foretell developments solely by invoking the dialectical law, he could only have said that the existing system would some time, somehow come to an end; he would have been unable to say when this negation would occur, whether very soon, or in a year, in ten or in a hundred years, or what form the ensuing 'synthesis' would take – military dictatorship with or without restoration of monarchy, or parliamentary democracy, or anarchy; any of these possibilities, and combinations of social, economic and political factors, would have constituted a 'synthesis'.

Or let us take an example from the history of warfare. In August 1914 the German army launched a powerful offensive on the western front, with initial success. A French counter-offensive halted – negated if you like – the German advance. German resistance – the second negation – enabled the Kaiser's army to retain and consolidate most of the gains made by the opening thrust, including nearly the whole of Belgium. The resultant 'synthesis' was stabilization of the front line and protracted trench warfare.

Events seemed to repeat themselves twenty-six years later, in May 1940. This time the Anglo-French counter-stroke was either non-existent or too weak to be an effective negation of the German attack, and Germany was immediately victorious. Something that a dialectician might call a negation came four years later: the Normandy landing and the ensuing expulsion of Hitler's army from France. Both in the First and the Second World Wars a military expert in possession of all relevant facts (comparative military strength, strategic competence and tactical skill of the army leaders, etc.) could have foreseen the actual outcome and could have explained why the campaign of 1940 ran an entirely different course from the 1914 campaign. And a dialectician could have pointed out *afterwards* that the sequence of events in both cases somehow conformed with the pattern of the twofold negation; but it would obviously have been impossible to make these forecasts and explain these differences solely on the strength of the law of the double negation. Furthermore, the chances of making an accurate prophecy would not in the slightest degree depend on whether the prophet believed in the validity of the dialectical law or not.

Similar considerations apply to Marx's prediction, in the penultimate chapter of the first volume of *Das Kapital*, of capitalist collapse and socialist revolution.[26] In this passage Marx explained that revolution was inevitable because the capitalist mode of production had become an obstacle to the development of the productive forces, and because intensified exploitation and mass misery would make the workers resolve to rise and destroy the system of wage slavery. Having formulated these conclusions, Marx went on to detect in the whole process of the genesis, the rise and the fall of capitalism the pattern of the Hegelian law of the negation of the negation. Pre-capitalist petty industry, based on the labourer's (i.e. the immediate producer's) ownership of the means of production, was the first stage of the triad. This state of affairs was negated by what is called the 'primitive accumulation of capital': the labourers were expropriated and eventually turned into proletarians who had to sell their labour power to the capitalist owners of the means of production. The capitalist order arising from this development was in existence (and still is, according to present-day Marxists) when Marx predicted its impending downfall, its negation by the proletarian revolution, which would lead to the expropriation of the expropriators and to *social* ownership of the means of production. The socialist transformation of society thus appeared as the culminating phase of the triad, the negation of the negation.

Marx's line of reasoning was apparently misunderstood by Eugen Duehring, the German scholar whose critique of Marxism Engels set out to refute. Duehring assumed that Marx's conclusions were based on the Hegelian triad, in the sense that Marx considered socialist revolution to be inevitable because it, and only it, could form the negation of capitalism and the 'higher unity'. Engels demonstrated that this was not so;[27] that Marx's prediction was not based on any dialectical law but on historical and economic analysis over the preceding fifty pages of *Das Kapital*; that the reference to the negation of the negation was not part of the argument. In Engels's own words: 'Only after he [Marx] has proved that the process has partially already occurred, and partially must occur in the future, he in addition characterizes it as a process which develops in accordance with a definite dialectical law. That is all.'[28]

Engels certainly proved his point; but in doing so he inadvertently demonstrated something else – the purely illustrative character of this so-called dialectical law and its lack of predictive value. Engels emphasized, in his polemic against Duehring, that Marx had clinched his argument without invoking the negation of the negation. In other words, this law did not in any way help Marx to reach his conclusions. We might add that it could not possibly have helped him to forecast (wrongly, as it turned out), the early demise of capitalism. Even if it were an established law of historical development – as Engels claims it is[29] – it would merely have enabled Marx, in this example, to conclude that the first negation (emergent capitalism destroying the individual property of the producer) would some time, somehow, be negated by the rise of another economic system. It would not have conveyed any information about when the second negation would occur, or what form it would take, or what the resultant socio-economic order would be like; for any combination of post-revolutionary features could be construed as the 'higher unity'. It is also clear from Engels's explanation that Marx, or for that matter any other believer in the inevitability of socialist revolution, could have arrived at the same conclusion if he had not believed in the validity of the twofold negation or of any other tenet of the dialectic.

It is curious indeed that in spite of the constant emphasis on the significance of dialectics, and on the crucial part these laws are said to play in history as well as in the human mind, Marxist textbooks hardly ever contain examples of a dialectical law actually being applied in order to reach a conclusion or decide on a course of action.[30] It may well be asked what use these laws are if they are only cited after things have been explained and argued in a straightforward, non-dialectical way, and if Marxist dialecticians (such as Engels) go to great lengths to refute the suggestion that a Marxist argument had been conducted and proved on the strength of a dialectical law.[31]

This question of the use (or uselessness) of the laws of dialectics has presumably often been asked in debates on diamat. One such discussion is related in a work of fiction – Solzhenitsyn's *First Circle*. Two inmates of a Soviet prison camp for privileged convicts (viz., experts in some field of technology) argue about dialectics in the middle of the night. Rubin, a former Party member who has fallen foul of the Stalinist establishment, has remained an orthodox Marxist and still believes in dialectics. His fellow prisoner, Sologdin, does not – at least not without important qualifications. At one stage in the discussion Sologdin says:

'If you deduce anything from these three laws . . .'
'We don't, I tell you!'
'Then what are they for? An ornament or something?'
'Will you listen to me! . . . Every decision is based on a concrete analysis of a given situation, got that? All economic teaching is based on the production unit . . . All social teaching on the analysis of the existing social circumstances.'

'Then what good are they, your three laws?' shouted Sologdin . . .
'You can do perfectly well without them, is that it? . . . If all you do is
repeat like a parrot: "negation of the negation" – then what the hell is
the use of them?'

At this point the two antagonists are interrupted by angry cell-
mates who are more interested in a good night's rest than in
dialectics, and we do not learn whether citizen Rubin ever
manages to explain the use of the three laws. The scene itself may
or may not have been taken from life; in any case, it is fair to
assume that the author, who knew his fellow intellectuals and their
problems, here speaks of an issue likely to be raised whenever a
critic of the established doctrine, in the USSR or in any other
communist country, feels safe to challenge it.

Engels, as his retort to Duehring shows, took great pains to
defend Marx against the charge of trying to predict the socialist
revolution with the help of the negation of the negation. Yet
Engels did not say in so many words that it was generally impossible to forecast events on the basis of that law; his assertion
that dialectics is a method 'of advancing from the known to the
unknown' seems to imply that he envisaged such a possibility.[32]
Strangely enough, Duehring's mistake about the meaning of the
negation of the negation in Marx's prophecy of revolution was
repeated, nearly sixty years later, by an orthodox Marxist: in *The
Theory and Practice of Socialism* (1936) John Strachey wrote that
Marx and Engels had discerned the 'general pattern' of the
negation of the negation in the history of human society, and he
added:

If this really is the pattern of history, exhibited in coil after coil, in
spiral after spiral, of ascending development, it must surely be possible
to predict the general character of the next phase? By producing the
present curve of development it must be possible to see how and when
society will return, though on a higher level, to a given point on a
previous spiral. Marx and Engels did not hesitate to put the matter to
this test. For example, they confidently predicted that the next phase
of historical development would return to the mass of the population
those means of production which had been gradually taken from them
during the last five hundred years.[33]

Ignoring the rebuke which Engels administered to Duehring, Strachey goes on to quote the relevant passage from *Das Kapital*; the context leaves no doubt that he, like Duehring, believed the prediction to be based on the dialectical law: of course, he, unlike Duehring, meant to praise and not to criticize Marx for it.

So no clear answer emerges from Marxist theory to the question of whether or not the so-called law of the negation of the negation can form a basis for predicting historical events. Marx and Engels certainly did not use it for that purpose. But dialectics is supposed to apply to all fields of knowledge, including natural science and mathematics. It is instructive to look at the examples from these sciences with which the dialecticians illustrate their theory. We shall begin with Engels, whose exposition in *Anti-Duehring* has served as a model for most authors of Marxist textbooks and other theoretical pronouncements on the subject of dialectics. It may be assumed that Engels has chosen the examples he thought most apt to demonstrate his views. It should also be borne in mind that Engels, like Mars, was a man of encyclopaedic learning and of considerable intellectual powers, and that he (unlike Marx!) was a very lucid writer. If the instances given by Engels, together with his reasoning, fail to establish the case for the validity and the relevance of dialectics, the explanation is most probably that such a case cannot be established.

In the preface to the 1885 edition of *Anti-Duehring* Engels claims that he and Marx had 'rescued conscious dialectics from German idealist philosophy' and had applied it 'in the materialist conception of nature and history'.[34] Engels amplifies this point in the (fragmentary) *Dialectics of Nature*, where he states that in developing the three laws of dialectics Hegel had approached the matter from the wrong angle:[35] his mistake lay 'in the fact that these laws are foisted on nature and history and not deduced from them'.[36] Engels goes on to point out that Hegel himself had given 'the most striking illustrations from nature and history of the dialectical laws'. In other words, in Engels's view Hegel had erred in developing these laws *a priori*, from the movement of ideas, instead of deriving them from observation and experience. Thus while Hegel gave examples from nature and history to illustrate the working of the laws whose validity he claimed to have deduced from *a priori* considerations, Engels with his examples tried to establish them, inductively, as empirical laws.

A famous example from nature is, according to Engels, so 'simple' that 'any child can understand [it]': when a grain of barley germinates, 'the grain as such', as Engels put it, 'ceases . . . to exist, it is negated, and in its place appears the plant which has arisen from it.' The plant grows, flowers, is fertilized, produces grains of barley, 'and as soon as these have ripened, the stalk dies, is in its turn negated'. The result of this negation of the negation would be more grains of barley, but 'not as a single unit but ten-, twenty-, or thirtyfold'.[37]

Although Engels believed his example to be simple enough for a child, a great many eminent men, including Marxist theoreticians, have apparently been unable to understand it. Karl Kautsky, for example, pointed out that to describe germination as the negation of the grain was tantamount to saying that a child was being negated by growing up to be an adult, although it remained the same person;[38] furthermore, the second negation in Engels's example was in no way connected with the synthesis, since the production of a large number of grains was not causally linked with the death of the stalk.[39] Generally speaking, the production of seeds and eggs and the death of the organism which produces them do not coincide: the former always precedes the latter. And we all know that an organism very often reproduces without perishing in the process.

Engels knew this, of course, but, oddly enough, failed to see that it invalidated his argument. This is how he disposed of the difficulty:

We are not concerned at the moment with the fact that with other plants and animals the process does not take such a simple form, that before they die they produce seeds, eggs or offspring not once but many times; our purpose here is only to show that the negation of the negation *really does take place* in both kingdoms of the organic world. (Engels's italics.)[40]

Could it be a rule of dialectical logic that an empirical law is regarded as proved if the sequence of events it asserts sometimes occurs but more often does not?

The dialecticians' standard examples from mathematics are no less absurd. Thus Engels argues:

Let us take any algebraic quantity whatever: for example, a. If this is negated, we get minus a. If we negate that negation, by multiplying minus a by minus a, we get plus a^2, i.e., the original positive quantity, but at a higher degree, raised to its second power . . . The negated negation is so securely entrenched in a^2 that the latter always has two square roots, namely a and minus a.[41]

In refutation of this kind of algebra it will suffice to quote Karl Popper:

Even assuming a to be a thesis and $-a$ its antithesis or negation, one might expect that the negation of the negation is $-(-a)$, i.e. a, which would not be a 'higher' synthesis, but identical with the original thesis itself. In other words, why should the synthesis be obtained just by multiplying the antithesis with itself? Why not, for example, by adding thesis and antithesis (which would yield 0)? Or by multiplying thesis and antithesis (which would yield $-a^2$ rather than a^2)? And in what sense is a^2 'higher' than a or $-a$? (Certainly not in the sense of being numerically greater, since if a equals $\frac{1}{2}$ then a^2 equals $\frac{1}{4}$.) The example shows the extreme arbitrariness with which the vague ideas of dialectic are applied.[42]

There is hardly an example presented by Engels or his fellow dialecticians that does not invite similarly devastating objections. Let us look at Engels's dialectical interpretation of the history of philosophy: according to him the philosophy of Antiquity was 'primitive, natural materialism'; as this old materialism could not clarify the relationship between mind and matter it was negated by idealism which taught the existence of a soul separable from the body – a doctrine which led to belief in immortality and to mono-theism. In the course of time this idealistic philosophy, too, 'became untenable and was negated by modern materialism', which combined the fundamentals of the old materialism with 'the whole thought-content of two thousand years' of history and of development of philosophy and natural science.[43] 'Modern materialism' appears to be equated with Engels's own interpretation of nature and of history, with the new philosophy of which, as Engels has told us, he and Marx were the only initial representatives.[44] Thus the emergence of materialist dialectics in the middle of the nineteenth century, being a case of negation of the negation, is adduced as further proof of the correctness of its own teachings: a kind of inverted ontological proof, no less tautological and no more convincing than the ontological proof of the existence of God.

Engels seemed to be aware that there was something wrong with his examples and that he had to twist and distort facts and the meaning of words in order to 'prove' that these laws actually operate. In *Anti-Duehring* he tries to answer some criticisms of the negation of the negation:[45]

Someone may object: the negation that has taken place in this case is not the real negation: I negate a grain of barley also when I grind it ... or the positive quantity *a* when I cancel it, and so on. . . . These objections are . . . the chief arguments put forward by the metaphysicians[46] against dialectics, and they are wholly worthy of the narrowmindedness of this mode of thought. Negation in dialectics does not mean simply saying no, or destroying it in any way one likes ... I must ... *so arrange* the first negation that the second remains or becomes possible. How? That depends on the particular nature of each individual case. If I grind a grain of barley ... I have carried out the first part of the action, but have made the second part impossible. Every kind of thing therefore has a peculiar way of being negated in such a manner that it gives rise to a development, and it is just the same with every kind of conception or idea. (My italics.)

This is a truly astonishing piece of question-begging. First we are told that 'nature is the proof of dialectics' and that the regular occurrence of the twofold negation in natural processes demonstrates this law's validity. Then Engels goes on to acknowledge the obvious fact that nature (as well as mathematics and, presumably, history) comprises numerous processes in which negation does *not* lead to a second negation and a higher synthesis. How does the dialectician dispose of this difficulty? He tells us that we must ignore the instances where the actual occurrence does not confirm the law of the negation of the negation, and that we should 'so arrange' the first negation that the second negation becomes possible.[47] In other words, in order to furnish the empirical 'proof' of the existence of this law we must first assume its validity: for if we don't believe in the negation of the negation to start with, we cannot 'arrange' the triad in such a way that the proof emerges. It is very strange indeed that a man of Engels's erudition and intellectual acumen should be guilty of this solecism.[48]

Thus the negation of the negation in no way lives up to the claim he makes for it – that it is 'an extremely general . . . law of development of nature, history and thought. . . .'[49] It is, in fact, neither a law nor a concept of universal validity; rather it is a formula vaguely describing a process – in history, nature, etc. – which sometimes takes place but more often does not. (It is probably less true, and certainly much vaguer, than the statement: 'In Manchester it rains on Easter Day', which will be found to be correct in some years but incorrect in others.) Or to quote Max Eastman's verdict, the phrase 'negation of the negation' is no more than 'a loose . . . analogy between certain curiosities of abstract thinking, and a way of viewing certain natural processes'.[50]

It seems pertinent to draw attention to a peculiar connotation of the negation of the negation. Some link is bound to exist between this dialectical formula and the age-old mythological-religious notion of death and resurrection, of a rejuvenated phoenix rising from the ashes, of a god achieving a more perfect reincarnation. The examples given by the Marxist dialecticians mostly lack plausibility; they are often far-fetched and artificial and sometimes altogether absurd. Far less unconvincing, as an example of the two-fold negation, than Engels's instances from mathematics or botany would be the ancient custom of killing and replacing the divine king or priest, the ritual which forms the point of departure for Sir James Frazer in his *The Golden Bough*: old age and decrepitude negate the divine life as enshrined in the material body of the incumbent. The killing both negates the process of gradual decay and also transfers the divine life to a young and vigorous successor,[51] thus establishing what dialecticians call a 'higher synthesis'. The Dalai-Lamaist belief in the Buddha's reincarnation as a healthy child could likewise be shown to fit the dialectical formula. But the most striking case of the 'higher synthesis' resulting from the negation of the negation is the death and resurrection of Jesus Christ. The crucificion negated the original incarnation: God became man but then ceased to be man; resurrection negated the negation, the killing of the divine Son of Man; the result is that the risen Christ now reigns in Heaven – with his resurrected body. It is difficult to believe that the Resurrection, as a perfect illustration of the negation of the negation, should not have occurred to Engels, Lenin and other atheistic dialecticians; it is not difficult, on the other hand, to understand their reluctance to explain the dialectical formula with the help of this example.

Quantity into quality

In the view of orthodox Marxists, the second main dialectical law, the 'transformation of quantity into quality and vice versa', is likewise derived from observation and capable of empirical confirmation. A typical transformation of quantity into quality occurs, according to Engels, when water changes from the liquid into the solid state at $0°C(32°F)$, or from the liquid into the gaseous state at $100°C$ $(212°F)$: here the rise and fall of temperature is seen as a quantitative change, while the transformation of water into steam or ice is a change in quality.[52] Marxist textbooks on dialectics contain various other examples of the same kind, mainly from natural science. For instance, in the molecular formulae of carbon compounds the quantitative addition of another element, and sometimes of several elements in the proportion of the original compound, produces a qualitatively different substance.[53] Similarly the addition of one proton or one electron in the nucleus of an atom spells transition to a different element.[54]

Marxist theorists, in particular Plekhanov, Lenin and Stalin, have made much of the fact that in most of these cases the qualitative change occurs not gradually but abruptly in one leap; and they have linked this with the observation that in society, too, the continuous gradual change in a certain direction is apt to lead to a

revolutionary eruption, a sudden 'qualitative' change. The following concise summary of this view is given in a communist
textbook:

In general, qualitative changes happen with relative suddenness – by a
leap . . . Continuous, gradual quantitative change leads at a certain point
to discontinuous, sudden qualitative change . . . If you are boiling a
kettle, the water suddenly begins to boil when boiling point is reached.
If you are scrambling eggs, the mixture in the pan suddenly 'scrambles'.
And it is the same if you are engaged in changing society. We will only
change capitalist society into socialist society when the rule of one class
is replaced by the rule of another class – and this is a radical transformation, a leap to a new style of society, a revolution.[55]

The 'dialectical' laws of nature are thus invoked to refute the
revisionist concept of a peaceful, gradual, evolutionary transition
from capitalism to socialism. But it is a characteristic of Marxian
dialectics that all kinds of actual development can be adduced as
proof of dialectical principles. The theory recognizes the obvious
fact that a change in quality does not necessarily occur as a sudden
leap. There is a qualitative difference between a thick layer of snow
and a snow cover six feet deep; yet the latter may be the result of
gradual, quantitative accumulation, without any leaps or abrupt
changes. Or to take an example from the Bible: when Jacob and
his house left Canaan to dwell in Egypt his was a large family of
seventy; when their descendants left Egypt to return to Canaan
they were a people. Gradual, quantitative increase had first turned
the family into a clan or a tribe, and had eventually produced a
nation. There were no discernible 'leaps' in this process of
quantity's being transformed into quality.

Marxist-Leninist theory has produced a socio-economic equivalent. In an essay Stalin wrote a few years before his death he
asserted that the law of 'transition from an old quality to a new by
means of an explosion' was fully effective in an 'antagonistic class
society', while social and economic developments in a non-
antagonistic society – the society resulting from socialist revolution
– would be gradual, without any breach of continuity; they
would proceed 'not by way of upheavals, but by way of gradual
changes, the old . . . changing its nature in adaptation to the new

... while the new does not simply destroy the old, but infiltrates into it, changing its nature and its functions, without smashing its form, but using it for the development of the new.'[56] Thus the transition from 'socialism' as the first post-revolutionary stage, during which a person's earnings would still depend on working performance, to 'communism' as the state of superabundance ('to each according to his needs') would be a peaceful and gradual one, not marked by abrupt leaps or revolutionary upheavals.

Engels and his fellow dialecticians are certainly right to the extent that there is a correlation between quantity and quality. It would indeed be difficult to think of a change in quality in which a quantitative change had not played some part. This 'transformation of quantity into quality' is undoubtedly a common occurrence; but is it a scientific law? If we tried to formulate it as a law expressing the relationship between quantitative and qualitative changes, we would merely produce a self-evident statement like: 'If a thing keeps changing in one direction (by getting bigger or smaller, hotter or colder, etc.) it will eventually become something different from what it was to begin with.'[57] Thus we get an assertion which is trite to the point of being meaningless. Like the dialectic triad, this law about quantity and quality will never help any one to reach any conclusion: it will never supply a criterion for making the right distinction, for it does not tell us in what circumstances a quantitative change will mean a change in quality. If water is heated to a certain point, it will turn into steam; if a boy keeps alive and growing, he will become an adolescent and then a man; if a tribe multiplies, it may become a nation. In order to know *when* these qualitative changes occur (if that can be determined at all) we have to study the laws of physics, of physiology, of sociology; to some extent the change in the term used is purely a matter of semantics. The fact that in all these cases a relationship exists between quantitative and qualitative changes is devoid of any theoretical or practical significance.[58]

The futility of operating with these dialectical laws stands out in relief in the feeble attempts which the Marxists sometimes make to demonstrate their validity. Thus in December 1939 Leon Trotsky wrote an article with which he intervened in a debate then going on in the ranks of the Socialist Workers Party, the American section of the Trotskyist Fourth International. After setting forth his interpretation of materialistic dialectics, and dealing at some length with the 'transformation of quantity into quality', he stated: 'To determine at the right moment the critical point where quantity changes into quality is one of the most important and difficult tasks in all spheres of knowledge including sociology.'[59] Inasmuch as this is true it merely illustrates the uselessness of the dialectical law. It is not invariably true: it is not normally difficult to determine at what point water has turned into steam or ice. But it is certainly difficult, if not impossible, to say when a boy has become an adolescent or an adolescent a man, or when a large tribe has grown into a nation. In all these cases observation and the laws of natural science or of sociology might yield the right answer; the dialectic is no help at all.

Another point is of interest here. The issue of this debate amongst the Trotskyists of the USA was the class nature of the Soviet Union. The party was divided on the question of whether the relentless bureaucratic degeneration of the Soviet state under Stalin had destroyed its proletarian character: was Russia still a 'workers' state' in December 1939, after the Moscow purge trials, after the pact with Hitler on the eve of the Second World War, after the Soviet invasions of Poland and Finland? In 'dialectical' parlance, the point at issue was whether the quantitative changes in the direction of counter-revolution or of a Soviet Thermidor had gone far enough to produce the qualitative change of liquidating the workers' state and substituting a bureaucratic, capitalist, quasi-bourgeois regime. Trotsky sided with those who held that the USSR was and would remain a workers' state so long as the means of production continued to be state property. The opposing faction included some militants who rejected dialectics,[60] but most of those who disagreed with Trotsky on this issue of the nature of the Soviet Union shared his belief in the dialectic and its laws. The application of the same dialectical rules and the same dialectical methodology evidently did not prevent the two sides from coming to opposite, and mutually incompatible, conclusions. This observation, incidentally, applies to all the numerous factional struggles, splits and schisms which have afflicted the Marxist (or Marxist-Leninist) movement for the past hundred years. The inner-party antagonists usually protest their loyalty to the dialectic, and each side accuses the other of abandoning dialectics and adopting, as the jargon has it, an 'undialectical' or 'metaphysical' approach.

The truth is that although Marxist literature is replete with the dialectical vocabulary, Marxists have never seriously tried to resolve any issue with the help of the dialectical laws. C. Wright Mills was right in saying that these laws are 'ways of talking about matters *after* these matters have been explained in ordinary ways of discourse and proof', and that 'Marx himself never *explained* anything by the laws of dialectics'.[61] The first volume of *Das Kapital* – the only volume Marx himself completed – contains two references to dialectics; both of these corroborate Mills's point.

One of these passages has already been discussed in this essay.[62] We have seen that Engels indignantly rejected Duehring's (indeed unfounded) allegation that Marx had had recourse to the dialectical law of the negation of the negation to prove the inevitability of capitalist collapse. In the other passage, which gave rise to a similar argument between Engels and Duehring, Marx deals with the question of when, and in what conditions, a sum of money turns into capital. He explains, by way of arithmetic and economic analysis, that a man who seeks to invest his money profitably must buy the labour power of not just one or two but several labourers (in his example, eight) to qualify for the designation 'capitalist'; otherwise his own living standard would not be higher than that of his workers. Having developed this argument Marx goes on to say that the result is a confirmation of the Hegelian law 'that merely quantitative differences beyond a certain point pass into qualitative changes'.[63] This Marxian reasoning, too, had been misunderstood by Duehring; he attributed to Marx the view that a sum would become capital by quantitative increase alone, i.e. by rising above a certain amount. Against this Engels pointed out that Marx had proved his contention on the strength of economic argument, without reference to the law concerning quantity's transformation into quality, and that he had merely remarked *afterwards*, in an aside as it were, that his conclusions showed the correctness of what Hegel had said about the relationship between quantity and quality.[64] Here, again, Engels obviously attached importance to the fact that Marx had clinched his argument without invoking any law of dialectics.

It would seem, then, that prisoner Sologdin in Solzhenitsyn's novel is not far wrong in describing the dialectical laws – or at least two of them, the negation of the negation and the transformation of quantity into quality – as useless ornaments.[65]

Now what about the 'vice versa' of the quantity—quality relationship – the alleged rule that qualitative changes lead to changes in quantity? This process is clearly not simply the reverse of the other one, of quantity turning into quality. Water getting hotter and hotter, and eventually turning into steam, is a change from quantity to quality; but steam condensing when the temperature is lowered, and re-assuming the liquid state, is likewise a case of quantitative change resulting in a change in quality. The same goes for melting ice and freezing water. Examples of quality turning into quantity are, indeed, not easy to think of; the rare examples given in Marxist writings are involved and obscure.

According to the Soviet *Textbook of Marxist Philosophy* (prepared in the early 1930s by the Leningrad Institute of Philosophy under the direction of M. Shirokov[66]) the process of capitalist industrialization illustrates the correlation of quantity and quality in both directions: 'The joint work of many workmen' in a factory 'is qualitatively distinct from small-scale craft. And this new quality creates a new quantity' in the shape of higher productivity and enormously increased output.[67] The *Textbook* concludes: 'That new quality which belongs to large-scale production . . . has created a new quantity; quality has gone over into quantity.'

In the view of the authors of the *Textbook*, a speech by Stalin on the success of collectivization in Soviet agriculture contains another example of the same 'dialectical transition from quality to quantity'. This is what Stalin is reported to have said:

The simple concentration of the peasants' implements within the collective farms had an effect not contemplated on the basis of our earlier experience. How was this effect manifested? In the fact that the transition to collective-farming methods gave an increase of the area under crop of from 30 per cent to 40 per cent and even 50 per cent. How do we explain this astounding result? By the fact that the peasants, who were powerless under the conditions of individualistic work, have been converted into a very great power by the concentration of their implements and by uniting into collective farms.[68]

There is no need to pursue the matter any further. The 'examples' of quality turning into quantity amply demonstrate the irrelevance of this aspect of the quantity—quality relationship and the uselessness of the law as a basis of investigation or prediction. Here again the dialectical terminology seems designed to obfuscate rather than elucidate the point at issue.

The unity of opposites

Marxists usually describe the 'interpenetration of opposites' as the most important of the three main laws; according to Lenin it is the 'kernel' of dialectics. Yet it often gets cavalier treatment in Marxist textbooks. Engels's *Anti-Duehring* devotes much space to the other two laws but mentions the interpenetration of opposites only in passing. The same is true of Strachey's *Theory and Practice of Socialism*. The terminological vagueness and ideological looseness which characterizes Marxist dialectics in general is most noticeable where theoretical writings enlarge on this particular law. Dialecticians assert that opposites interpenetrate in the sense that each phenomenon or process somehow includes its own opposite. But instead of 'interpenetration' they often speak of the 'unity' or even the 'identity' of opposites; and there is also some confusion between the terms 'contradictory' and 'opposite'. Where examples are given of the way this law operates we find that it overlaps with the negation of the negation.

Hegel considered the unity of opposites to be a phenomenon of universal validity:

Positive and negative . . . are at bottom the same: the name of either might be transferred to the other . . . Debts and assets are not two particular, self-subsisting species of property: what is negative to the debtor, is positive to the creditor. A way to the east is also a way to the west . . . The north pole of the magnet cannot be without the south pole, and vice versa . . . Similarly, in electricity the positive and the negative are not two diverse and independent fluids . . . Inorganic nature is not to be considered merely something else than organic nature, but the necessary antithesis of it. Both are in essential relation to one another. . . .[69]

Class relations in capitalist society are often cited by Marxists as an example of interpenetration. The Soviet *Textbook of Marxist Philosophy* (which has been quoted above in a different context) puts it like this:

In capitalist society, the bourgeoisie is connected with the proletariat, the proletariat with the bourgeoisie; neither of these two classes can develop without the other, because the bourgeoisie cannot exist without exploiting the labour of others and the hired proletariat cannot exist without selling its labour power to the capitalist, seeing that itself it does not possess the means of production.[70]

Thus bourgeoisie and proletariat exist and act only inasmuch as they complement each other; the existence of either depends on that of the other.

On the face of it this interpenetration of opposites again expresses a characteristic of certain phenomena, a reciprocal or complementary relationship between contradictory aspects, but, like the negation of the negation and the transformation of quantity into quality and vice versa, it is not a law; it does not state that certain combinations of circumstances will produce certain consequences. Marxists have, however, tried to formulate general rules based on this particular relationship between opposites, and on the notion of conflict between them. The following 'definition' appears in another communist standard textbook, *Foundations of*

Marxist Philosophy, by a group of Soviet Academicians and other scholars, headed by F. V. Konstantinov:

> The law of the unity and the struggle of opposites states that all things, phenomena and processes comprise contradictory aspects and tendencies which are in conflict with each other; the struggle of the opposites imparts an internal impulse to development and leads to the growth of the contradictions which, at a certain stage, are resolved by the passing of the old and the emergence of the new.[71]

This is obviously too vague and too abstract to be called a law. It could never form the basis of a conditional prediction. The formula also contains a false generalization: it is simply not true that '*all* things . . . comprise contradictory aspects and tendencies which are in conflict with each other'. Most concrete, inanimate objects comprise no such aspects or tendencies (which 'opposites' could be said to 'struggle' in a teapot or in a ham sandwich?). A further defect is the imprecise wording: 'contradictory aspects' and 'opposites' are not necessarily the same thing, yet they are equated in that definition and, indeed, in most dialectical disquisitions. The second half of the definition seems to be a paraphrase of another law of dialectics, that of the negation of the negation.

Last and most important, the definition covers, at most, certain kinds of contradictions and interpenetrating opposites, viz. those occurring in animate nature, in human society and history and perhaps in human thought. For it is only in these fields that a conflict or struggle leading to 'the new' replacing 'the old' (and outdated) can materialize. Whether we can really speak of contradictions or opposites in inanimate nature is open to doubt. It has been argued by some critics that these so-called contradictions exist not so much in the things themselves as in the human mind and in the words in which human feelings and thoughts are couched. The communist textbook from which the above definition is taken indignantly rejects this argument, denouncing the 'frantic attempts' by 'modern bourgeois philosophers' to disprove 'the dialectical doctrine of the contradictions' and to 'transpose the contradictions into human consciousness and thought'.[72] Be that as it may, it would seem impossible and, indeed, somewhat comic to speak of 'conflict' or struggle between such 'identical opposites' as (to take some of Hegel's examples) the north and south pole of a magnet or inorganic and organic nature.

Lenin who, as we have seen, regarded the interpenetration of opposites as the kernel of dialectics, listed examples from various fields of science; he considered these pairs of opposites to be typical:

In Mathematics: Plus and Minus; differential and integral calculus.
    In Mechanics: Action and reaction.
    In Physics: Positive and negative electricity.
    In Chemistry: Combination and dissociation of atoms.
    In Social Science: The class struggle.[73]

Only the example from social science would be covered by the definition given in the communist textbook on Marxist philosophy: this is the kind of contradiction which could conceivably be resolved by 'the disappearance of the old and the emergence of the new'. As for the examples from mathematics and natural science, no Marxist-Leninist dialectician has as yet, to the best of my knowledge, seriously suggested that there is a conflict or struggle between plus and minus, or that positive and negative electricity fight one another until the more progressive of the two (whichever that may be) eventually emerges victorious and eliminates its defeated opponent. Thus there seems to be some confusion among dialectical materialists as to the meaning and scope of this law of the unity and the struggle of opposites.

Confusion is not made any less confounded by the dialecticians' habit of varying their terms and using words with different meanings to express the same idea. Contrary to normal usage, terms like 'interpenetration', 'unity' and 'identity of opposites' are treated as synonyms. For instance, Lenin, in his essay 'On the Question of Dialectics', speaks of the 'identity of opposites' but adds: 'It would be more correct, perhaps, to say "their unity", although the difference between the terms identity and unity is not particularly important here. In a certain way they are both correct.'[74] And 'interpenetration', presumably, also means much the same. What does one make of this cryptic pronouncement? Such opposites as proletariat and bourgeoisie may be said to interpenetrate in a fashion: that makes sense, though nothing of importance seems to follow from it. And if one suspends one's dislike of the flabbiness of dialectical terminology, one could also accept the use of the term 'unity' in this context: proletariat and bourgeoisie, taken together, somehow embody the totality of what Marxists call 'capitalist relations of production'; they are, so to speak, the two sides of the coin of bourgeois industrial society. But in what sense are antagonistic classes, or any other opposites, identical? Are communism and capitalism identical? Or class struggle and class collaboration?[75]

All or nearly all attempts by the spokesmen of diamat to explain this mysterious relationship of opposites add to the existing confusion. Although the unity of opposites is stated to be the kernel, the essential aspect of dialectics, we are also told by Lenin and his disciples that this all-important unity is 'conditional, temporary, transitory and relative', while the *struggle* of opposites is 'absolute'.[76] We are further informed that to regard unity or identity as a 'reconciliation of opposites' is a 'direct perversion of Marxism' and a Menshevik heresy, aimed at playing down class hostility.[77] This suggests that 'reconciliation' denotes a closer relationship than 'unity' or 'identity'. More bewildering still is a quotation which the *Textbook* of the 1930s regards as appropriate for elucidating the phenomenon: it is an extract from a speech by Kaganovich, Stalin's erstwhile right-hand man:

What exactly does the unity of opposites mean in the ordinary language of our party? The unity of opposites in actuality means not to be afraid of difficulties. Not to be afraid of those contradictions of life which spring up on our journey, but instead to conquer them with Bolshevik energy and staunchness.[78]

Which must have made the meaning of the unity of opposites crystal-clear to even the dimmest member of the Soviet Communist Party.

Contributions to this debate have also come from the late Mao Tse-tung. They show that however great the ideological differences may be between the Marxists-Leninists of Peking and those of Moscow, there is complete unity (the unity of opposites?) about the interpretation of the dialectical law. Thus in a speech before the Supreme State Conference of the Chinese People's Republic in 1957 Mao dealt with the unity of opposites in terms which partly repeat and partly paraphrase the formulae of the Muscovite textbooks. He went on to distinguish between 'antagonistic' contradictions, which he declared to be typical of capitalist and earlier societies and which could only be resolved by revolution, and the 'non-antagonistic' contradictions prevailing under socialism – contradictions to be 'resolved one after the other by the socialist system itself'.[79] This distinction recalls, and seems to be based on, an assertion made by Stalin in the context of another dialectical law, viz. that qualitative changes are abrupt and explosive in antagonistic societies, but gradual and continuous in non-antagonistic ones.[80] But while it is fairly clear what Stalin means by 'antagonistic' and 'non-antagonistic' societies (though not all will share his professed view that the USSR is a non-antagonistic society), Mao's terminology is rather more obscure. The main difficulty stems from his unorthodox use of such words as 'contradictions' and 'opposites'. For example, in the same speech he refers to economic planning and to the – pretty obvious – fact that the production plan must aim at ensuring the satisfaction of the needs of society. In Mao's diamat language this is called 'resolving the contradiction between production and needs'. This is how he explains the matter:

Every year our country draws up an economic plan in order to . . . achieve a balance between production and needs. Balance is nothing but a temporary, relative unity of opposites. By the end of the year this balance . . . is upset by the struggle of opposites; the unity undergoes a change, balance becomes imbalance, unity becomes disunity, and once again it is necessary to work out a balance and unity for the next year . . . Sometimes, contradictions arise and the balance is upset because our subjective arrangements do not correspond to objective reality; this is what we call making a mistake. The ceaseless emergence and ceaseless resolution of contradictions is the dialectical law of the development of things.[81]

The actual process described in this passage is straightforward enough, yet the dialectical jargon has obscured it to the point of near-incomprehensibility. For example, why are 'production' and the 'needs of society' supposed to be 'opposites'? And in what sense can they be said to 'struggle' when a new annual plan has to be drawn up? The whole point of this confusing vocabulary seems to be to sacrifice intelligibility to a demonstration of the universal validity of the dialectical law.

Mao's treatment of concepts like freedom and democracy shows the same tendency to squeeze everything into the pattern of dialectical formulae. In another passage in the same speech he obviously meant to convey that the need for discipline imposes certain limitations upon individual freedom, and that democracy involves acceptance of majority decisions taken by an elected central body. The Chairman put it like this:

Within the ranks of the people, democracy is correlative with central-ism and freedom with discipline. They are the two opposites of a single entity, contradictory as well as united ... This unity of democracy and centralism, of freedom and discipline, constitutes our democratic cen-tralism. Under this system, the people enjoy extensive democracy and freedom, but at the same time they have to keep within the bounds of socialist discipline. All this is well understood by the broad masses of the people.[82]

Maybe it is, but it is almost certain that the broad masses would understand it better still without the dialectical mumbo-jumbo (although the masses, or at least some individual Chinese, might then become aware of a 'contradiction' Mao Tse-tung had not mentioned: the contradiction between the theory and the reality of freedom and democracy in Communist China). It is, of course, always possible to complicate simple notions with the help of an esoteric phraseology. The Concise Oxford Dictionary defines 'grey' as the 'intermediate between black and white'. Mao and his fellow dialecticians would no doubt define it as a shade or colour expressing 'the unity and the struggle of black and white'.

The upshot is that this law of the interpenetration (or unity, or identity) of opposites is as useless as the other two main laws of dialectics for solving problems or reaching conclusions. The voluminous writings in which Marxist dialecticians have expounded their so-called science contain one solid (but non-original) suggestion for scientists, historians, politicians, etc., a method which Marxists have described as dialectical but which is really simply a matter of common sense: the ability and willingness to view phenomena not in isolation but as interlocking parts of a continuous process of evolution.

The Trotsky-Burnham controversy

Confusion, lack of semantic precision and *non sequiturs* mark most attempts by Marxist theorists to demonstrate the practical value of any of the dialectical laws. Engels was not the only outstanding Marxist thinker to commit elementary errors of logic in 'explaining' the working of these laws. In the debate between Trotsky and his followers in the USA about the class nature of the Soviet Union the great revolutionary put forward the most incongruous arguments and examples.[83] This is how he tried to prove his thesis that people, and even animals, sometimes apply the law of the transformation of quantity into quality unconsciously: 'A housewife knows that a certain amount of salt flavours soup agreeably, but that added salt makes the soup unpalatable. Consequently, an illiterate peasant woman guides herself in cooking soup by the Hegelian law of the transformation of quantity into quality.'[84]

What this example really illustrates is not the use of dialectics in daily life but – once again – the extreme vagueness and arbitrariness of dialectical terminology. A rule which every good cook (male or female, literate or illiterate, peasant or town-dweller) follows is that certain ingredients to a meal are good when added in moderation but noxious in excessive quantities. *Mutatis mutandis* this rule applies to many other fields of life, and it has nothing to do with quantity turning into quality. Many people like a hot bath; above a certain temperature the bath water might be unpleasantly hot for some but just right for others or, alternatively, at a lower temperature the water is too cold for some but enjoy-able for others. Is that a change in quality? According to Engels such a change occurs when water turns from the liquid into the solid or the gaseous state. In Trotsky's view the quality of the soup changes when the soup gets too salty – and, presumably, the quality of the bath when the water gets too hot or too cold: the 'qualitative' change would depend on the subjective taste and inclinations of the individual consumer. The difference between quantity and quality is blurred in Trotsky's examples; the terms become meaningless.

But this is not the full extent of the absurdity in Trotsky's reasoning. The passage about 'unconscious dialecticians' continues:

Even animals arrive at their conclusions not only on the basis of the Aristotelian syllogism but also on the basis of the Hegelian dialectic. Thus a fox is aware that quadrupeds and birds are nutritious and tasty. On sighting a hare, a rabbit or a hen, a fox concludes: this particular creature belongs to the tasty and nutritive type, and – chases after the prey. We have here a complete syllogism, although the fox, we may suppose, never read Aristotle. When the same fox, however, encoun-ters the first animal which exceeds it in size, for example a wolf, it quickly concludes that quantity passes into quality, and turns to flee.

This 'example' shows into what logical muddle a highly intelli-gent person can subside when devotion to ideological orthodoxy obliges him to regard dialectic as a form of logic. Experience and/or instinct tells the fox that hares and chickens are edible and tasty. Experience and/or instinct tells him that wolves are dangerous to foxes. In either case the conclusion which determines the fox's reaction to the appearance of the animal in question can take the form of a syllogism. Quantity or size do not enter into it. Trotsky's assumption that an animal must be afraid of another animal whose size exceeds its own may or may not follow from Hegelian dia-lectics: it certainly does not square with the facts of zoology. A wolf does not run away from a horse – quite the reverse. A sparrow does not fear a pigeon, nor does a duckling flee from a swan. Trotsky's dialectical fox would, presumably, take to his heels at the sight of a harmless, herbivorous cow but would dis-regard, while fleeing from the ruminant, a venomous little adder in the grass. If the fox, before dying from the snake bite, retained some lucidity of mind he might sadly reflect that rather than relying on Hegelian, Marxian or Trotskyite dialectics he would have been better employed in learning the hard facts of zoology: then he would have known that the transformation of quantity into quality is an absolutely useless criterion in judging another beast's appetites, that a larger animal can be quite innocuous and a smaller one quite deadly.

So much for the attempt – rare in Marxist literature – to give concrete examples of conclusions reached on the basis not of formal but of 'dialectical' logic. The passage concerning 'unconscious dialecticians' originally formed part of an 'Open Letter to Comrade Burnham'. In his reply James Burnham said that he at first thought this passage was only some kind of joke, but then became convinced that it was also meant seriously. It certainly was. Trotsky, a brilliant and witty writer, never missed the chance of a humorous aside, but he would never write a lengthy paragraph just for the sake of being funny. In this case he evidently wished to prove what he considered to be an important point. What he really proved is that a man of genuis can talk nonsense when trying to make sense of Engelsian dialectics.

There are sound reasons for dwelling especially on Trotsky's interpretation of diamat. For one thing, he was one of the greatest Marxist theoreticians of the twentieth century – probably the greatest after the disappearance of Luxemburg and Lenin. Second, he was a sincere revolutionary and a convinced Marxist, unlike Stalin and his underlings, cynical opportunists who never hesitated to twist Marxist principles when it suited their tactical ends; for them, dialectics proved an appropriate method of hiding the grossest betrayals behind pseudo-revolutionary verbiage. Trotsky never preached what he did not believe in; and for all his juggling with the dialectical vocabulary he never used dialectics to propagate theories or policies he knew to be inconsistent with Marxist doctrine. Lastly and most importantly, Trotsky's formulae and the way in which he conducted the debate on dialectics indicate that, in his subconscious, Marxist orthodoxy had assumed the character of religious dogma. His stand in the 1940 debate, and in particular his reactions to Burnham's heresies, reflect the transition from Marxism to Marxianity, which had then been in progress for nearly half a century.[85]

In his reply to Trotsky's 'Open Letter', James Burnham paid tribute to his antagonist's stylistic brilliance and his 'unconquerable devotion to the socialist ideal'.[86] At the same time he exposed Trotsky's obvious ignorance of more recent developments in philosophy. In the 'Open Letter' Trotsky had written: 'I know of two systems of logic worthy of attention: the logic of Aristotle (formal logic) and the logic of Hegel (the dialectic) . . . Perhaps you will call my attention to those works which should supplant the system of dialectical materialism for the proletariat? . . . None exist.'[87]

Burnham retorted: 'Comrade Trotsky . . . where have you been all these years? Since Hegel wrote . . . science has progressed more than during the entire preceding history of mankind. During that same period . . . logic has undergone a revolutionary transformation . . . Do you wish me to prepare a reading list? It would be long. . . .'[88]

Burnham went on to list a number of works, including *Principia Mathematica* by Russell and Whitehead ('the historic turning point in modern logic'), and added: 'In all these works you will find scarcely a single reference to Hegelian (or Marxian) dialectics.'

Trotsky never bothered to answer Burnham's arguments. He merely remarked, in a letter to political friends, that Burnham's paper was a rehash, 'with some "modernized" illustrations', of what critics of dialectical materialism had written in the nineteenth century:[89] 'The thousand and first professorial refutation has no more worth than all its precedents.'[90] But an oblique reference in another letter to friends to what Burnham had said about post-Hegelian philosophy is highly significant. Trotsky commended articles written by two members of the anti-Burnham faction in the American Party who had criticized Burnham's eulogy of *Principia Mathematica*. He went on to stress the importance of the philosophical debate within the Party: 'We should now continue systematically and seriously our theoretical campaign in favour of dialectical materialism.' Evidently he no longer held that no post-Hegelian system of logic was worthy of attention. The impression one is left with is that Trotsky knew little or nothing, to start with, about modern developments in logic. He would anyway not have been prepared to judge logical symbolism on its merits: on learning that this contemporary work was incompatible with Marxian dialectics he decided that a campaign must be waged against it. In the same way a member of the hierarchy of the medieval Church might have pronounced his anathema against a new doctrine he was not acquainted with, simply because he knew it to be inconsistent with established dogma.

A number of passages in Trotsky's 'Open Letter' are redolent of the terms in which some ecclesiastical authority might warn the faithful against the dangers of heretical teachings. Thus, after discussing Burnham's challenge to 'the philosophy of scientific socialism', Trotsky continued:

Since in the course of the factional struggle the question has been posed point-blank, we shall say, turning to all members of the party, especially the youth: beware of the infiltration of bourgeois scepticism into your ranks . . . Bear in mind that the method of scientific socialism is dialectical materialism. Occupy yourselves with serious study! Study Marx, Engels, Plekhanov, Lenin and Franz Mehring. This is a hundred times more important for you than the study of tendentious, sterile and slightly ludicrous treatises on the conservatism of Cannon. [Cannon was leader of the anti-Burnham majority in the Socialist Workers Party.[91]]

To suggest the drawing up of an *index librorum prohibitorum* might have been the next step.

Burnham's response was the typical one of a man who had resolved to defy the dogma: 'You issue many warnings to the young comrades of our movement. I add an ominous warning to the list: beware, beware, comrades, of anyone or any doctrine that tells you that any man, or group of men, holds a monopoly on truth, or on the ways of getting truth.'[92]

In the debate on the class character of the Soviet state which led to the clash between Trotsky and Burnham about dialectics, both sides started from the same set of premises. Like all Marxists, they accepted the doctrine of the state as an instrument of class rule, which meant that the bourgeoisie was the ruling class in a capitalist state while rule by the proletariat was the chief characteristic of a 'workers' state'; they were also agreed that the Russian October Revolution had established a proletarian regime but that the bureaucratic degeneration of the state apparatus had reached extreme proportions by the end of the 1930s. There the agreement ended. Trotsky and the majority of the US Socialist Workers Party maintained that owing to the Soviet bureaucracy's failure to restore private property in production, the USSR was still a workers' state – despite glaring inequalities, repression, massive slave labour, etc.: therefore – and this was the crux of the problem in the context of the 1939–40 world situation and the Soviet–Finnish war – it was still the revolutionary duty of socialists in the USA and elsewhere unconditionally to defend the Soviet Union. Much dialectical jargon was employed by Trotsky in this argument. He spoke of the 'contradiction' between the social basis of the Soviet state and the bureaucratic character of the ruling caste, and of the degeneration of the proletarian regime, which had not yet passed 'from the quantitative stage to the qualitative'. He described Marxism without the dialectic as 'a clock without a spring' and stressed the importance of the dialectical laws for this controversy; but he failed to demonstrate in what way his conclusions were based on these laws.

The Socialist Workers Party minority faction, led by the dialectician Max Shachtman and the non-dialectician (or 'metaphysician', according to Engels) James Burnham, rejected the slogan of the defence of the USSR. Shachtman and Burnham regarded Soviet foreign policies as starkly imperialist and refused to attach any importance to state ownership of the means of production, seeing that the state apparatus itself was firmly in the hands of Stalin and his clique. They pointed out that the Soviet state and party bureaucracy both controlled the country's production machinery and decided on the distribution of the social product – largely in favour of its own members and hangers-on; hence the 'state-owned' means of production were really the property of the ruling bureaucracy. This reasoning was in line with the Marxist interpretation of nationalization under a bourgeois regime. In a capitalist state, the theory said, enterprises such as the postal services, the railways or the coal mines do not become national property when they are 'nationalized' but pass from individual or company ownership into the collective ownership of the ruling capitalist class as a whole. In the USSR, Trotsky's opponents in the inner-Party debate argued, there had been a development in the opposite direction. Genuinely socialist property, as established after the October Revolution, had become the collective property of the new ruling class, the state and party bureaucracy, which had expropriated the Soviet working class both politically and economically.[93] Those members of the Shachtman-Burnham group who still used the dialectical vocabulary asserted that this emergence of a new ruling class was a typical case of quantity passing into quality. The progressive degeneration of the workers' state had reached the point where the workers' state as such had disappeared and had been replaced by a new type of state, a state-capitalist, or bureaucratic, or 'managerial' state, as James Burnham was eventually to call it.

In rejecting the reasoning of Shachtman and Burnham, Trotsky did not deny the economic and political dominance of Soviet bureaucracy: indeed it was he who, during the preceding fifteen years or so, had untiringly drawn attention to, and denounced, the growing might of the bureaucrats and the disfranchisement of the workers. But he contended that the bureaucracy was not a 'class' in the sense in which Marxists understood the term. Hence it could not be a ruling class: it was a ruling oligarchy and, as such, a transitory phenomenon. Trotsky professed to be almost certain that the existing set-up in the USSR would not continue much longer: there would be either a return to capitalism – the reintroduction of private property in industry and agriculture – or else a political revolution leading to the dethronement of the Stalinist bureaucracy and the restoration of proletarian democracy.[94] 'Might we not,' Trotsky wrote in September 1939, 'place ourselves in a ludicrous position if we affixed to the Bonapartist[95] oligarchy the nomenclature of a new ruling class just a few years, or even a few months, prior to its inglorious downfall?'[96] Here again the dialectical method proved to be a poor vehicle for historical prediction.

James Burnham, who at that time accepted Marxist sociology but rejected dialectics, maintained that the revolutionary answer to the concrete questions about the nature and the defence of the USSR must depend on a marxist analysis of objective factors in which dialectical formulae could play no part. He was undoubtedly right in disputing both Trotsky's prophecy about the impending demise of bureaucratic rule in the USSR and his insistence on the relevance of dialectics for resolving the issues of the nature of the Soviet state and of its defence by socialists in the event of war. Both sides in the controversy might well have accepted Trotsky's pronouncement on the 'contradictory' nature of the USSR where positive features – a nationalized and planned economy, which is progressive from the Marxist point of view – coexisted with the reactionary bureaucratic superstructure: this would not decide the issue of the proletarian character of the Soviet state, since capitalist society, too, comprises both 'progressive' and 'reactionary' elements.[97] Neither the so-called law of the transformation of quantity into quality, which Trotsky invoked in the course of the argument, nor any other dialectical law or concept provided a method of settling the matter one way or another.

The psychological significance of Marxist dialectics

The dispute about the social character of the USSR ended in a split among Trotsky's followers in the United States, the Burnham-Shachtman faction founding the break-away Workers' Party. And there was a curious aftermath. James Burnham, who had cogently argued against the relevance of dialectics in the context of revolutionary Marxism, suddenly effected an about-turn: in May 1940, a few months after the conclusion of his debate with Trotsky, he announced his break with Marxism and left the new party he had helped to create. In his letter of resignation he declared that he had been wrong and Trotsky right in *one* respect: 'Dialectical materialism, though scientifically meaningless, is psychologically and historically an integral part of Marxism.'[98] He went on to outline his newly acquired, non-Marxist views, which subsequently led him to write *The Managerial Revolution*.[99]

In this letter Burnham did not explain what he meant when he said that dialectical materialism was 'psychologically' an integral part of Marxism. A passage in *The Managerial Revolution* seems to indicate that, like Eugen Duehring and John Strachey, he mistakenly thought the Marxist belief in the inevitability of socialism was based on the Hegelian triad and the negation of the negation.[100] But whatever the real meaning of Burnham's statement, it is, in a sense, profoundly true to say that diamat is *psychologically* essential to Marxism. Indeed, the truth of this statement is even more obvious today than it was in 1940 when Burnham made it.

The history of post-Marxian developments in Marxist theory is largely a history of elaborate attempts to explain the failure of Marx's predictions to come true. The dialectical notion of contradiction and negation as fundamental aspects of progress, and of history proceeding in a zigzag or spiral movement, together with the haziness and obscurity of the dialectical vocabulary, have proved particularly apt for explaining away the refusal of history to bear out Marxian prophecies. And while the adoption (with some modifications) of Hegelian dialectics by the founding fathers of 'scientific socialism' was perhaps largely an accident,[101] it must seem doubtful whether Marxism as an ideology would have survived, let alone spread and grown more powerful, if its principal spokesmen and propagandists had not been able to fall back on dialectical terms and tenets in defence of the original doctrine.

In the early development of a religion dogmatic orthodoxy often emerges or gains strength in the fight against what fundamentalists consider to be heresy. In the early history of Marxism *after* Marx and Engels it was the 'revisionist' challenge, about the turn of the century, which introduced dogmatism into the theoretical system. Revisionism, as expounded by its chief protagonist Eduard Bernstein, was a rational reaction to one of the first collisions between Marxist assumptions and the apparent trend of history. Marx's predictions seemed to have been falsified in several respects: there had been no major recession in the preceding two decades and consequently no mass unemployment; working-class standards of living had risen owing partly to a rise in real wages and partly (in Germany) to the social welfare legislation initiated by Bismarck in the 1880s; the middle layers in society, the people between big capitalists and workers, were not disappearing but, on the contrary, becoming more numerous and moderately prosperous. Bernstein's main conclusion was that the class struggle was bound to lose intensity and that socialism would be the end-result not of violent upheavals and civil war but of a peaceful process of gradual transformation.

The ensuing controversy was doubly concerned with the problem of dialectics. Bernstein had linked his 'revision' of Marxian economics and Marx's historic determinism with an attack on dialectical materialism.[102] The defenders of orthodoxy in turn tended to see an intrinsic connection between Bernstein's rejection of dialectics and his economic and political heresies, and to over-emphasize, in their anti-revisionist polemics, the importance of materialist dialectics.[103] Besides, the dialectic furnished a ready-made answer to the revisionists' critique of orthodox Marxism: the rise in living standards and the slackening of the class war at the close of the nineteenth century were part of one of the brief regressive phases in the march of history: this temporary negation of the trend towards intensification of the class struggle and towards increasing working-class misery would soon be negated, and the next stage would be marked by the return, at a higher level, of acute class confrontation – and so on, until the final showdown.[104]

The dispute within the Trotskyist ranks about the class nature of the USSR was a sort of repetition, on a smaller scale, of the debate held some forty years previously, between revisionists and orthodox Marxists. The issue was again an unfulfilled Marxist (or rather, in this case, Marxist-Leninist) prophecy. This time it concerned post-revolutionary developments. The seizure of state power by the Russian proletariat (which, in the view of all Leninists, had occurred in October 1917) should, according to the theory, have heralded the end of all class distinctions, the end of all coercion and repression and the gradual disappearance of the state as such. When twenty-two years later Trotsky and many of his followers, in the USA and elsewhere, differed on the question of the Soviet Union's social character, it was clear – and agreed on both sides – that another prediction had gone awry. Class distinctions, which had largely vanished in the era of 'war communism' between 1917 and 1921, had returned with a vengeance, and the 'workers' state', so far from withering away, had grown into a brutal instrument of totalitarian repression. In the debate Trotsky and the other defenders of the thesis of the 'degenerate workers' state' used the dialectical terminology to good effect; once again one of the chief spokesmen of the opposition denied the relevance of Marxian dialectics; once again the net result of the controversy was the strengthening of dogmatic rigidity – at least in one camp that claimed to represent Marxist orthodoxy.

It can be said that in this debate acceptance of dialectics was indeed a psychological precondition for accepting the 'Marxist' thesis that the totalitarian monster which had issued from the October Revolution was still, in 1940, a 'proletarian dictatorship' – i.e., by definition, a regime in which the ruling proletarian majority wields state power while adhering to the principles of democracy in its inner counsels. Only the dialectical phraseology of contradictions, recurrent negation, unity of opposites, the zigzag progress of history, etc., could outweigh, for some people, the factual evidence to the contrary.

While Burnham and his faction were at loggerheads with Trotsky about the character of the Soviet state, they did not dispute his view that world capitalism was doomed and would be overthrown either during or shortly after the war which was then in progress. The Russian experience put in question the propensity of proletarian revolution to pave the way to the perfect, classless society, but there seemed to be no reason to doubt, in 1939–40, that world capitalism was, indeed, in its last throes. Everything that had happened during the preceding decade tended to confirm this, and there was no need for a Marxist to resort to abstruse dialectical formulae to prove a point on which all communists, many socialists and, indeed, not a few non-socialists, were agreed.[105] But when after the war, and especially in the 1950s and 1960s, capitalism confounded the prophets of doom by prosperity and unprecedented expansion, dialectics came back into its own. The dialectical jargon was indispensable for explaining the inexplicable. As a strictly scientific theory Marxism should have become extinct when practically all its assumptions and predictions had been proved wrong. It was dialectics which helped the creed to survive – as a strictly non-scientific ideology.

The post-war period of capitalist prosperity, not unnaturally, produced a reaction among the idealistic young (i.e. *not* specifically the young workers) of emotional revulsion against the 'consumer society', the commercialization of life, the cult of selfishness, the widespread indifference towards surviving poverty and squalor, especially in the Third World, and other 'unacceptable' features of capitalist societies which are *not* beset by grave economic problems. There was – and is – no logical link and no affinity between this rebellious mood of active protest and the revolt of the starvelings against a bankrupt, decaying, exploitative system foretold by Marx and the Marxists. Yet this protest movement against what the protesters regarded as the perverted values of capitalist society was somehow channelled into the stream of Marxist militancy. This was not done by rational, convincing argument but by a process of psychological conditioning or religious conversion, for which diamat and the laws of dialectics were semi-intelligible yet irrefutable dogmas. To become or remain a Marxist one had to accept the dialectical theology, not because dialectics was an essential part of Marx's socio-economic or political theories, but because belief in dialectics alone would enable the mind to disregard the divergence of theory and reality.

Marx and Engels were not dogmatists. They did not claim to be in possession of the ultimate and complete truth – indeed, the rejection of the very concept of eternal truth was inherent in their view of both history and science. 'Genuinely scientific works', Engels wrote in the polemic with Eugen Duehring, 'avoid such dogmatic-moral terms as "truth" and "error".' Marx and Engels would not have had any use for the Leninist habit of classifying concurrent opinions as 'correct' and dissenting ones as 'absolutely false', or for Lenin's description of their own doctrinal system as 'a single block of steel'. They did not see this system as the last word, the theory to end all theories, but rather as a philosophy reflecting the transient position of one of the antagonistic forces of the society in which they lived. But when, in the twentieth century, history undeniably departed from the route sketched out by Marxist theory, the latter-day disciples proceeded to explain that all that had happened was, when viewed 'dialectically', fully in line with the original forecasts. The greater the gap between theoretical prediction and reality, the stronger the emphasis on dialectics as a method of finding the ultimate – Marxist – answer.

It is, in a way, ironical that dialectics was used as an instrument of creating a dogmatic doctrine, since the dialectical theory, inasmuch as it is intelligible, is basically incompatible with dogmatism. On the other hand, it was specifically the philosophical aspects of Marxism which lent themselves to conversion into dogma. It is obvious that writings of the 1850s and 1860s on contemporary economic and political problems cannot retain full relevance in the second half of the twentieth century. The teachings that were derived from such out-of-date analyses have to be constantly modified and supplemented, which is what even orthodox Marxist theoreticians have kept doing for the past eighty years or so. But 'dialectic logic' as expounded by Engels or Lenin's epistemology, being largely non-empirical, can more easily withstand the erosion of historic development and scientific change. A passage in Burnham's reply to Trotsky aptly describes this spurious irrefutability of dialectics:

I can understand . . . your recourse to dialectics in the current dispute. There is little else for you to write about, with every appeal you make to actual events refuted the day after you make it, with each week's development in the war smashing another pillar of your political position. An argument about dialectics is 100 per cent safe, a century ago or a century hence. . . .[106]

The conceptual vagueness and elasticity which enables the dialectic to absorb new ideas and discoveries, and thus to resist refutation, is reflected in the way in which the attitude of Soviet science towards the theory of relativity has changed in the course of time. In Lenin's *Collected Works* Einstein is only mentioned once, and in passing; Lenin derided the notion of a fourth dimension. Furthermore, Einstein built, to some extent, on the ideas of the Austrian physicist Ernst Mach, the arch-villain of Lenin's *Materialism and Empirio-Criticism*. In the circumstances the Soviet scientists' initial reaction could not have been other than highly sceptical, if not hostile. Thus the first edition of the *Great Soviet Encyclopaedia* which appeared in the early 1930s conceded that the theory of relativity was 'a step forward in the development of physics' but went on to say that the theory had been 'exploited by reactionary bourgeois philosophy', which was partly Einstein's own fault; Einstein's analysis of space-time was not exhaustive, and there was some inconsistency in his philosophical position, where 'materialistic and dialectical views are intermixed with Machist postulates which prevail in nearly all of E's philosophical utterances'.[107]

Things had assumed a different aspect by the time the second edition of the *Encyclopaedia* appeared in the mid-fifties. This was the time of the 'thaw' after Stalin's death. Einstein's theories had gained wide acceptance, and the Soviet scientists who had solved the problems of nuclear fission and fusion could not very well deny the importance which Einstein's ideas and formulae had for post-war scientific achievements. The criticism levelled at Einstein and his work in this edition is accordingly subdued. There is no mention of 'Machist' deviations. Einstein's achievements are stated to be 'of deep progressive significance'; while he had never stated his philosophical views in consistent form, his theory had philosophical implications. By establishing the connection between space and time, the theory of relativity

confirms the teaching of dialectical materialism on the reciprocal connection and interdependence of all aspects of material reality. By posing concrete problems of the dialectics of form and content, concrete and abstract, absolute and relative . . . the theory of relativity confirms Engels's statement that natural science is the touchstone of dialectics.[108]

Finally the Soviet *Dictionary of Philosophy* by M. Rosenthal and P. Yudin (an English translation was published in 1967) abandons all criticism. Under 'Relativity' we read:

The philosophical conclusions of the theory of relativity fully confirm the correctness of the ideas of dialectical materialism and of the assessments of the development of contemporary physics which were given by Lenin in his *Materialism and Empirio-Criticism*. The idealist and positive trends in philosophy have tried to use the theory of relativity to substantiate their claim that science is subjective and that physical processes depend on observation. The actual meaning of the theory of relativity is that physical processes are independent of the choice of the system of calculation . . . The theory of relativity provides a picture of objective processes and is a more exact reflection of reality than classical mechanics.

There is no mention of inconsistency in Einstein's philosophical views, and he is not held responsible for the fraudulent misuse of his theories by 'reactionary bourgeois' philosophers. The dialectical method apparently permits a wide range of contrasting judgements.

C. Wright Mills in his book *The Marxists* paid tribute to Karl Marx's analytical method as 'a signal and lasting contribution to the best sociological ways of reflection and inquiry available';[109] he went on to give a brief exposition of Marxian dialectics, which he concluded with this verdict:

The 'dialectical method' is either a mess of platitudes, a way of double-talk, a pretentious obscurantism – or all three. The essential error of the 'dialectician' is the . . . confusion of logic with metaphysics. . . . As a guide to thinking, 'dialectics' can be more burdensome than helpful, for if everything is connected, dialectically, with everything else, then you must know 'everything' in order to know anything, and causal sequences become difficult to trace.[110]

This, roughly, is the gist of the assessment given in this study. Marxian dialectics (where it does not simply mean flexibility of mind and readiness to view things in their development and not as static phenomena) is partly tautological, partly unintelligible, partly vague and ambiguous, partly absurd. It has no value in the search for knowledge and truth: on the contrary, it serves merely to confuse issues and sidetrack arguments. Yet it is not part of present-day Marxist ideology for nothing. For the members of the hierarchy (of all Marxist persuasions) it has important uses. By turning Marxism into a 'reinforced dogmatism' (to borrow Karl Popper's phrase) it wards off attacks and criticisms levelled at the creed and at the pronouncements and actions that purport to be based on the creed; it helps to justify repressive and undemocratic measures taken by 'Marxist' regimes, as well as their expansionist foreign policies. It furnishes explanations for the persistent refusal of history to conform to the Marxist (or Marxist-Leninist) scheme of things. Last but not least, thanks to its lack of terminological precision, to its ambiguity and its partial incomprehensibility, it tends to convert Marxist philosophy into an esoteric, semi-occult science which contains elements of the mysterious and the *credo quia absurdum*.

There is a revealing sentence in one of the articles in which Trotsky, in the last year of his life, stressed the supreme importance of dialectics for the policy of the revolutionary party: in December 1939 he wrote: 'To demand that every party member occupy himself with the philosophy of dialectics naturally would be lifeless pedantry.'[111] Yet in his 'Open Letter' to Burnham, written three weeks later, he exhorted all party members, and especially the young, to familiarize themselves with the writings of the classical authors of dialectical materialism.[112] The inconsistency is more apparent than real. The call to study dialectics was addressed to the members of the Socialist Workers Party, as it then was – a small, élite vanguard comprising mainly intellectuals. The statement that not all party members should be urged to study dialectics refers to 'party' in a more general context: what Trotsky had in mind was the mass membership of the large working-class party which he hoped the Socialist Workers Party, and fraternal parties in other capitalist countries, would eventually become. The meaning (possibly subconscious in Trotsky's case) is that the esoteric science of dialectics is for the select few, for the 'vanguard of the vanguard', as the small Trotskyist groups in the 1930s would call themselves.[113] The proletarian rank-and-file of the future mass party would, of course, have to endorse the party's programme and ideology, including the dogma of diamat, without having studied or understood the latter: they must take it on trust from the leading cadres.

This is, in fact, the position in the Communist Party and other Marxist parties. The relationship between the leaders and the led is not greatly different from the relationship between the priests and the laity in one of the Christian Churches. To the average practising Christian the concept of the Holy Spirit is presumably exactly as much of a mystery as the interpenetration (or identity, or unity) of opposites must be for the average member of any communist party, whether inside or outside the communist world.

Notes

Diamat and Dogma

1 For instance, M. Cornforth (*In Defence of Philosophy*, London 1950) calls the formulation of Marxist dialectics 'a discovery of epoch-making importance', which had introduced into philosophy 'the class outlook of the modern proletariat'.

2 *Anti-Duehring* (London 1969), pp. 168–9.

3 By John Strachey in *The Theory and Practice of Socialism*, Left Book Club edition (London 1936), p. 381.

4 Some twentieth-century Marxists and near-Marxists (Lukács, Sartre, *et al*) consider dialectics to be applicable only to history or human affairs in general, but not to nature or natural science. This restriction is not accepted by the academic establishment in the USSR and the other communist countries.

5 Z. A. Jordan, *The Evolution of Dialectical Materialism* (London 1967), pp. 12–13, quotes Karl Korsch and other Marxist theorists as denying any necessary link between philosophical and historical materialism.

6 Cf. John Plamenatz, *German Marxism and Russian Communism* (London 1961), pp. 9–16. I share Plamenatz's view on dialectics but must dispute his assertion that Marxists 'are not very interested' in dialectical materialism (p. 10).

7 Eduard Bernstein went further and claimed that whatever Marx and Engels accomplished had been achieved not

by means of, but in spite of, the dialectical method.

8 About this term, cf. pp. 107ff. above.

9 *Anti-Duehring*, p. 33. This is also the method Marx described as his own in the preface to the second edition of *Das Kapital* in 1873.

10 Cf. pp. 126ff. above.

11 Ironically a striking example of what could be termed 'undialectical thinking' in this sense is the attitude of some Marxist dialecticians during the Second World War. They revived the Leninist policy of 'revolutionary defeatism', which is based on the concept of reciprocal interaction between the revolutionary struggle and military defeat. Events in Russia in 1917, and in Germany, Austria and Hungary in 1918-19, showed that this policy may have made sense in the First World War. The same policy was utterly absurd, from the point of view of the revolutionary working class, between 1939 and 1945, when the defeat of Poland, Norway, the Netherlands, Belgium, France, etc., at the hands of Nazi Germany did not produce revolutionary situations in the defeated countries but led to the setting up of fascist or semi-fascist, rabidly anti-Marxist regimes. Instead of ('dialectically') evaluating the crucial differences between the two world wars in respect of background, genesis, issues and circumstances, these Marxists (in Britain the Communist Party between September 1939 and June 1941; the Independent Labour Party and various Trotskyist and other extreme left-wing groups throughout the war) mechanically equated the Second World War with the First and declared the same policy to be applicable. Had the workers of the capitalist countries of the anti-Hitler alliance taken the Marxists' advice, Europe might have become Fascist and Marxism as a movement might not have survived.

12 Cf. *Anti-Duehring*, p. 170. People with no knowledge of and no interest in philosophy, who invariably use their non-dialectical common sense, would be equally surprised to learn that they had been metaphysicians all their life.

13 *Anti-Duehring*, p. 33.

14 Earlier editions took a different view and denounced the theory of relativity as 'undialectical'; *see* pp. 146ff.

15 Matters would then seem to have improved since 1878, when Engels had complained that 'naturalists who have learned to think dialectically are few and far between' (*Anti-Duehring*, p. 33); yet over forty years after Lenin another exponent of dialectical materialism, Maurice Cornforth (*In Defence of Philosophy*, p. 59), echoed Engels by stating that 'scientists have seldom been able to think dialectically'.

16 This ideological self-righteousness, exemplified by the habitual use of such words as 'correct', 'incorrect', 'false', is another instance of Marxist theoretical inconsistency. One would have thought that writers who regard everything as being in flux, who attach a positive, constructive value to contradictions and maintain that every phenomenon is closely bound up with its own opposite, would refrain from apodictic judgements; that they would be ready to see all sides of an argument and to concede that a problem can be viewed from various angles. Not so: Marxists, and in particular Leninists, never hesitate to declare categorically that a certain way of looking at a matter is 'absolutely correct', that dissenting opinions (whether on philosophical, theoretical or topical political issues) are 'absolutely incorrect' or 'absolutely false'. Lenin himself knew no difference between philosophical argument and political polemics. In his philosophical work (*Materialism and Empirio-Criticism*) he treated scientists and philosophical writers he disagreed with to the kind of invective he habitually dished out to his political opponents. Typical phrases in the course of philosophical argument are: 'Listen, Mr Machist: lie if you must, but don't overdo it!' or 'The pedant Petzoldt ... with the smug satisfaction of the philistine, chews the cud of Avenarius's biological scholasticism.' Lenin's reasoning in this book is almost entirely theological: *see* the essay 'Marxism and Marxianity', in this volume, p. 57 and n. 90.

17 Some Marxist dialecticians have criticized the Hegelian triad as too artificial. They prefer the phrase 'negation of the

negation' which Hegel also used and which does not differ in content from the triad.

18 Further examples below. Marxist theorists do not usually enlarge on the question of whether communism in its turn will eventually be negated by an opposing movement.

19 Cf. the example given above (p. 107); to choose a more compact and short-term example: French Revolution, ascending phase, 1789–94; Thermidorian reaction and Directory, 1794–9; Bonapartist synthesis (cf. pp. 109–10 above).

20 Cf. the 'trial and error' method outlined by Karl Popper in *Conjectures and Refutations*, 3rd edition (London 1969), pp. 312ff.

21 Darwin's concept of evolution underwent far-reaching modification but was in no way affected by the vehement theological attacks levelled against it.

22 *Conjectures and Refutations*, p. 322.

23 Which is implicitly confirmed by Engels when he states (*Anti-Duehring*, p. 33) that 'nature is the proof of dialectics'.

24 Max Eastman (*Marxism, Is It Science?*, London 1941, p. 180) was right in saying this about the triad: 'It is astonishing how much of the change and motion in the world, as well as the relations among abstract ideas, if you examine them with a sufficiently casuistic determination to believe so, and particularly if you refrain from defining the word *opposite*, can be made to fit into this mould.'

25 The events of the English Revolution in the mid-seventeenth century, together with the Restoration, could similarly be interpreted as stages of a dialectical triad. As for the events after the French Revolution, a different triad could be conceived of, in which the Bonapartist regime figures as part of the revolutionary negation of eighteenth-century royalist France, and the Bourbon restoration – constitutional monarchy on the basis of the post-revolutionary economic order – as the negation of the negation, or the synthesis.

The fact that two (or more) completely different sequences can be squeezed into the pattern of the dual negation illustrates Karl Popper's characterization of such theories

(*Conjectures and Refutations*, p. 36): 'It is easy to obtain confirmations, or verifications, for nearly every theory – if we look for confirmations.'

26 *Capital*, 8th edition (London 1902), II, pp. 788–9.
27 *Anti-Duehring*, pp. 155ff.
28 *Anti-Duehring*, p. 161.
29 *Anti-Duehring*, p. 168.
30 We shall come across one such example in Marxist literature, but there the application of the laws of dialectics leads to an obvious absurdity; cf. pp. 133ff. above.
31 In the polemics with Duehring, Engels also rejected and refuted his opponent's suggestion that Marx had made use, in a different context, of the dialectical law of the transformation of quantity into quality: cf. pp. 124ff. above.
32 *Anti-Duehring*, p. 161.
33 *See* p. 386.
34 *See* p. 15.
35 *See* pp. 26–7.
36 As Jean-Paul Sartre remarks in *Critique de la Raison Dialectique* (Paris 1960, p. 127), the logical process is really one of induction rather than deduction.
37 *Anti-Duehring*, pp. 162–3.
38 *Der Historische Materialismus* (Berlin 1927); quoted in I. Fetscher, *Der Marxismus* (Munich 1967), p. 176.
39 In the reproduction of humans and other mammals only one of hundreds of millions of spermatozoa emitted by the male in coition fertilizes the ovum – the others perish. In Engelsian parlance, 'negation' is the fate not of the millions that die but of the one sperm that survives and initiates procreation. As Humpty Dumpty put it, 'When I use a word it means just what I choose it to mean – neither more nor less,' – an apt illustration of the way the dialecticians use the word 'negation'.
40 *Anti-Duehring*, p. 163.
41 *Anti-Duehring*, p. 164.
42 *Conjectures and Refutations*, p. 323; cf. also Edmund Wilson, *To the Finland Station* (London 1941), pp. 191–2.

43 *Anti-Duehring*, pp. 165–6.
44 Cf. p. 115 above and n. 34.
45 *See* p. 169.
46 About this term, cf. p. 105 above.
47 As Engels himself does, for example, where reproduction is not linked with any kind of negation; cf. p. 116 above.
48 Another passage from Solzhenitsyn's novel illustrates the problem. The author evidently had some experience of the quibbles by means of which dialecticians try to get round their difficulties. In the discussion on dialectics (pp. 113–14 above) the sceptic, Sologdin, asks the orthodox Marxist, Rubin:

> 'Does negation of the negation *always* take place in the course of a development or not always?' Rubin felt a momentary hesitation.
> 'Basically it does . . . For the most part.'
> 'There we have it,' Sologdin shouted. 'There is your jargon: "basically", "for the most part". That is the way to snarl things up so that you can never find the ends! . . . Why can't you give me a straight answer: *when* does negation of the negation take place and when doesn't it?'
> Rubin was doing his best to collect his wits for this useless and yet somehow important discussion: 'But what can be the practical importance of knowing when it does and when it doesn't?'
> 'That's marvellous! What is the practical importance of one of the three laws from which everything else follows! . . .'
> 'You are putting the cart before the horse . . . None of us would dream of analysing a concrete situation simply by applying to it a ready-made dialectical law. That is why we don't have to know "when it does" and "when it doesn't"!'

49 *Anti-Duehring*, p. 168.
50 *Marxism, Is It Science?*, p. 138.
51 One-volume edition (London 1950), p. 300.
52 *Anti-Duehring*, p. 151.
53 *Anti-Duehring*, p. 153.
54 M. Cornforth, *Dialectical Materialism* (London 1961), I, pp. 83–4.
55 *Dialectical Materialism*, I, p. 83.

56 'Marxism and the Problem of Linguistics' in *The Essential Stalin* (London 1973), pp. 407–44; cf. Z. A. Jordan, *The Evolution of Dialectical Materialism*, p. 266.

57 Cf. a similar formula in C. Wright Mills, *The Marxists* (Harmondsworth 1963), p. 128.

58 To quote another critic (Z. A. Jordan, *The Evolution of Dialectical Materialism*, p. 202): 'The law [of quantity changing into quality] provides no factual information and, in fact, it makes no difference whether we accept this law or not. It lacks any informative content and even a modicum of precision.'

59 *In Defence of Marxism* (London 1966), pp. 64–5.

60 E.g. James Burnham, who soon afterwards broke with Marxism and became the author of *The Managerial Revolution* (London 1943).

61 *The Marxists*, p. 128.

62 *See* pp. 112–13 above.

63 *Capital*, pp. 294–6.

64 *Anti-Duehring*, p. 150.

65 *See* pp. 113–14 above.

66 English translation published by Gollancz.

67 *See* p. 324.

68 *See* p. 324.

69 *Logic* (Oxford 1892), p. 222.

70 *See* p. 162.

71 The quotation is taken from pp. 240–1 of the German translation, *Grundlagen der Marxistischen Philosophie*, which appeared in East Berlin in 1965.

72 *Grundlagen der Marxistischen Philosophie*, p. 232.

73 'On the Question of Dialectics', *Collected Works* (Moscow 1961), XXXVIII, p. 359.

74 *Collected Works*, p. 359.

75 It was this 'identity of opposites' which the ex-Marxist George Orwell meant to satirize when he coined the Party slogans of 1984: 'War is Peace'; 'Freedom is Slavery'; 'Ignorance is Strength'.

76 *Textbook of Marxist Philosophy*, p. 186.

77 *Textbook of Marxist Philosophy*, p. 186.

78 *See* p. 189.

79 *Selected Readings from the Works of Mao Tse-tung* (Peking 1967), p. 358. The speech was given on 27 February 1957 and published in the *People's Daily* on 19 June 1957, with the title 'On the Correct Handling of Contradictions Among the People'.

80 *See* pp. 121–2 above.

81 *Selected Readings from the Works of Mao Tse-tung*, p. 361.

82 *Selected Readings from the Works of Mao Tse-tung*, pp. 358–9.

83 *See* pp. 122ff. above.

84 *In Defence of Marxism*, p. 106.

85 Cf. the essay on that subject in this volume, p. 5ff.

86 *In Defence of Marxism*, pp. 232ff: the pamphlet consists of a collection of Trotsky's articles and letters written in 1939–40, with Burnham's reply added as an appendix.

87 *In Defence of Marxism*, pp. 91ff.

88 *In Defence of Marxism*, pp. 236–7.

89 *In Defence of Marxism*, p. 196.

90 Burnham lectured on philosophy at New York University. Later Trotsky described Burnham as a 'strutting petty-bourgeois pedant' and an 'educated witch-doctor'.

91 *In Defence of Marxism*, p. 98.

92 *In Defence of Marxism*, p. 246.

93 A conception later elaborated by several Marxists and ex-Marxists, including Burnham in *The Managerial Revolution* and Milovan Djilas in *The New Class* (London 1957).

94 Which, according to Trotsky, prevailed during the first years of the Soviet regime.

95 A term which, in Marxist theory, denotes a regime of in-direct class rule, based on a temporary balance between the contending classes but committed to the upholding of the socio-economic *status quo*.

96 *In Defence of Marxism*, p. 17. Thirty-odd years later most of Trotsky's disciples still regard the Soviet Union as a degener-ate workers' state, ruled by an ephemeral bureaucratic oligarchy; what is more, even the East European satellites are

considered to be degenerate workers' states, without ever having been the genuine article – non-degenerate workers' states. Each of these degenerate workers' states was, presumably, the result of a degenerate revolution, made by a degenerate proletariat.

97 In 1905, when tsarist Russia was at war with Japan, Lenin declared that Marxists should side with Japan, whose progressive capitalism was preferable to the Tsar's semi-feudal regime.

98 *In Defence of Marxism*, p. 257.

99 It is not an original work: its basic idea is borrowed – without acknowledgement – from the book of an Italian ex-Trotskyist, Bruno Rizzi, published on the eve of the Second World War in Paris, under the title *La Bureaucratisation du Monde*. A lucid summary of Rizzi's book and of Trotsky's reaction to it is to be found in Isaac Deutscher's *The Prophet Outcast* (Oxford 1963), pp. 463–4. For some reason Rizzi's work failed to make an impact comparable with that of *The Managerial Revolution*.

100 *See* p. 48: Marxists were using an argument which 'is a deduction from the metaphysical theory of "dialectical materialism". It is held that Hegel's metaphysical logic of thesis, antithesis and synthesis somehow guarantees that out of the clash of the two antithetical classes, *bourgeoisie* and proletariat, socialism will issue.' This is *not*, in fact, the belief of orthodox Marxists.

101 Cf. pp. 103f. above.

102 Bernstein and his friends regarded socialism as desirable but not inevitable.

103 It would be wrong to assume that in general right-wing socialists did not accept dialectics while the left-wing did. Karl Liebknecht, who stood on the extreme left in Germany and became a co-founder of the German Communist Party, had no use for dialectics; Plekhanov and the Russian Mensheviks were mostly staunch defenders of Marxian dialectics.

104 If the development of the last 150 years in regard to living

standards is seen as a whole, a zigzag movement can, indeed, be discerned, but the general tendency is the opposite of what Marxist theory assumed it would be: not a steady process of increasing misery, with brief spells of alleviation, but rather a secular change, with ephemeral setbacks, in the direction of a general improvement in the condition of the working classes under capitalism.

105 After his break with Marxism Burnham continued to believe in the inevitability of capitalist collapse. His *The Managerial Revolution* contains a number of predictions which turned out to be just as incorrect as the numerous forecasts made by Marxist dialecticians and which were eventually abandoned by Burnham himself (cf. B. D. Wolfe, *An Ideology in Power*, London 1969, p. 377, n. 2).

106 *In Defence of Marxism*, p. 235.

107 Quoted in Milovan Djilas, *The Unperfect Society* (London 1969), pp. 76–7.

108 *The Unperfect Society*, p. 78.

109 *The Marxists*, pp. 127f.

110 *The Marxists*, pp. 128–9. Cf. the characterization of diamat philosophy by B. D. Wolfe, *An Ideology in Power*, p. 350, as 'little more than verbal casuistry'.

111 *In Defence of Marxism*, p. 58.

112 *See* p. 137 above.

113 The present author belonged to one such group at the time.

The Decline and Fall of the Soviet Empire

The problem of assessing Soviet foreign policy

In a Fabian tract published in 1955 Michael Stewart (later to serve as Foreign Secretary in Harold Wilson's Government) had this to say about the USSR's post-war foreign policy: 'If we examine the record of events since 1945, there is one conclusion that we cannot escape. The Soviet Union has repeatedly shown that she will snatch anything that is within her grasp, and which she believes can be snatched without starting a world war.'

The view that the Soviet Union is bent upon territorial expansion but would make no aggressive move which might provoke war with another major power has been, since the late 1940s, the rationale of West European and American diplomacy concerning relations with the communist powers. The essence of this policy is the formation and maintenance of defensive alliances – NATO, CENTO, SEATO – designed to deter communist aggression. The same interpretation of Soviet and, *mutatis mutandis*, Chinese foreign policy is prevalent among Western historians and political writers. This 'orthodox' Western view of the origins of the Cold War is succinctly summarized in *The Semblance of Peace* by Sir John Wheeler-Bennett and Anthony Nicholls, in these words:

. . . Russia's foreign policy, as disclosed during the [Second World] War and practised thereafter, was a re-embodiment of those imperial ambitions which in the glory of the tsarist expansionist period had led to the Crimean War, the colonization of the Transcaucasian territories and of Manchuria, the penetration of the Balkans and the Middle East, and the threat to Britain's 'lifeline' to India. To this old-fashioned imperialist policy was added the further threat of the proliferation of communism in Europe . . .

It was in recognition of the threat inherent in this policy that, with supreme reluctance, the Western powers were constrained to accept the Soviet challenge and to make a brave and essential response of free men against aggression. It was completely irrelevant to the issue that both sides had very shortly before been engaged in a life-and-death struggle against a common aggressor from another quarter.[1]

In opposition to this orthodox thesis a 'revisionist' school (to use the terminology first applied by American scholars) has emerged both in the USA and in Britain.[2]

Its central thesis is that the growing antagonism between Soviet Russia and the West after 1945 was chiefly due to the attitude of President Truman who, basing his policy on America's monopoly possession of the nuclear bomb, had abandoned the wartime course of East—West co-operation and had systematically tried to elimin- ate Soviet influence in Eastern Europe: Truman's reckless and aggressive anti-communism had compelled Stalin to consolidate, in defence of the USSR's territorial integrity and of her revolutionary heritage, the Soviet position in Eastern Europe; the result had been Europe's division into two armed camps, represented by the North Atlantic Treaty and the Warsaw Pact.

What is the truth in this controversy? Are Mr Stewart and the 'orthodox' school right about the Soviet Union's propensity to 'snatch' foreign territory and commit other aggressive acts when- ever this can be done safely? If so, in which historical epoch and in what circumstances has this propensity been most marked? What determines the Kremlin's present-day policy, and in what direc- tion is this policy likely to develop? Is the West's policy of defensive alliances still relevant?

These are the questions the present study will try to answer.

The roots of Soviet expansionism

It is impossible to deny that the USSR has repeatedly, and not only from 1945 onwards, committed acts of aggression. In fact against those 'revisionist' scholars who argue for the complete exculpation of the Soviet Union regarding the Cold War it must be pointed out that the most blatant acts of Soviet expansion, by force or by threat of military action, occurred between September 1939 and June 1941, that is to say, between the outbreak of the Second World War and Hitler's invasion of Russia. Soviet aggrandizement after 1945, whether or not it was provoked by Western actions or gestures, was essentially the consolidation and extension of what the USSR had acquired, by war or military-political pressure, in 1939 and 1940.

Soviet foreign policy since 1939

The Soviet Government, which in the mid-thirties had been a champion of 'collective security', i.e. joint action with the Western capitalist democracies against the German menace, had switched to a policy of friendship and collaboration with Nazi Germany at the very moment when the latter, having completed its military preparations, was on the point of unleashing a war which, by any standard, was one of unprovoked aggression. Substantial gains of territory were, for the USSR, the fruits of this collaboration.

Following the German-Soviet pact of August 1939, which provided for the partition of Poland, the Soviet Union occupied and annexed, with Germany's connivance, large slices of Polish territory. Nazi Germany also connived when the USSR bullied into submission, and then annexed, the three Baltic republics – Lithuania, Latvia and Estonia – and when, after a war of aggression against Finland, she grabbed one-tenth of Finland's territory, including the second biggest town, Viborg. Last, in the summer of 1940, again with Hitler's consent, the Soviet Union obtained from Rumania, under threat of war, the cession of two provinces, Bessarabia and Northern Bukovina.

There is no doubt that these annexations, whatever their motives, were violations of international law and of specific undertakings embodied in the 'non-aggression pacts' between the USSR and her neighbours. The same goes for Russia's post-war expansion. In January 1942 the USSR adhered to the Atlantic Charter (previously agreed between Churchill and Roosevelt) which committed the signatories to 'seek no aggrandizement, territorial or other', to countenance 'no territorial changes that do not accord with the freely expressed wishes of the peoples concerned', and to 'respect the right of all peoples to choose the form of government under which they will live'. It is true that the Soviet endorsement of the Charter carried an obscure reservation about adapting its principles to 'the circumstances, needs and historic peculiarities of particular countries'. Whatever this clause may mean, it can certainly not be interpreted as conferring the right on the signatories to infringe every one of the provisions of the Charter. This, however, is precisely what the Russians did when they not only held on to all they had gained in 1939 and 1940, but also acquired vast additional territories. Some of these gains were made at the expense of the USSR's own satellites and friends – which invalidates the 'revisionist' argument that the Kremlin had to act in response to a Western threat to Soviet security. Thus a case could have been made for handing over East Prussia to Poland: East Prussia had been under Polish suzerainty from the fifteenth to the seventeenth centuries and parts of it were inhabited by people who speak a Slav dialect akin to Polish. Yet the Soviet Union herself annexed half of that province, which had never in history been a Russian possession, including the old German capital of Koenigsberg (then renamed Kaliningrad). Russia also annexed Ruthenia which the allied Czechoslovak Government was prevailed upon to cede in 1946: another acquisition which could not conceivably enhance Soviet 'security'. Lastly the USSR, again in breach of the Atlantic Charter, embarked on a far-reaching programme of satellization by imposing her own economic and political regime (with some local variations) on most of the neighbouring countries of Eastern Europe.[3]

Whether or not it is true – as the revisionists contend – that

Western actions, attitudes and inconsistencies have contributed to the outbreak of the Cold War, it must be emphasized that neither the USA nor any West European power did anything that conflicted with the terms of the Atlantic Charter. There were no Western acts of expansion or satellization after 1945. Generally speaking, while all great powers, and many medium and small ones, have at some time or other pursued policies of aggression and conquest, Russia and China are the only great powers to have conquered and annexed territory since the end of the Second World War – Russia in Eastern Europe, China in Tibet. In fact they are the only great powers even to have attempted territorial aggrandizement.[4]

Another aspect of Soviet territorial acquisition that deserves attention in this assessment of the Soviet record is that the expansionist moves were all made within the space of about nine years, from the outbreak of the Second World War to the end of its aftermath. Between 1921 (the end of the civil war) and 1939 the Soviet leadership had concentrated on consolidation and internal reconstruction. Only one minor military encounter outside Soviet territory occurred during that period. When Nationalist China moved in 1929 to deprive Russia of the 'Chinese Eastern Railway' – one of the assets the communist regime had inherited from the Tsar's empire – Soviet troops entered Manchuria to restore the previous position. This was a piece of gun-boat diplomacy, the normal reaction, in those days, of any great power to a similar 'provocation'; it was hardly consistent with communism's anti-imperialist ideology, yet not an act of aggression within the conventional meaning of the word.

The Soviet campaign of territorial expansion began in 1939 with the occupation of Eastern Poland and ended with the satellization of Czechoslovakia in February 1948. There was one further expansionist move in 1948: the Berlin blockade, designed to push the Western Allies out of the former capital of the Reich and to incorporate the Western half of the city in the Soviet zone of occupation. The attempt was abandoned the following year but half-heartedly renewed some years later, between 1958 and 1961, in a different form; it was finally dropped – or so it would seem at the time of writing – with the signing of the East—West German 'General Relations Treaty' in December 1972. We shall, in due course, deal with other instances of Soviet aggression after 1948, such as the invasion of Hungary in 1956 and of Czechoslovakia in 1968. At this stage it will suffice to point out that the purpose in these cases was not further expansion but rather the prevention of developments which might have led to the reduction of the total area under Soviet control.

While Michael Stewart was certainly right in characterizing Soviet post-war foreign policy as expansionist, it would be too sweeping to assert, in the light of historical fact, that this propensity to expand has been apparent across the whole range of the USSR's diplomacy. The truth is that there does not seem to be a mainspring, a single motive determining all phases of Soviet foreign policy. Throughout the Soviet state's existence dynamic and restrained policies have alternated, in accordance with the changing pattern of internal and world situations. When Hitler set out to re-draw the map of Europe in 1938–9, the Soviet leadership grasped the opportunity of recovering territory lost after 1917: a passive phase of consolidation and conservation of the *status quo* gave way to a dynamic policy of annexation, eventually comprising regions beyond the boundaries of the last Tsar's dominions. This dynamic phase had run its course some years after the end of the Second World War, partly, perhaps, because the Soviet Government feared that further expansion might entail a risk of world war, and partly, maybe, because the USSR's overriding need was to absorb into her system and digest what she had swallowed between 1939 and 1948. Since 1948 Soviet policy has mainly been one of consolidation of wartime and post-war gains; in the process the USSR has felt at times constrained to resort to armed intervention (as in 1956 and 1968) to avert the danger of losing those gains and, as we shall see, of losing much else besides.

Aggression and communist ideology

Some Western anti-communists who broadly agree with the 'orthodox' interpretation of the history of East—West relations claim to discern a link between Soviet foreign policy and the ideological and other peculiarities of the system; for example, a policy of conquests for the attainment of world communism is said to follow logically from Marxist-Leninist doctrine. Writers holding this view sometimes date Soviet expansionism back to the civil war which followed the October Revolution, and point out that the reconquest by the Bolsheviks of the Tsar's multi-national empire between 1917 and 1921 was accomplished by military force, and often against the will of the non-Russian nations, some of whom had actually established independent non-communist states. These writers also feel that the imposition of communism on Soviet-occupied Eastern Europe proves their point.

It is certainly true that the Russian communists, both during and after the civil war, frequently disregarded the principle of national self-determination. In some cases they violated their own explicit commitments; for instance, by invading the Caucasian state of Georgia in March 1921, seven months after the solemn recognition of the independent Republic of Georgia by the Moscow Government. But this merely means that the Russian Bolshevik leaders did exactly what the Tsar's Government (and, indeed, most if not all other governments) would have done at the time, without incurring much opprobrium. The denial of independent statehood to subject nations and the oppression of minorities in general are not features peculiar to communism.

They are, in fact, blatant violations of communist principle, and in direct conflict with Lenin's explicit teachings.[5] By flouting the right of self-determination (which includes the right of a minority nation to secede from the larger unit), the Bolsheviks infringed a sacred tenet of their creed. While the civil war was in progress, the temporary occupation of a regime against the wishes of the inhabitants might have been justified as an operation designed to deny the enemy a territorial base – just as the occupation of hostile territory is permissible in an external war. But communist theory provides no justification for the Bolsheviks' policy of retaining and consolidating, after the civil war, communist rule and Great Russian domination in the non-Russian parts of what used to be the tsarist empire, and of suppressing the national aspirations of the peoples concerned.[6]

The belief that Leninists would, in accordance with their doctrine, favour territorial conquest as a means of promoting the cause of world communism is based on a misinterpretation of the theory. Of course, the world-wide triumph of communism *is* the avowed aim of Marxism-Leninism. Yet this doctrine does not preach the imposition of the communist system on unwilling nations by armed force. It does not advocate the 'export' of communism. Both Marx and his Bolshevik disciples considered revolutionary war to be both possible and permissible; Bolshevik doctrine also envisaged wars of intervention by a socialist country against a capitalist state in which a proletarian rising was in progress. Thus in 1915, on the assumption that the revolution would, to begin with, be victorious in one country only, Lenin (who was far from being a champion of 'peaceful coexistence', as present-day Soviet propaganda has it), proclaimed:

After expropriating the capitalists and organizing its own socialist production, the victorious proletariat of that country will arise *against* the rest of the world – the capitalist world – attracting to its cause the oppressed classes of other countries, stirring uprisings in those countries against the capitalists, and in case of need using armed force against the exploiting classes and their state.[7]

In practice this has never happened. The conditions under which (according to Lenin) revolutionary intervention might have been called for did not prevail when the Soviet Union attacked Finland in 1939, when she annexed the Baltic states or forced Rumania to surrender Bessarabia and part of Bukovina in 1940. Even communist propaganda did not pretend on these occasions that Soviet action had been undertaken in support of a working-class revolution in the annexed territories. Likewise when China invaded and annexed Tibet in 1950, the Peking Government did not claim that Chinese forces had entered Tibet to back a socialist rising. China simply asserted that Tibet was, historically, Chinese territory, over which she was entitled to exercise her sovereignty.

What, in fact, happened in Eastern Europe in 1939-40, and in

Asia in 1950, was that a communist great power took aggressive action to recover territory which, several decades earlier, had belonged to its pre-revolutionary predecessor. In both cases a communist power committed aggression against a weaker neighbour for purposes of territorial expansion.[8] It is true that the economic and political system of the conquering power was, in each case, extended to the newly acquired territory, but this was purely the unavoidable concomitant of annexation.

There was no revolutionary element, either, in the USSR's policy of expansion after the Second World War. This was simply the continuation of the process whereby the Great Russians, in centuries gone by, had acquired their colossal empire and had established a relationship with other nations which, as Lenin pointed out in the context of the late nineteenth and early twentieth centuries, bore all the marks of imperialist domination.

During the early years of Soviet power the Bolsheviks' chief aim was the spread of communist revolution to the advanced capitalist countries. This was not to be achieved by military action but by encouraging and promoting autochthonous proletarian risings. The Soviet leaders pursued this line not just in obedience to international doctrine but also, and perhaps primarily, for pragmatic reasons of self-preservation. They were convinced that the survival of their regime depended on the triumph of socialist revolution in Central and Western Europe, that the revolution would either conquer in most of Europe or perish in Russia. When, in the middle twenties, it became clear that neither had happened or was likely to happen in the near future, Stalin's theory of socialism in one country gained ascendancy. Russia went ahead with the development of modern industry, and her rulers became increasingly indifferent to the progress of the cause in the international arena. Eventually, and paradoxically, the USSR's ruling bureaucracy began to acquire a stake in the international *status quo*. What the Soviet leaders called the 'building of socialism' was, in truth, the forced industrialization of a comparatively backward country. The success of this drive depended on commercial and technical co-operation with the highly developed capitalist countries – the USA, Britain, France, Germany. From these the Soviet Union sought to – and did – obtain capital, machinery, know-how, technical aid and guidance. Violent upheavals in the Western world were apt to imperil this co-operation, and with it the prospects of economic rehabilitation and rapid industrialization in Russia. At this stage the Soviet leaders, and the leaders of world communism who took the cue from them, rationalized their altered hopes and fears by re-interpreting the international scene: they evolved new theories about the 'relative stabilization of capitalism' and explained to the masses that world revolution had ceased to be a short-term objective.

In the field of international relations this new Soviet conserva-tism was reflected in a return to old-fashioned power politics. Having lost interest in communist world revolution, the Kremlin rulers exerted a restraining influence on the communist parties abroad. Often in a revolutionary situation – for example, in Spain and France in 1936 – the communists exercised a moder-ating influence within a left-wing alliance.[9] In general the political directives the Kremlin issued to foreign communist parties were dictated by the Soviet Union's great power interests. Hence the many twists and turns of the communist general line throughout the world, always parallel with the shifting and changing objectives of Soviet foreign policy.

Communist power politics

The late Konni Zilliacus, an ardent champion of East—West understanding and a strong believer in the peaceful intentions of the Soviet ruling oligarchy, contended that ever since Stalin's rise to power in the 1920s Russia's affairs had been conducted on 'non-doctrinal' lines, that Stalin's diplomacy during and after the Second World War was 'straight, old-fashioned power politics', and that Stalin's successors had also been guided by their country's imperial interests and not by the interests of world communism.[10]

From this correct assessment Zilliacus drew highly dubious conclusions. In his view the abandonment of Marxist revolution-ary ideals signified that Soviet foreign policy had become innocuous and peaceable. It could be argued that the opposite might be the case. The paradoxical truth is that the West cannot trust the Soviet rulers to pursue peaceful external policies just because their decisions and actions are determined not by Marxist but by old-style concepts of power.

If orthodox Marxist-Leninist principles had always been the motive force of Soviet (and Chinese) foreign policies, the Western and other capitalist powers would have nothing to fear, and the need for defensive alliances against the threat of communist aggression would never have arisen. The conditions which, according to the doctrine, might justify military action in support of proletarian revolution have never materialized, or at least not since the end of the First World War. As for the international crises of the Cold War period, they occurred precisely because power politics and not Marxism-Leninism held sway in Moscow. When, in 1950, the Russians gave the North Koreans the green light for an assault on the South there was no question of North Korea's intervening to aid a revolutionary rising in South Korea. The Korean War was just an old-fashioned war of conquest, an attempt to extend the Soviet sphere of influence by armed force. There was nothing revolutionary about it. In 1948, and again between 1958 and 1961, the Russians and their East German puppets tried to oust the Western Allies from Berlin, not in this case by force of arms but by the devious exertion of pressure. They did not even try to argue that what they demanded was desired by the working masses of that city; indeed, there was no denying the obvious fact that the workers of West Berlin abhorred communist rule and opposed any change in the *status quo*. The Russian-East German bid was just another piece of un-Marxist power politics.

Aggression and morality

The foreign policies of the Soviet Union and of Communist China are not aimed at spreading socialism, although the widening of the area of state-directed economic planning is usually a by-product of the success of these policies. The two powers are not fighting for the sovereignty and independence of small nations: what they do or instigate in Asia, Africa, Latin America or the Middle East is designed to widen their spheres of influence. Their intervention in areas of conflict outside their own territories are not part of a world-wide struggle between capitalist-imperialist reaction and socialist progress: they are bids to expand by annexation or satellization, or to gain influence at the expense of a rival power – which, in the case of Russia and China, often means at each other's expense.

The communist powers thus play the game of world affairs according to the rules of power politics and not of Marxist-Leninist doctrine. Neutralists in the West who are opposed to NATO and SEATO, without being fellow-travellers, usually point out that the communist countries are not the only ones to play at power politics: they may have committed aggression, but they have neither invented aggression nor do they monopolize it. If the Soviet Union, in Michael Stewart's words, 'will snatch anything that is within her grasp', Britain and France (so the neutralists say) did quite a lot of snatching in the course of the eighteenth and nineteenth centuries. If aggression is not confined to the communist camp, why call for a system of collective security to deter just the communists? In other words, what is the justification of NATO-type defensive alliances?

Much the same questions could have been (and sometimes were) asked in the 1930s, when the peace of Europe and the world was threatened by Nazi Germany and Fascist Italy. In fact the Fascists and the Nazis often, and quite plausibly, denounced the 'hypocrisy' of Western statesmen and spokesmen who fulminated against German and Italian aggression while their own countries were still enjoying the fruits of colonial aggression committed in previous centuries. The moral indignation displayed by Western war and peacetime propaganda against the aggressive acts and designs of the dictators was, indeed, spurious. There is no difference, in terms of international ethics, between the colonial conquests made by Britain, France, the Netherlands and Portugal – and, for that matter, Imperial Russia – in the eighteenth and nineteenth centuries and the expansion within Europe which, in our century, has been the aim of German and Soviet aggression. The short answer to the neutralist arguments is that moral judgements are irrelevant in this matter. We are faced with the fact that the kind of expansion upon which, at various times during the present century, the rulers of Germany and Soviet Russia have embarked, is apt to threaten the independence and integrity of other countries – incidentally at a period in history which is marked by the withdrawal of the colonial powers from their overseas possessions and by the emergence of the ex-colonies as independent states. It is natural and logical for the threatened nations to take all available diplomatic and military steps in their own defence, just as it would have been natural for the African, Indian and other victims of Western colonial expansion to mobilize all military and political resources in resisting their European conquerors.

Generally speaking, it should be made clear from the start that no moral condemnation of individual rulers or statesmen is implied when a country's foreign policy is described as aggressive, or when the appraisal of historic events has led to the conclusion that a government has failed to honour its pledges. All great powers and many smaller ones have, at some time or other, been engaged in territorial expansion. In some cases such policies may be dictated by personal motives, such as the personal or dynastic ambitions of a despotic ruler. The ephemeral empires of Alexander the Great, of Napoleon and Hitler are examples that come to mind. But as a general rule it may be assumed that governmental policies are a reflection of what is commonly called the 'national interest' – that they are pursued because they appear to serve the interests of at least an influential social stratum of the country concerned. Indeed, it is only on this assumption that an analysis of a foreign government's political motivation, and predictions regarding future developments, are possible.[11]

The same approach is valid for an appraisal of Western foreign policy. The moderation of Western statesmen in the recent past (Britain's and the USA's respect for the principles of the Atlantic Charter, for example) has nothing to do with the individual character of these statesmen. It simply expresses the historical fact that in the second half of the twentieth century the main capitalist powers have ceased to be interested in territorial gains in Europe or elsewhere. In other words, in appraising world political problems it is impossible to judge antagonistic policies in terms of good or evil, or to make a moral distinction between the defenders of the *status quo* and those who wish to upset it. Time and circumstances, not ethical imperatives, determine the peacefulness or aggressiveness of a country's external policies.

The temptation to apply moral criteria seems to be particularly compelling when it comes to assessing communist policies and their motivation. Certain critics of the Soviet and other communist regimes never tire of quoting – and largely misinterpreting – Lenin's dictum that it is necessary for revolutionary socialists 'to use any ruse, cunning, illegal method, evasion, deceit'. This was addressed, primarily, to revolutionaries in opposition, not to communist governments in their dealings with their capitalist counterparts. Lenin was telling the Party militants (many of whom, whatever their errors, were dedicated men and women with a noble vision, naturally reluctant to resort to subterfuge and deceit) that they were fighting a powerful and ruthless enemy, and that in this struggle they would be facing hopeless odds unless they, too, were prepared to be ruthless. But however he may have meant it, there is no doubt that he and the Bolsheviks did employ such methods when seeking and gaining power; and many political parties and individual politicians throughout the world and throughout history, whether communist or not, have done the same. Lenin himself later used the most obnoxious stratagems in order to retain and strengthen his power. His successors did likewise; so did, and do, communist and non-communist rulers of many lands. Nor are knavish tricks in international relations a peculiarity of any particular type of regime. There is nothing specifically communist about immorality in politics.

It is not only the anti-communists who tend to apply moral yardsticks or to attribute aggressiveness to the character of the individual ruler or rulers, instead of seeing it as a reflection of the economic, political and geographical conditions prevailing at a given time. Some communist partisans and fellow-travellers who, in Stalin's days, were never at a loss for an explanation and an excuse for Russia's ever-changing policies and for all the horrors and brutalities of the period, later admitted that evil things did happen under Stalin's dictatorship, but maintained that all evils had died with the dictator. Now, it is, indeed, highly probable that the nature and intensity of the purges, the extermination of real or presumed opponents, the abductions and assassinations of exiles, defectors, etc., somehow reflected a vicious streak in Stalin's character. If Stalin had been a different kind of person some features of his regime might have been different, although during his rule, too, 'liberal' phases alternated with harsh ones. But the general trend of the USSR's foreign policies would have been the same. It was not affected by Stalin's death in 1953, by Malenkov's removal in 1955 or by Khrushchev's downfall in 1964.[12]

Totalitarianism and aggression

Like the aggressor states of the 1930s, the communist powers of today are totalitarian dictatorships. Some Western critics of communism think there is a definite link between the totalitarian character of these regimes and their propensity for acts of aggression. There is no evidence for this. Dictatorships will feel less inhibited than are liberal democracies when it comes to waging wars of aggression and conquest. In the past aggressive wars have often been launched by dictators, but not invariably so. In the eighteenth and nineteenth centuries several European powers with liberal institutions and a democratic-parliamentary system of government were engaged in large-scale colonial conquest. Whoever was responsible for the First World War, it was not a totalitarian regime. None of the great powers that clashed in 1914 was totalitarian in the modern sense. Germany and Austria were less democratic than Britain or France, but they were more free and democratic than tsarist Russia. And even Russia was not 'totalitarian' in 1914: she had a rudimentary parliamentary system and a modicum of civil liberties.

An evident relationship between dictatorship and aggression

did, however, emerge in the inter-war period. About half-way through this period the 'Briand-Kellogg Pact', which outlawed war as an instrument of national policy, was concluded: it was signed in 1928 and became operative in 1929, when nearly all independent countries in the world, including all major powers, had ratified it. Ironically the conclusion of this anti-war pact preceded a series of aggressive actions, beginning in the early thirties; and it is surely of some significance that the perpetrators of all these acts were totalitarian or semi-totalitarian governments – all of them, incidentally, signatories to the Briand-Kellogg Pact. In 1931 Japan invaded Manchuria. In 1934 Nazi Germany insti-gated a coup in Austria which, if successful, would have imposed Nazism and German domination on that country four years before this actually happened. In 1935 Germany tore up the Versailles Treaty and introduced conscription. In the same year Italy invaded Ethiopia. In 1936 German troops marched into the Rhineland, in violation of the Locarno Pact. In 1937 Japan in-vaded China proper. In 1938 Germany annexed Austria and forced Czechoslovakia, under threat of war, to surrender the Sudetenland. In the spring of 1939 Germany occupied Bohemia and forced Lithuania to cede the Memel territory, while Italy invaded and occupied Albania. Later that year Germany invaded Poland, thus launching the Second World War, and Soviet Russia invaded eastern Poland and Finland. In 1940 Germany occupied five neutral countries; Russia annexed the three Baltic Republics and parts of Rumania; Italy invaded Greece. In 1941 Germany occupied Yugoslavia and Greece and then invaded Russia. At the end of the same year Japan attacked the USA and Britain.

This is in stark contrast to the record of the 'democracies' during that period. They did not resort to armed force or go to war, except in self-defence or in aid of a victim of aggression. Unavoid-ably they found themselves in alliance with the totalitarian USSR, which had committed aggression in the recent past. On the other hand, the only parliamentary democracy fighting on the Axis side was Finland, and here unique circumstances prevailed: Finland had joined Germany in a vain attempt to recover territory which Russia had forced her to cede in 1940. Apart from Finland the Axis was, indeed, a coalition of totalitarian aggressor states.

We have seen that the advanced Western countries which happened to have parliamentary regimes had no motive for adopting expansionist policies: they were satiated and eager to maintain the *status quo* – even ready to make concessions to appease the dictators for the sake of preserving peace and the essence of the *status quo*. But why did aggression become the prerogative of dictatorship? More specifically: why did all major powers with dictatorial regimes wage wars of aggression in the 1930s and 1940s?

There are several possible explanations. A natural corollary of dictatorship is militarism; and the combination of militarism and opportunity for aggression, together perhaps with collective feelings of frustration born of former setbacks or an imagined lack of 'living space', tends to produce a chauvinistic mood of expansionist adventure. Such factors might account for the aggression of Germany, Italy and Japan in the 1930s, but hardly for the expansionist policy pursued by the USSR from 1939 onwards. Another explanation, sometimes offered by Marxists, is that capitalist 'have-not' countries, whose ruling classes favour territorial expansion for economic reasons, will tend to turn Fascist, or at any rate dictatorial, because a dictatorship will normally find it easier to cope with the problems of material and psychological preparations for war. Again this explanation might hold good for pre-war Germany, Italy or Japan; but the Soviet Union was not a 'have-not' country and had been a dictatorship long before she resorted to aggression – in the mid-thirties she advocated the maintenance of the *status quo*, the League of Nations and 'collective security' against the danger of German and Japanese aggression.

The USSR, clearly, is in a category by herself. Her motives for turning aggressive and expansionist after the outbreak of the Second World War are not in any way linked with a turn towards totalitarianism or to a desire for more 'living space'. How, then, can we explain the paradox that the USSR, satiated and normally a defender of the *status quo*, is yet apt to resort to aggression during certain periods and in certain circumstances?

The USSR and the Cold War

Soviet expansionism since the Second World War

Michael Stewart's assessment of the USSR's post-war policy is certainly correct in regard to its negative aspect. The Soviet Union refrains from 'snatching anything' if this could lead to world war – or, practically speaking, to war with the USA. In this respect the USSR differs fundamentally from the dictatorships of the thirties: Nazi Germany, Fascist Italy and Japan could not be deterred; they risked war – and actually found themselves at war with other world powers. The Soviet Union can be deterred by the prospect of a major confrontation; she sought to avoid war with Germany between 1939 and 1941 and with the USA and her allies after 1945. Fear of getting involved in a war with America prompted the withdrawal of Soviet troops from Iran in the spring of 1946, the abandonment of two attempts to force the West out of Berlin in 1948–9 and again in 1958–61 and the removal of nuclear missiles from Cuba in October 1962. If war with Hitler was not averted, it was not for want of trying on Stalin's part.

Yet if Russia was careful not to provoke a major war after 1945, she managed to get away with a vast 'peaceful' increase in power and territory. Within three years of the end of the Second World War the USSR had established, by annexation and satellization, a substantial puppet empire in Eastern Europe. No parallel development had taken place in the West. There was no annexation of German, Austrian or Italian territory by any of the West European powers. France temporarily administered the Saarland – as she had done after the First World War – but restored it after a plebiscite in which the inhabitants had opted for a return to Germany. France would have had a better claim to the left bank of the Rhine than the Russians had to Koenigsberg: the territory west of the Rhine had once belonged to France, and in the days of Napoleon that river was still generally considered to be France's 'natural' eastern border. But no such considerations affected the post-1945 settlement, under which Germany's frontiers with France, Belgium, Holland and Luxembourg followed the line laid down at Versailles a quarter of a century before. After her defeat in the Second World War Germany lost, to her eastern neighbours, over a quarter of what had been her territory under the Versailles Treaty, but not an inch in the West. Her Western neighbours did not seek to punish her by claiming frontier revision. Nor did Britain try to recover Heligoland which, after being ceded by Britain to Germany in 1890 (in exchange for Zanzibar), was used by Germany as a key base in naval warfare in both world wars.

Unlike the Soviet Union, the main Western powers did not try to turn their military preponderance in the liberated regions into political domination. After the collapse of the Nazi 'New Order' Western Europe returned to the pre-war pattern: a number of independent states with parliamentary regimes re-emerged. The USA made no attempt to convert France, Belgium or Holland into puppet states, and even the defeated and temporarily occupied Axis countries, (West) Germany and Italy, eventually resumed full sovereignty. All European countries outside the Soviet orbit were able to pursue their own policies, free from outside interference; and these policies, as the Americans discovered to their chagrin, often diverged sharply from the political line Washington would have liked to see adopted in Western Europe.

There was another significant contrast between the Soviet and the Western attitudes after 1945. Between the end of the war and 1948 the USA reduced its armed strength from 11 million to $1\frac{1}{2}$ million men, and Britain reduced hers from five million to 750,000 men. Russia did not demobilize below a level of four million. In 1948 the USSR possessed armed forces larger than those of all the rest of the world put together – not counting China, where communists and nationalists were then locked in civil war. The USSR's strength, and the presence or proximity of her forces, played a decisive part in the extension and consolidation of the Soviet sphere of influence in Eastern and Central Europe.

The propaganda war

While this dual process was going on – growing Soviet power in Eastern Europe; disarmament and return to peacetime conditions in the West – the propaganda apparatus of the Soviet Union and the other countries of the Soviet bloc unleashed a savage anti-Western campaign. Immediately after the war Britain was the main target of the attack; later, from 1947 onwards, the USA became the No. 1 enemy. The other Western countries, and in particular the colonial and ex-colonial powers, were not spared. America was accused of arming for war, of turning European countries into puppet states, of having broken wartime and post-war pledges – in short, of all the things the Russians themselves had done and kept on doing. When the British gave freedom to India and Burma, and the Dutch to Indonesia, Soviet propaganda asserted that the independence of these new countries was a sham and that their leaders were imperialist stooges: Britain, it was claimed, was still ruling India and Burma by indirect methods, while the Indonesians had merely exchanged their Dutch masters for American ones.[13] At the same time Soviet leaders and spokesmen insisted that Bulgaria, Poland, Rumania, Hungary, etc., were truly sovereign and independent – naturally friendly towards the socialist Soviet Union and grateful for her help, but in no way Soviet-dominated.

Satellite propaganda chimed in enthusiastically. The Poles held Britain and France partly responsible for Poland's destruction in 1939, but praised the Soviet Union for having 'liberated' the country in 1944. The East German communist rulers accepted without demur the Soviet-imposed Oder-Neisse frontier with Poland, but launched a jingoist campaign against French moves to integrate the tiny Saarland economically with France, denouncing this as an imperialist violation of Germany's sacred soil. In similar terms they attacked Britain for using Heligoland (whence the civilian population of a few thousand had been evacuated) as a target for practice bombing.

Furthermore Soviet and satellite propaganda 'explained' and justified all acts of aggression and all expansionist manoeuvres of the USSR just before, during and after the Second World War, including the Stalin-Hitler pact, the partition of Poland, the invasion of Finland and the annexation of the Baltic countries and Rumanian territory. This, incidentally, is still the official position throughout the communist camp. Even at the height of 'de-Stalinization', following the Twentieth Soviet Communist Party Congress in 1956, criticisms of Stalin's conduct never extended to his foreign policy. He was blamed for failing to anticipate the German invasion and to make adequate defensive preparations, but not for conniving at Hitler's onslaught on Poland, or for the war against Finland, or the subsequent annexations. Official communist historiography still regards the Munich Agreement as an abominable crime but Soviet collaboration with Nazi Germany from 1939 to 1941, and all the Soviet rulers did during that period, as apt to serve the cause of world peace and of socialism. And, indeed, it could not be otherwise. However much Stalin's successors may criticize the 'personality cult' and certain aspects of his domestic policy, or of the part he played during the war, they cannot possibly condemn the actions by which Soviet Russia acquired the foreign territories she still holds and intends to keep.

Western reaction: the fight for Berlin

Moscow's expansionist policies in the first three years after the end of the Second World War produced Soviet domination over a number of East European countries. These policies did not involve a risk of war because (as Stalin had correctly calculated) the Western powers, and in particular the USA, deemed resistance to the communization of such countries as Poland, Hungary and the Soviet zone of Germany impractical. Western resistance did become effective when the Soviet Union tried to spread her creed and her rule, not in neighbouring Eastern Europe but in the direction of the Asian no-man's land. In 1945 the Russian leaders took advantage of the presence in Iran of Soviet troops (dating back to 1941) to set up a communist puppet regime in Persian Azerbaijan. Vigorous Western support for Persia's protest, and strong pressure on the part of the USA caused the Russians to withdraw from this province in May 1946, whereupon the communist regime in Azerbaijan collapsed. Soviet expansion was checked in Greece by force of arms; here the USSR was not officially and directly involved, so there was no danger of an outright confrontation. The activities of the communist guerillas were countered by military measures combined with Western economic and military aid to the Greek Government. In France and, particularly, in Italy the communist threat took the form of a constitutional-parliamentary challenge: it seemed possible for communist parties to be voted into power. Here again the USSR as such was not involved, and the only means the other Western powers had of influencing events was to halt the swing of opinion towards communism by granting material aid which contributed to economic rehabilitation. In the event the communists did not, in either country, come anywhere near winning a parliamentary majority.[14]

A new chapter in post-war East—West relations opened with the so-called 'Berlin blockade' in the summer of 1948. This time the Russians, acting officially and on their own behalf (not by proxy, as so often before and after) made a direct attempt at wresting territory from Western control. It was not another thrust into no-man's land like the Persian coup, or subversion by proxy as in Greece, or aggression by proxy as two years later in Korea. Rather it was a deliberate, calculated Soviet move to force US, British and French troops out of West Berlin and to make the Western sector of the divided city part of the Soviet zone of occupation. The Russians did not resort to military action, partly, no doubt, because this might have precipitated war and partly because they believed military steps to be unnecessary. They felt sure that the cutting of road and rail links between Berlin and the West would force a Western withdrawal. When the Western Allies countered by organizing an air lift the Russians did not impede it, again out of fear of provoking a military confrontation but also because they thought the Western operation would fail anyway. The air lift, however, proved successful beyond expectation. Combined with the Western counter-blockade of rail freight into Soviet-occupied Germany, it caused the Russians to shelve their plan of removing the Western presence from Berlin. In March 1949 the blockade was lifted.

Another Berlin crisis was started by the Soviet and East German communists towards the end of 1958. On that occasion they sought to gain by stealth what they had failed to obtain by unilateral action and a show of force a decade earlier. Their proposal for turning West Berlin into a 'neutral and demilitarized free city' (while East Berlin was to remain the East German capital) was rejected by the West; had it been accepted it would have led to the erosion of the Western powers' presence in Berlin. When the communists realized, almost three years after the inception of this crisis, that they had again miscalculated the West's reaction, they played their last trump card: in August 1961 the Berlin Wall went up and the hole in the Iron Curtain disappeared.

In some way the building of the Wall was an admission of defeat, of the communists' failure to persuade or compel the Western powers to abandon their positions in Berlin. But the Wall also created the conditions of future economic success for the East German regime. The communists' wish to push the Western allies out of Berlin sprang from two motives: first, they wanted to liquidate a Western enclave in communist territory which constantly demonstrated 'capitalist' material superiority and which served the West Germans and their allies as a base for propaganda by radio and television. The second and more urgent reason was to stop the mass migration of workers, and especially of skilled workers and technicians to the West, a process that had continued ever since the partition of Germany and had reached panic proportions in 1960–1. The building of the Wall achieved some of its purposes. Together with the 'death zone' established all along the East-West German border, it halted the drain of valuable labour and thereby laid the foundations of substantial economic advance in the German Democratic Republic. By preventing East Germans and East Berliners from visiting West Berlin, the Wall also lessened the impact of Western economic efficiency. It could not eliminate anti-communist radio and TV propaganda from West Berlin; in fact, the existence of the Wall as such proved a powerful propaganda weapon in Western hands. But in this field the East subsequently obtained some relief through the 'general relations treaty' concluded between the East and West German Governments in December 1972. From the communist point of view this was a genuine compromise, especially in regard to West Berlin. By officially recognizing the links between the German Federal

Republic and West Berlin the East Germans buried, at least for the foreseeable future, their schemes for removing the Western presence from Berlin. In return they benefited from a side-effect of the treaty, the toning-down of West German propagandistic hostility which in the past twenty-five years had been a highly disturbing element in East German economic and political life.

Satellite Crises: Korea, Indo-China, Africa, Cuba

The communist *coup d'état* in Prague in February 1948, which made Czechoslovakia a Soviet satellite, and the 1948–9 Berlin blockade combined to produce a result which Stalin could not have intended: the consolidation and formalization of Western solidarity. The North Atlantic Treaty, initialled shortly after the events in Prague and signed shortly before the end of the Berlin blockade, proved a turning point in post-war East—West relations. The significance of NATO lay not so much in its official purpose: Western solidarity, which forms the Treaty's basis, was effective before its conclusion, and the *casus foederis* might never arise. Yet this demonstration of Western unity of purpose ushered in a new climate in Western foreign policy; its main aspect was the determination, particularly on the part of the USA, to contain communism on an international scale. The failure of the Berlin blockade was *one* result of the greater firmness of resolve which characterized the new era; another, possibly, was Russian inactivity in the face of Yugoslavia's defiance after the latter had broken away from the Soviet camp in 1948: Stalin then made threatening noises and might have struck (as Khrushchev did in similar circumstances in Hungary in 1956, and Brezhnev in Czechoslovakia in 1968, when Western intervention would not have been practical) if he had been sure that Soviet or satellite invasion of Yugoslavia could not trigger off an American military response.

In the summer of 1950 the USSR sanctioned the North Korean invasion of South Korea. In the choice of this particular front line the anxiety to avoid a global confrontation again played a part. Two years previously the American occupation troops had withdrawn from South Korea; this withdrawal, together with ambiguous statements by some prominent US politicians and generals, led the Russians to believe that the Americans had lost interest in the area and might not even oppose military action designed to unify the country under communist rule. When the Soviet leaders realized their mistake they did not themselves intervene militarily, not even when the North Koreans were faced with the threat of total defeat; it was then the Chinese who acted to stave off disaster. The outcome was not the victory the communists had hoped for, nor the liquidation of the communist regime in the North, which at one time had seemed within the USA's reach, but a return to the *status quo* of a partitioned Korea.

The Korean conflict was the first international confrontation in which Communist China took the stage as the main antagonist of 'Western imperialism'.[15] She played a similar part in the Indo-Chinese wars which ended (or at least appeared to end) in 1975 in communist take-overs in all three Indo-Chinese states, Vietnam, Laos and Cambodia. In Vietnam and Laos both the Soviet Union and China backed the communist side; Cambodia, on the other hand, testified to the effect of the Sino-Soviet rift in the international field: Peking wholeheartedly supported the communist Khmer Rouge while Moscow remained ostentatiously distant.

The USSR and China had clashed before in the Nigerian civil war (1967 to 1970), the former backing the Lagos federal government and the latter the breakaway state of Biafra. Later the two great communist powers were, more openly, on opposite sides in Angola, where Russia (and Cuba) lent material and military assistance to the Popular Movement for the Liberation of Angola (MPLA), while China sided with the National Front for the Liberation of Angola (FNLA) – which also received support from some Western powers. In 1976 the MPLA prevailed in most of the country and formed a government which achieved a measure of international recognition. But that was not the end of the fighting in this former Portuguese colony and it would be premature to say, at the time of writing (November 1977), that Angola has definitely become a member of the pro-Soviet communist camp.

These collisions between the USSR and China in the international arena have nothing to do with the ideological differences (such as they are) between the Chinese and the Soviet Communist Parties. These clashes were, on both sides (as well as on the part of other intervening powers), old-fashioned exercises in power politics and nothing else. It would, therefore, be wrong to assume that, for example, the regime in Angola, while it maintains its links with the USSR and Cuba, will organize its economic life in accordance with the official Soviet interpretation of Marxism-Leninism, or that a different course would have been followed if, after the withdrawal of the Portuguese, the internal struggle had not been won by the MPLA but by the NFLA or UNITA, the third independence movement.

The accession of Cuba to the communist camp cannot be described as a result of Soviet expansionist policies. Castro's victory in 1959 was a windfall for Russia, just as Yugoslavia's defection had been for the West eleven years previously. Cuba's espousal of Marxism-Leninism was apparently something neither the USSR nor Mao's China had planned or worked for. Nor is there any reason to assume that the Cuban missile crisis in October 1962 was the outcome of Soviet long-term planning in Cold War strategy. The Russians were simply trying to derive maximum advantage from the fact that a Latin-American country on the USA's doorstep had unpredictably become a friend and ally. The communization of Cuba cannot, therefore, be seen as the continuation of the USSR's post-war drive to extend her sphere of influence.

Communist imperialism and its prospects

Peaceful coexistence?

The communists' half-hearted second bid for West Berlin, which for all practical purposes ended with the building of the Wall in 1961, has been the Soviet camp's last outright expansionist move to date. Since then there has been a comparative easing in East—West relations, a *détente*, formalized in the 'Final Act' of the Helsinki Conference on Security and Co-operation in Europe. The conference had been convened at the Soviet Union's suggestion, and the final declaration was signed by thirty-five heads of state or government on 1 August 1975. This declaration, a lengthy and detailed yet vaguely worded document, ratified the frontiers established in Europe after the Second World War. It forbade frontier changes by force, as well as the seizure or military occupation of 'part or all of the territory of any participating state'. This confirmation of existing frontiers was in line with Soviet wishes; so was the acceptance, by all signatory powers, of the separate existence of two German states.

Soviet insistence on a treaty clause proclaiming the inviolability of frontiers is an indication that the Soviet Government does not – or, at least, did not at the time – contemplate any frontier changes or acquisitions of foreign territory. Circumstances can, of course, alter very suddenly. For instance, when the Soviet Union signed the Atlantic Charter in January 1942 she undertook to seek 'no aggrandizement, territorial or other', and to countenance 'no territorial changes that do not accord with the freely expressed wishes of the peoples concerned'.[16] A few years later the USSR, and with her connivance another East European communist state, annexed vast tracts of territory whose native inhabitants had not been consulted but expelled.

If the ratification in Helsinki of the post-1945 frontiers was a Western concession to the Soviet Union, the latter reciprocated by agreeing to a number of provisions by which the signatories promised to encourage the free movement of ideas, information and people across state boundaries and to respect 'human rights and fundamental freedoms, including the freedom of thought, conscience, religion or belief'. The incorporation in the Helsinki text of these undertakings has not so far made a discernible difference with regard to the degree of political or religious repression in the USSR, but it has strengthened the Western position, in that it has enabled the non-communist signatories to claim that the human rights situation within Soviet territory is not a purely internal matter, since by withholding fundamental rights and freedoms from its own citizens – including political dissidents – the Soviet Government is violating an express provision of an external treaty.

But whatever the practical policies of the governments which were represented at Helsinki (or at the aftermath in Belgrade), there is no doubt that a certain limited *détente* has materialized. It is not the first time this has happened. There was a similar prolonged pause in the confrontation between Soviet Russia (then the only communist state in the world) and the Western powers between the wars. Then, too, the Soviet leaders pursued a policy of 'peaceful coexistence' with the capitalist world. This was most marked between 1933 and 1939, between the victory of Nazism in Germany and the outbreak of the Second World War. During that period the USSR joined the League of Nations, established diplomatic relations with the United States and concluded defensive alliances with France and Czechoslovakia. Many Western observers allowed themselves to be convinced that Russia would never resume her drive for territorial gain and the widening of her sphere of influence and that she had, once and for all, abandoned the traditional expansionist ambitions of the tsarist regime.

We know now that these conclusions were wrong. Yet the opinion is again widely held in the non-communist world that the Soviet Union, a 'satisfied' power, will not embark again on conquest and satellization, that she would not have a motive for doing so even if Western military organization and the Western arsenal did not act as a deterrent. What this view implies is that the need for defensive alliances such as NATO has disappeared, at least in so far as these are directed against a potential threat emanating from the USSR and not, for example, from Communist China.

Is this optimistic view of the East—West relationship justified? Are there more solid reasons now to believe in the permanence of peaceful coexistence than there were before the Second World War? The crucial question is whether a situation is likely to arise which furnishes the Soviet leadership with a motive for aggressive action.

Soviet aggression, as we have seen, does not stem from

Marxist-Leninist doctrine which, as currently interpreted by official ideologues, is the state religion in all communist countries. The totalitarian character of a regime does not by itself create the proclivity to commit aggression. A ruling class or caste which is bent on war might be inclined to smooth its path and facilitate the preparation for and the waging of war by replacing democratic institutions, where they exist, by dictatorial ones. But the motive for expansion must exist independently of the nature of the regime that pursues expansionist designs.

The question of whether the USSR, if she could disregard the Western deterrent and the threat of nuclear war with the USA, would be likely to embark again upon a policy of systematic expansion is impossible to answer in the abstract. But a situation could be visualized in which the temptation to take aggressive action – not so much for expansion as for maintaining the *status quo* of Soviet domination – might be extremely strong for the Soviet rulers. This follows from a characteristic of the Soviet state which has not yet been mentioned: the USSR is a colonial empire. To be more specific, it is the largest surviving colonial empire, and the only one that is also a great nuclear power. The time has come to spell out the implications of this fact.

The Soviet colonial empire

The colonial character of the Russian empire was the basic element in the Soviet Government's decisions to undertake armed intervention in Hungary in 1956 and in Czechoslovakia in 1968. The link between Soviet colonialism and the crisis in the Soviet bloc which erupted on those two occasions is brought to light by something the late Walter Kolarz wrote in 1964. In an essay headed 'The Hungarian Anti-Colonial Revolution' he had this to say about the motives prompting Soviet action in Hungary:

The offensive of Soviet tanks and aircraft against the Hungarian people was a desperate effort to maintain the cohesion of the Soviet colonial empire . . . The loss of Hungary might have had the most far-reaching consequences on Soviet power and prestige inside the USSR . . . The Ukraine would have become the neighbour of a democratic country of the Western type. This . . . would have had a tremendous psychological effect on the Ukrainian people. But had the Hungarian example been imitated in Rumania and Bulgaria, this might have affected the Soviet Union even more immediately and more dangerously. The overthrow of Rumania's communist regime . . . would have had immediate repercussions on the two million Moldavians – a people speaking a Rumanian dialect, and separated from Rumania only by the river Pruth . . . Finally in the Soviet-occupied Baltic countries the impact of the Hungarian events was such that the official spokesman of the communist regime admitted quite openly that they had stimulated political opposition . . . The Communist Party Secretary of Lithuania told the Lithuanian Soviet Parliament at the beginning of December 1956: 'The armed rising of the reaction against the democratic regime in Hungary has encouraged the reactionaries in our Republic . . . the bourgeois-nationalist elements and their various helpmates, started to raise their heads.' Similar complaints were made by the Latvian Party Secretary . . . who asserted that nationalist propaganda in Latvia had increased.

Soviet anxiety that the example of Hungary would be contagious played a decisive part in determining the brutal Soviet action in Hungary. . . .[17]

Considerations of this kind must have applied *a fortiori* when the Soviet rulers decided to intervene in Czechoslovakia twelve years later. The Carpatho-Ukrainian territory, on which both Hungary and Czechoslovakia border, was once part of Czechoslovakia and was annexed by the Soviet Union after the Second World War. The people of this Slav province would naturally be even more strongly impressed by events in Czechoslovakia than by what happened in non-Slav Hungary. Furthermore the danger of, for example, a Rumanian breakaway from the Soviet bloc (though not necessarily in the form of an overthrow of Rumania's communist regime) was certainly more acute in 1968 than it had been in 1956. It is, in actual fact, conceivable that the USSR's action against Czechoslovakia did have the result of deterring Rumania from overstepping certain limits in asserting her independence.

The view that the USSR is an imperialist power and a colonial empire in which the Great Russians (just over half the total population of the Soviet Union) play the part of colonial masters is, of course, hotly disputed by official Soviet theory, which claims that the non-Russian nations of the USSR remain voluntarily, and indeed enthusiastically, within its borders. Yet unless one accepts the communist definition of colonialism as a facet of *capitalist* development (i.e. as something that, by definition, cannot occur under communism), there is no sense in which British, French, Dutch or Portuguese territorial expansion in recent centuries could be regarded as colonialist while Russian aggrandizement could not be so described. The features normally associated with colonialism are all inherent in the relationship between Russia proper and the minority nations of the Soviet Union: concentration of power in the hands of the metropolitan rulers, political impotence of the nation-states and republics of which the USSR is composed, national oppression and discrimination, coupled with systematic Russification of the non-Russian regions, economic inequality and exploitation.[18]

In denying the charge of colonialism Soviet propaganda usually points to the massive social and material benefits which Russian rule is said to have conferred on many backward peoples, especially since the October Revolution. Such claims are largely valid. So are similar claims made by the conventional type of Western colonialist about rising standards of living and of health in African and other colonial or ex-colonial territories. The main difference is that old-style Western imperialists are not normally able to conceal the fact that the colonial masses were resentful of European domination and not invariably appreciative of the progress introduced by the conquerors. The Soviet communist rulers, who have perfected the police state and the system of doctrinal uniformity, manage to keep up the pretence of fraternal accord, and even of equality, between the Russians and the subject nations.

The colonial nature of the Russian empire has to some extent been obscured by its genesis. Like other colonial empires, the Russian empire has been built by the conquest and subjection of a variety of peoples, some more, some less backward than the Great Russians of Muscovy. But unlike the modern empires founded by the British and other West European nations, the Russian empire has expanded by absorbing one contiguous area after another:

hence, this process has not been generally recognized for what it is – the acquisition by the Great Russians, by military force, penetration or diplomacy, of colonial territories inhabited by non-Russians. These peculiarities of Russian colonial expansion were expounded in 1964 by Edward Crankshaw in his foreword to Kolarz's *Communism and Colonialism*, from which the quotation (on pp. 188–9) was taken. Mr Crankshaw wrote:

The existence of the British empire . . . was always plain for all to see. All the imperial territories were far removed from the tiny island from which their conquerors came. The Russian imperialists had the inestimable advantage of interior lines. The gradual extension of the tsarist empire rarely called for a sea voyage, an expedition: the Russians simply spread outwards, consolidating each step before moving to the next, and firmly binding their latest acquisition through military, police and bureaucracy to the metropolitan centre. They did this under the tsars, they did it again under Lenin, and once more under Stalin when, in 1945, they began to move into Eastern and Central Europe.

Crankshaw also dealt with the communist thesis that the relationship between the Russians and the minority nations ceased to be imperialistic after 1917:

Lenin was once a genuine anti-imperialist, and he attacked tsarist imperialism and British and French imperialism . . . But when, after the success of his revolution, he became a responsible Head of State he had second thoughts. When Georgians, Ukrainians, Azerbaijanians and others proclaimed their sovereign independence and set up their own governments he knew at once that it was the duty of the Russian Bolsheviks . . . to bring what had once been component parts of the tsarist empire into the communist fold. Such action was all the more imperative since the Russians depended on Azerbaijan and Georgia for their oil, on Turkestan for their cotton, on the Ukraine for much of their bread and a great deal of their steel.

The imperialist nature of the Soviet state is not affected by the provision of the USSR's Constitution which grants the component republics the right to secede from the Union and to establish themselves as fully independent states.[19] The right of secession exists – on paper. It is significant that the legislative organs of the Soviet Union have never bothered to lay down a constitutional procedure whereby the Union republics could assert this right. Territorial separatism has, in fact, always been considered a crime in the USSR – particularly during the purges of the thirties, when the indictment often included the charge of activities designed to 'dismember' the Soviet Union. Many people were sentenced to death and executed for actions which – even if they had committed them – should have been considered lawful under the Constitution. It is safe to say that it is just as impossible now as it was in the 1930s for any part of the USSR peaceably to achieve separation from the Union and sovereign independence.

The survival of Soviet colonialism – anachronistic in the present world political context – is probably due to the 'compactness' of the Russian empire. The British, the French, the Dutch and the Portuguese, sometimes under pressure but often willingly and indeed eagerly, have divested themselves of their overseas possessions. Western colonialism survives precariously in southern Africa: but there, too, its days seem numbered. The winds of change have had no comparable effect on the position within the Soviet Union. It would appear that the 'interior lines' which facilitated Russia's imperialist expansion have so far enabled the Great Russians to keep anti-colonialist trends at bay and to go on administering from its European centre this vast, compact landmass. The imposition of a uniform governmental doctrine, of a uniform economic, political and administrative system, would have been impossible, for instance, in a far-flung, scattered empire like the British, had the British attempted it. In the vast, coherent territory that is the Soviet Union, economic, political, ideological and even cultural integration has not appeared unattainable, and stereotype propagandistic indoctrination may even have partly succeeded in inculcating a synthetic sense of common nationhood.

The dangers of decolonization

If it is true that geographical compactness and 'interior lines' have facilitated the preservation of the multi-national empire, it is equally true that these features make it impossible for the ruling sections at the centre to do anything but try to preserve the empire intact at all costs. Where the metropolis and the colonies are adjacent, and have been welded into one administrative and political unit, decolonization becomes something too perilous to contemplate, for it is apt to lead to complete disintegration. The liquidation of the Western and Japanese colonial empires did not (contrary to Leninist predictions) result in social and economic collapse in the 'imperialist' metropolitan countries. But while the dissolution of their empires did not tend to disrupt the political structure of the ex-colonial powers, the general upsurge of nationalism – of which the colonial peoples' striving for independence forms one aspect – did produce secessionist movements, based on genuine or spurious claims to separate nationhood, in the 'minority' regions of, for example, Britain, France and Spain. The indisputably multi-national Soviet Union is naturally more vulnerable in this respect than the countries of Western Europe. Decolonization (i.e. the grant of independence to any non-Russian part of the Soviet empire – say, the Baltic provinces or Tajikistan or the Ukraine) would stimulate separatism throughout the USSR and even in Russia proper. For the 'Russian Federation' or RSFSR itself comprises a huge, heterogeneous territory without natural boundaries. The most likely end-result would be the complete fragmentation of what is now the Soviet Union. Hence the Western alternative of attaining prosperity and retaining stability after releasing the colonial possessions from tutelage does not present itself to the rulers of the USSR. To combat the anti-colonial virus must be a matter of life or death for any Russian government, whatever its political or social complexion.

The urge to maintain the cohesion of the Soviet empire accounts, at least in part, for the dictatorial character of the Soviet regime and that of its tsarist predecessors. Many, if not most, multi-national states suffer from an inherent weakness. Friction occurs even in such countries as Belgium, Canada and (to a lesser extent) Switzerland, where democratic equality is assured and national discrimination proscribed. States that are essentially 'colonialist' – in that power is vested in the ruling section of the ruling nation – cannot allow the reins of dictatorial repression to slacken. Thus the Habsburg Dual Monarchy, similar in structure and composition to the Tsar's empire, could not survive the liberalizing trends of the nineteenth and early twentieth centuries. Liberal and nationalist tendencies, both within the USSR and among the satellite peoples, now threaten the stability and existence of the Russian empire. Without a strong central power, ruthlessly determined and able to crush and uproot all separatist aspirations and activities, this gigantic, multiform creation would long ago have suffered the fate of the Habsburg empire.[20] We are here faced with another intrinsic difference between the Russian and the Western colonial empires: the latter could, by virtue of geographical distance and lack of territorial contiguity, combine a more or less paternalistic authoritarianism in the (overseas) colonies with parliamentary democracy and civic equality in the metropolis; but totalitarian uniformity is an indispensable feature of a compact colonial empire like the Russian one.

As Walter Kolarz pointed out (in the passage quoted on pp. 188–9), the threat to the survival of the multi-national Soviet state comes mainly from the satellite system in Eastern Europe. At the end of the Second World War Stalin and his associates, anticipating post-war hostility between the USSR and the capitalist West, proceeded to construct a *cordon sanitaire* in reverse (a 'protective glacis', as George Kennan called it) in the areas the Soviet army had occupied. The Soviet Union, alone among the victorious powers, annexed vast stretches of foreign territory and established, along her Western borders, a chain of communist-ruled states subservient to Moscow's dictation. But this protective belt, once it had been created, was itself in need of protection, not so much from the constantly emphasized threat of 'capitalist aggression' but from the dangers born of the reluctance of the hitherto independent East European nations to remain within the Soviet orbit. Capitalist aggression never materialized – and probably never will. But satellite rebellion against Soviet domination has become a stark fact of the post-war world: with the single exception of Bulgaria, every East European satellite of the USSR has either broken, or attempted at least once to break, the Soviet stranglehold. Three attempts of this kind were crushed by Soviet armed power. Thus in addition to totalitarian uniformity (absolute in the USSR but qualified in the satellite states), military power is an essential characteristic of the Soviet system: armed force may be necessary, both to suppress the stirrings of national self-assertion within the Union and to prevent defection from spreading among the satellites. To avert the danger of an anti-colonial tide rising within the USSR the Kremlin must combat fissiparous tendencies in the European satellite empire. This is the basic significance both of the events in Hungary in 1956 and of the crisis caused by Czechoslovakia's 'liberalization' in 1968.

There can be no doubt that the Soviet rulers must be seriously worried about the prospects of keeping the empire intact. Nationalism in the satellite states, and in the non-Russian regions of the USSR, is but part of a world-wide phenomenon. However tightly the peoples of the Soviet Union are sealed off from the outside world, they cannot be kept unaware of the rise of national consciousness even in the more backward parts of the world. Ironically Soviet propaganda itself is driven by the exigencies of the Cold War to draw attention to the anti-colonial struggle and the emergence of independent states in what used to be colonial territory in Africa and Asia, and thereby to bring it home to the non-Russian minorities of the USSR that their own national status is, in fact, a colonial one. The native populations of the Ukraine, of Kazakhstan, of Latvia and (Soviet) Georgia are being constantly reminded of their natural solidarity with the peoples of Rhodesia and South Africa in their struggle for liberation. In the end at least the intellectual élite among the non-Russian ethnic groups will inevitably realize to what extent national self-determination is withheld from them.

The Soviet satellite dilemma

The East European satellite system was probably established by the Soviet rulers as a preliminary step leading to annexation – in the same way as the three Baltic republics were reduced to satellite status in 1939 and annexed the following year. Full-scale annexation would have been in line both with theory and with Soviet thinking, and the intention is reflected in such measures as the appointment of Soviet 'advisers' who were attached to the police forces, the armies, and ministries of economic affairs of the satellite states and given authority to intervene. Sometimes prominent Russians were placed in key positions within the satellite administration. The most remarkable case – actually a direct attempt to impose a satrap on a satellite country – was that of Soviet Marshal Rokossovsky, one of the outstanding Russian army leaders in the Second World War, who happened to be of Polish descent: in 1949 he was made Polish Minister for War and member of the Politbureau of the Polish United Workers (i.e. Communist) Party.

Yet it soon became clear that outright annexation (demotion, that is, from semi-colonial to full colonial status for the communist-ruled East European satellites), was not at that stage a practical proposition. National consciousness was strong enough to produce resentment about the country's subordinate position and definitely too strong to make it possible for annexation to be achieved without a major upheaval: the most loyal communist governments were unable to persuade the people to countenance the abandonment of the trappings of independence.

Since the end of the Second World War the Soviet rulers must repeatedly have found, to their chagrin, that so far from being able to enforce the incorporation of the East European states in the USSR, they were hard put to it to preserve Soviet hegemony in Eastern Europe. The year 1948 marked a kind of dual turning point: the completion of the satellite belt and the first defection. In February 1948 Czechoslovakia exchanged her leftish coalition government for a fully-fledged communist one and thus became a member of the Soviet bloc. A few months later Yugoslavia was expelled from the Cominform, and subsequently anathematized by the USSR and the other communist governments. It is a matter for speculation whether at that juncture Stalin contemplated military action and, if so, why he decided against it. It must be borne in mind that from the outset Yugoslavia was not a satellite in the fullest sense of the word. Communism had come to her (as to Albania) mainly through the efforts of native communist resistance fighters and not on the bayonets of the Red Army, as in Poland, Hungary, Bulgaria and East Germany. Unlike Ulbricht, Dimitrov, Gottwald, Bierut and others, Tito and the other leaders of the Yugoslav Communist Party were not Moscow-trained bureaucrats who had lived in the Soviet Union as exiles during the purges of the thirties, had duly admired the great Stalin and endorsed his zig-zag pre-war and wartime policies and had then returned home to be installed in office by the occupying power. The Yugoslavs were not subjugated: military action to prevent them from defecting would have meant a campaign not to reassert Russian domination but to enforce it for the first time. Besides, Yugoslavia has no frontier with the USSR; armed intervention in or after 1948 would have had to start from a satellite territory: to crush Tito the Soviet Union would have had to launch an inter-satellite war, in which Hungary, Rumania, Bulgaria and possibly Albania would have had to invade Yugoslavia. Perhaps Stalin considered some such move but dreaded its unpredictable consequences. It is also possible that he procrastinated in the hope of an anti-Tito palace revolution in Belgrade. Once this had failed to materialize and the conflict had come into the open it would have appeared to Stalin that it was too late to act, because to strike at Yugoslavia might then have meant military confrontation with America and her allies.

The second attempt to overthrow Soviet colonial rule, and that of the Kremlin's local henchmen, was the spontaneous rising of the East German workers in June 1953. This was inevitably a failure. The Soviet Union's course of action was quite clear: there can have been no doubt in the minds of the Russian rulers and of the Soviet commanders in East Berlin that this rising must be quelled. The challenge here came only from the masses and not even partly from Party and Government leaders, as in Yugoslavia or, later, in Poland, Hungary, Albania, Rumania and Czechoslovakia. The issue of the East German rising was far more clear-cut than the issue of any other crisis in the satellite camp: the East German rebels did not just demand independence from Moscow or the right to build 'democratic socialism' their own way; they wanted to go over to the other side of the Iron Curtain, to shed communist rule and become part of a reunified 'bourgeois' Germany, in which Bonn-style parliamentary democracy (with or without denationalisation, which would have been a secondary issue) extended to the whole of the country. This was obviously something the Russians had to stop at all costs. Besides, Soviet intervention presented no strategic or logistical problems. The Soviet garrison on the spot could put down the rising without reinforcements from outside, and for once the Russians were justified in claiming that local 'leaders' had solicited intervention.

We shall probably never know exactly why, in each subsequent satellite crisis, the Soviet rulers have reacted as they have; why they decided in favour of intervention in Hungary and Czechoslovakia but against intervention in Poland in 1956, Albania and (so far) Rumania. It may be assumed that there were divided counsels on each occasion and that much heart-searching preceded the actual decision. The crucial question on which the decisions have depended must always have been to what extent the development in the satellite country has imperilled the cohesion of the Russian empire and jeopardized the prospects of its survival. In principle each defection or threat of defection, or even each single self-assertive act of defiance by a satellite, tends to weaken imperial security up to a certain point. So whenever a decision has had to be taken on whether to intervene or not, the issue would have hinged on an appraisal of the consequences of military action – or inaction. Could military action be relied on to be swift and effective? On the other hand, would not its advantages (from the Soviet imperialist point of view) be outweighed by the harmful political repercussions in the world at large, i.e. in the communist countries, among the working masses anywhere, in the communist parties of the West, in the Third World? In the case of Czechoslovakia the detrimental consequences were foreseeable and probably largely foreseen by the Soviet leaders when they decided to intervene; they must, therefore, have felt that action was nonetheless imperative and that the evil consequences – such as Russia's loss of prestige and the blow to world communism – were the price that had to be paid for avoiding the disastrous consequences of inaction.

Whatever may be thought of the Russians' attempt to justify the invasion, the danger of Czechoslovakia's defection from the 'socialist camp' and the Warsaw alliance was quite real. The liberal reforms initiated by Dubček and his colleagues were apt to usher in a democratic climate of free debate, including the right of open dissent – a political situation in which a future move to opt out of the communist bloc could not be excluded. But the threat inherent in Czechoslovakia's possible defection was not a military one: it was a threat to the cohesion of the Russian colonial empire. Strategically speaking, the position of Czechoslovakia would hardly be relevant in a full-scale nuclear war. And the theory that Russia wanted to protect herself from the threat of a conventional West German attack along, *inter alia*, West Germany's frontier with Czechoslovakia can be discounted.

Soviet intervention was thus not prompted by military considerations. Nor did concern for ideological purity play a part. If Russia insisted on Press censorship in Czechoslovakia, or on the Party's monopoly of power, she was not moved by the wish to enforce respect for Marxist-Leninist orthodoxy – which, incidentally, prescribes neither Press censorship nor one-party rule. Behind the Soviet demands was the Kremlin leaders' awareness that the logic of the process of democratization in Czechoslovakia was likely to produce a constitutional reality in which the continued adherence to the communist bloc would have depended on the fluctuating state of public opinion. This prospect the Kremlin could not tolerate.

When deciding on intervention the men in the Kremlin must have looked at the problem in the light of the experience of inter-state relations within the bloc since the end of the war. In East Germany in 1953 and in Hungary in 1956 intervention had proved effective in the short and long terms. Non-intervention in Poland in 1956 had paid off: in retrospect it must have seemed that Khrushchev was lucky in his gamble at that stage.[21] But failure to intervene in Yugoslavia, in Albania and in Rumania had lost the USSR two of her eight East European satellites and had weakened her hold on a third. With Czechoslovakia going the same way, half of the Soviet satellite empire as it was at its zenith in the spring of 1948 would have gone. It is understandable that the Soviet rulers, or at least the majority of those who mattered, should have concluded that the time had come to stop the rot, lest the very structure of Soviet colonial power should crumble. Hence the decision to strike, regardless of world reaction. Czechoslovakia's defection had to be prevented and if the obstreperous Rumanian leadership could be brought to heel in the process, so much the better.

The seeds of East—West conflict

There is a further question the Soviet rulers must ask themselves before deciding on intervention within the satellite empire: what would be the impact of armed action on the international situation in the context of the East—West antagonism? In present circumstances neither of the two superpowers wishes to risk a nuclear conflict with the other; the USSR would not, except under extreme duress, take any action in any part of the world that would be likely to involve her in war with the USA. Now, the invasions of Hungary in 1956 and of Czechoslovakia in 1968 were *defensive* operations, inasmuch as they were designed to preserve but not to extend the Soviet Union's territorial possessions and sphere of influence. This is the principal reason why these interventions were not likely to lead to a confrontation with the West.

Yet the potential chain reaction described by Kolarz might well, in certain circumstances, induce the rulers of the multi-national USSR to resort to an aggressive – albeit preventive – operation that might spark off a global conflict. There is an instructive precedent: Austria's policy in 1914. One of the national minority groups in the Habsburg empire was the Bosnian Serbs who looked on the Kingdom of Serbia as their true motherland. The resultant irredentist movement was one of the factors threatening the cohesion of the multi-national Dual Monarchy. The outrage at Sarajevo in June 1914 seemed to offer the Government in Vienna the long-awaited opportunity of crushing Serbia and thereby striking at the roots of Slav irredentism. Austria struck – and in the process provoked the First World War which eventually caused the downfall of the Habsburg empire and brought the Slav national aspirations to fruition.

There are elements in the Central European situation today which could give rise to developments along similar lines. Some 17 out of a total of 70 million Germans form part of the Soviet satellite belt in Eastern Europe. Their allegiance is not to the Soviet camp, the communist cause, the East German state, but overwhelmingly to Germany – to the reunified Germany they long for. Obviously the East Germans' desire for reunion with their West German fellow countrymen conflicts with the interest the Soviet Union has in keeping the German Democratic Republic within the communist orbit. The separation of this territory from the satellite system would have a destructive effect on this system and ultimately on the multi-national Soviet state itself. Yet the striving of the majority of East Germans for national reunification and, implicitly, for integration with the non-communist West, will persist as long as the Federal Republic exists and prospers. And despite the German Democratic Republic's economic progress in recent years the West German Federal Republic is still vastly more prosperous; its workers enjoy a higher living standard than their East German class brothers. This dangerous attraction which the West German state has for the East Germans accounts for the fierce hostility which Soviet Russia has, until recently, displayed towards the Bonn state – a hostility quite out of proportion to the military threat which West Germany, no longer a world power and without nuclear arms, could possibly present to the Soviet Union.

Since a centre-left West German Government some years ago embarked on its *Ostpolitik*, tension has visibly eased between West Germany on the one hand and Russia and the East European communist countries on the other. The danger of confrontation, as a product of the failure to solve the German problem, now seems remote. But the process has not gone far enough to be irreversible. If a right-wing government committed to a return to Adenauer's policy were to take office in Bonn in a few years' time (by no means an unlikely prospect), a situation could arise in which the Russians felt that the existence or the policy of the Federal Republic, or the particular role played by West Berlin, might lead to another upheaval in East Germany and, eventually, to a change of regime and East Germany's defection from the Eastern bloc. In that case the Soviet leaders might feel tempted to take *offensive* action for *defensive* ends and strike at West Germany or West Berlin in order to remove the potential causes of a crisis in the East German and East European set-up. They might be tempted; they could, however, be deterred by fear of Western retaliation and might, therefore, refrain from an action they would normally deem essential for the preservation of Russia's Eastern European hegemony and her empire. On the other hand, the Soviet rulers might come to the conclusion that for the sake of preventing the disintegration of the satellite and Russian empires the risk of an East—West confrontation must be accepted – just as the Austrian Government in 1914 risked world war because they thought it imperative to remove a danger threatening the existence of the Habsburg multi-national empire. If that happened the world would be faced with the threat of nuclear war resulting from the anachronistic survival of a colonial empire in the post-colonial era.

The Chinese enigma

For some years past it has been fashionable in certain Western circles to regard not Soviet Russia but communist China as the main, if not the only, potential aggressor. These circles argue, not altogether incorrectly, that China's more dynamic foreign policy and her apparently greater readiness to run risks is, or was originally at least, one of the issues in the rift between the two big communist powers.[22]

Without going into the details of the cause and the nature of the Sino-Soviet conflict it can certainly be stated that China, though she, too, professes to abhor nuclear war, has shown far less caution than the USSR in her conduct of foreign affairs. Another parallel with the pre-1914 European power set-up might serve as an illustration.

If the Soviet Union is to be compared with the multi-national

Habsburg empire, the role played by Communist China today bears similarities to that of the Kaiser's Germany: she is a late-comer among the great powers; she has but recently acquired a new political physiognomy as a state; and she is not (unlike the USSR) a big colonial power. There is a similar expansionist trend and a similar, somewhat synthetic sense of mission, albeit based on completely different political and social philosophies. Communist China does not demand 'living space' or 'a place in the sun', but she has evolved a variant (really a distortion) of the Marxian concept of world revolution. The slogans of 'the east wind pre-vailing over the west wind' and of 'the villages surrounding the towns' – on a world scale – reflect the Maoist theory that the socialist revolution will triumph first in backward, colonial and ex-colonial territories and not in the highly industrialized capital-ist countries: and this theory in turn expresses the geographical and strategic perspectives of China's policy of aggrandizement and the extension of her spheres of influence.

In 1972 the Peking Government switched to a policy of con-ciliation and the establishment of normal diplomatic and trade relations with the major capitalist powers. That Government's conduct of foreign affairs is often enigmatic and unpredictable; the significance and the prospects of any change of course are difficult to assess. On the assumption of a rational motivation, the main reason for the *rapprochement* with the West would seem to be the enmity between the two great communist powers, which varies in intensity but has now lasted too long to be regarded as a tem-porary estrangement.[23] The Chinese leaders may simply have decided to take steps that would obviate the threat of a war on more than one front. This would mean that China's aggressive designs, such as they are, may now be aimed at a different poten-tial opponent. On the other hand, she has no apparent strong motive for going to war against the Soviet Union – or, for that matter, against any other power, with the possible exception of India; even a renewed frontier clash between China and India is no more likely now to lead to general war than it did in 1962. And as China is not a colonial empire her territorial integrity is not threatened by upheavals in peripheral or adjacent areas. On balance the USSR, more vulnerable in this respect, is still more likely than China to resort to the kind of military action which would make a major war inevitable.

Conclusion: the end of the Russian Empire

The dilemma that has confronted, and still confronts, the Kremlin over the recurring crises in the satellite states throws into relief the futility of the attempt to preserve indefinitely a system which history has doomed to extinction. The Russians may succeed in keeping Hungary, Czechoslovakia and Rumania within the fold for years to come, but in doing so they will prepare the ground for future crises. Each new intervention will provoke a nationalist backlash – directly among the peoples of the satellite bloc and indirectly in the USSR's minority regions.[24] In the end the last remaining empire, the Russian, is bound to succumb to the tide which has swept away the British, French, Dutch and Portuguese empires. Repression may delay the end: a breach in the dike may be repaired, but at the cost of weakening the whole structure.

How long will it take for history to run its course and close the chapter of colonialism? No exact prediction, of course, can be attempted, but perhaps an historic parallel is instructive. As far as Soviet colonialism is concerned the first blow was struck when Yugoslavia, from 1948 onwards, defied the Soviet Union with impunity. Success for her stand was assured in 1955 when Khrushchev, in a drastic reversal of Stalin's policy, offered to restore friendly relations without insisting on Tito's return to the satellite fold. In terms of imperial history, Russia's acquiescence in Yugoslavia's full independence may be compared with Britain agreeing, in the Irish Treaty of December 1921, to grant a substantial measure of independence to what then became the Irish Free State and is now the Republic of Ireland. Soviet acceptance of the Yugoslav defection has probably marked the beginning of the end of the Soviet colonial empire, in the same way as the repeal of the Union with the larger part of Ireland heralded the dissolution of the British Empire. The Unionist die-hards who insisted at the time that Dominion status for Ireland would lead to the disintegration of the Empire were not proved wrong by history. A slow and gradual process was then initiated; over a quarter of a century elapsed between the Anglo-Irish Treaty and the departure of the British from India which marked the end of what the Empire had meant in history. The process of imperial disintegration will last longer for the USSR because the Russian, unlike the British, imperialists are bound to put up, for the sake of self-preservation, a last-ditch resistance to decolonization. It may well take the remainder of this century; but whenever the end comes history will record that it was the manifestation by the rulers of Yugoslavia of the spirit of both national and ideological independence which set in motion the process culminating in the decline and fall of the Russian empire.

Notes

The Decline and Fall of the Soviet Empire

1 *The Semblance of Peace: The Political Settlement After the Second World War* (London 1972), p. 556. Other formulations of the orthodox view are to be found in Arthur Schlesinger Jr, 'Origins of the Cold War', *Foreign Affairs*, 46 (Oct. 1967), pp. 22ff, and Desmond Donnelly, *The Cold War and its Origins in 1917* (London 1965).

2 Cf. D. F. Fleming, *The Cold War and its Origins* (New York 1961); David Horowitz, *The Free World Colossus* (New York 1965); Coral Bell, *Negotiations from Strength* (London 1965); Gar Alperowitz, *Atomic Diplomacy: Hiroshima and Potsdam* (New York 1965).

3 This Soviet satellization drive did not prove wholly and permanently successful. Some of the satellites dropped out of the Soviet orbit completely; in other East European countries the Kremlin's control ceased to be absolute; other satellites again tried to shake off the Russian grip but failed. Though none of the countries concerned have restored private capitalism, Soviet influence in that region is certainly less firm today than it was in the late forties. It is worth noting that desatellization, where it occurred, was not due to voluntary relaxation of control by Moscow but to a successful act of defiance by the local communist leadership: the moral, from the Kremlin's point of view, may well be that satellization is no substitute for annexation (cf. pp. 195ff. above).

4 The USA has sometimes been accused of aggression – in Cuba (Bay of Pigs), Guatemala, Indo-China and the Dominican Republic. Yet, whatever the rights and wrongs of these interventions, the purpose of American action was, in every instance, the containment or subversion of communism and not the acquisition of more territory (colonial or non-colonial).

5 Lenin actually described the recognition of the Ukraine's right to secede from *post*-revolutionary Russia as a criterion of a communist's internationalist sincerity; cf. *Collected Works* (Moscow 1965), XXX, p. 295. *See also*, on the nationality problem in communist theory and practice, the work of a Soviet author, Ivan Dzyuba, *Internationalism or Russification? A Study in the Soviet Nationalities Problem* (London 1968), especially pp. 57ff.

6 Numerous examples are given in Dzyuba's book, *Internationalism or Russification?*

7 *Collected Works*, XXI, p. 342.

8 Military considerations probably played a major part: Russia in 1939–40 and China in 1950 were anxious to improve their initial strategic positions in possible future wars with Germany and India respectively.

9 Cf. George Orwell, *Homage to Catalonia*, on the non-revolutionary role of the Spanish communists during the civil war. In Chile the communists apparently played a similar part in Allende's 'Popular Unity' Government from 1970 to 1973.

10 Cf. *A New Birth of Freedom* (London 1957), pp. 67ff.

11 In the case of Soviet Russia it has, in fact, been argued by, *inter alios*, Arthur Schlesinger Jr ('Origins of the Cold War', p. 47) that Stalin's paranoia played a crucial part in the transition from wartime collaboration to the Cold War.

12 In some respects Stalin practised more restraint than his successors; he refrained from intervention in Yugoslavia in 1948 while Krushchev and Brezhnev took military action against restive satellite governments in 1956 and 1968 respectively.

13 This propaganda line, which was later abandoned, did not stop the Soviet Government from establishing diplomatic links with the newly independent states.

14 In 1949 Zilliacus described the speeding-up of Marshall Aid

to Italy early in 1948 as American 'intervention'. Semantics aside, in the Italian general elections in April 1948 the communist-dominated Popular-Democratic Front polled just over 30 per cent of the total votes cast: it is extremely unlikely that even in the absence of US aid the communists would have won an overall majority of votes or seats.

15 China's occupation and annexation of Tibet that same year was one of the 'safe' expansionist moves directed against a weak country which could not expect outside help.

16 Cf. p. 163 above.

17 In *Communism and Colonialism* (London 1964).

18 For details, *see* (in addition to Kolarz's book, *Communism and Colonialism*): Hugh Seton-Watson, *The New Imperialism* (London 1961); Robert Conquest, *The Last Empire* (London 1962); and in particular Ivan Dzyuba, *Internationalism or Russification? A Study in the Soviet Nationalities Problem.*

19 Article 17 (of the 1936 Constitution).

20 Recent developments in Yugoslavia – a far smaller and less diversified country than the Soviet Union – illustrate this point. The slackening of totalitarian rigidity allowed national and autonomist aspirations, even among the leading communist cadres of the federated republics, to come into the open. The need to combat such trends and the inherent dangers of disintegration apparently decided Tito to return to stricter dictatorial centralism and to ideological puritan conformity.

21 About Khrushchev's possible motives for intervening in Hungary in 1956, after *not* having intervened in Poland earlier that year, *see* A. B. Ulam, *Expansion and Co-existence* (London 1968), p. 594.

22 Cf. the 'paper tiger' controversy between Mao and Krushchev.

23 On the projection of the Sino-Soviet conflict into the international arena, *see* pp. 184–5 above.

24 Since 1964 (when Kolarz described the impact of the Hungarian events of 1956 on some non-Slav nationalities in the USSR; cf. pp. 188f.) there have been frequent reports of growing unrest among the national minority groups in various parts of the USSR.

Farewell to Revolution: *Revisionist Trends in Contemporary Communism*

In that twilight . . .

For the true Marxist believer the eve of the Second World War was a time with an ambiguous message compounded of utter despair and highest hope. The cause had suffered a series of terrible defeats. In Germany, where socialism had apparently been on the agenda for many years, the most barbarous form of anti-socialist tyranny had triumphed and destroyed a strong and well organized labour movement. Both in France and in Spain socialist prospects had seemed bright in 1936; but all chances were crushed in the three years that followed, by a reversal of party-political fortunes in one case, by left-wing defeat in civil war in the other. Fascist Italy had conquered and annexed Ethiopia, one of the last remaining non-colonial territories in Africa. Reaction and total-itarian dictatorship had spread to Austria, then to Czechoslovakia. Nazi Germany had become the dominant power in non-com-munist Europe. And the Soviet Union, once the faithful Marxist's land of hope and glory, was in the agony of the purges and seemed to be shedding more and more of the axioms of the faith.

And yet it was somehow, for the orthodox Marxist, 'bliss to be alive' in that twilight of the late thirties. The blows and reverses of the preceding years were one facet of contemporary reality; another was the glorious vindication of Marxism – in its predic-tions. According to the communist creed, the process leading to the birth of a new social order must be a 'dialectical', zigzag movement, in which advance alternates with retreat, progress with spells of reaction. From the true Marxist's point of view the European climate of reaction and retrogression in 1938–9 was something analogous to the rule of Anti-Christ just before the final triumph of the Kingdom of God. The decay of the capitalist system and its 'superstructure', reflected in catastrophic slumps, mass unemployment, poverty and starvation in the midst of plenty; in the spread of totalitarian barbarity, with its racialist and pseudo-cultural absurdities; in the brutalization of political life and of class warfare; in the growing rapaciousness of some capitalist powers (Germany, Italy, Japan) and the drift to 'imperialist' war: that was just how the founders and apostles of 'scientific socialism' would have visualized the death agony of world capitalism. The approaching war would bring the consummation of the revolutionary hopes that had seemed so near fulfilment at the end of the First World War and the beginning of the inter-war period.

Most Marxists, and not a few non-Marxists, also felt that where parliamentary government and democratic freedoms had been destroyed they would never be restored under capitalism, and that liberal bourgeois regimes would crumble where they still existed. The pluralist society had begun to disintegrate between the wars – or so it seemed at the time. The only conceivable alternative to socialism was the rule of the 'Iron Heel', which would retain capitalist private property but would combine a substantial measure of economic planning with extreme totalitarian repression.

Theory and practice of 'imperialist' war

The Second World War had long been expected, predicted and even analysed in advance by communists of all shades. Consensus prevailed among them as to its basic character: it was clearly a typical 'imperialist' conflict, a predatory war of conquest –

essentially a repetition of the 1914–18 war. There were the Axis states and Japan fighting the old colonial powers for territory and spheres of influence. Britain, France and the USA would be striving to maintain the imperialist *status quo*, i.e. they would defend, and if possible extend, their colonial and semi-colonial empires and their positions of power. That was all in accordance with the Marxist-Leninist textbook. So would the outcome be: the overthrow of world capitalism and the socialist transformation of the international community.

Yet when war did come it caused much ideological confusion in the Marxist camp. The official Comintern line changed immediately after the outbreak of war. On the assumption that the USSR would be Nazi Germany's enemy from the start and an ally of the Western capitalist powers, the communists had, before war was declared, preached out-and-out resistance to German expansion. They argued that following a German act of aggression, a war against Hitler's Reich would be a just, 'anti-Fascist' war of defence, and not imperialist in character – even if the anti-German camp were to include 'imperialist' powers. This Soviet and Comintern view was hotly disputed by other left-wing Marxists (Independent Labour Party (ILP), Trotskyists, etc.), who reminded the Moscow-oriented communists that in 1914 Lenin had scornfully dismissed the Entente powers' claim that they were defending the independence of small nations. In the Bolshevik view (which was later endorsed by all Comintern parties) the First World War was 'imperialist' on the part of all belligerents.[1] When it turned out, in September 1939, that Russia, far from fighting on the Western side, was benevolently neutral towards Hitler's Germany, the Communist Party line swung back to Lenin's 1914 position of 'revolutionary defeatism'; the communists now declared that all warring powers were waging an imperialist war. After the German attack on the USSR in June 1941 the Comintern parties returned to their pre-war assessment of the international situation and proclaimed that Soviet Russia as well as her (capitalist) allies were fighting a just, defensive and progressive war against Fascist aggression.[2] The left-wing non-Stalinist groups, such as the ILP, did not follow suit. They continued to oppose the Western governments and the war, and were promptly denounced as German agents by the pro-Moscow communists.

The events of the war failed to bear out the Leninist expectation that defeat would facilitate revolutionary risings. In Italy after Mussolini's overthrow in 1943 (not by the workers but by the king and an anti-Duce faction within the Fascist Party) internal clashes did occur but these did not culminate in a proletarian revolution. There were civil wars in two countries of the victorious alliance: in China, where the struggle had started long before the war but had been suspended for the duration of the fight against Japan, and in Greece, where the communists tried to seize power, not in the hour of defeat but when victory over the external enemy was in sight. In none of the countries at war did revolutionary workers or a revolutionary party do what the Bolsheviks did in 1917 when they took advantage of their country's military plight to step up, and win, the struggle for power. In short the Second World War did not lead anywhere to 'socialist revolution'. In some countries – notably Yugoslavia – communists became a leading force in the anti-German resistance and eventually took power on the strength of the positions thus gained. But primarily the huge increase, during and after the war, in the total area under communist rule in Europe was a by-product of Soviet military expansion and occupation.

Thus when the guns fell silent in 1945 the revolution had still not come; the faithful Marxist, however, saw little cause for despondency. There were fresh grounds for optimism. Hitler's New Order had collapsed and an independent labour movement and working-class rights been restored in the liberated territories. Capitalism had survived the war, but for how long? Nothing that had happened shook the Marxist belief in the inevitability of an early end to world capitalism. Economic slumps loomed ahead, with hunger marches, riots and other forms of intensified class struggle. Inter-'imperialist' rivalry would recur, as after the first war, with new international crises producing new revolutionary situations. If orthodox left-wing socialists did not repeat their former mistakes, counter-revolution would not again prevent a proletarian victory.

Yet doubts arose, soon after the war, about the Leninist view of imperialism. The behaviour of the victorious powers did not fit into the theoretical pattern. As the redistribution of the world and its riches had allegedly been the main object of the war, the 'imperialists' should have followed up their victory by grabbing whatever they could of the possessions of the vanquished. This is not, in fact, what happened. Japan, predictably, had to give up the fruits of previous conquests; this signified, in substance, the failure of her attempt to turn China into a Japanese colony. Yet China did not afterwards become an American or British colony. The winding-up of Italy's African empire did not benefit the Western 'imperialists' either: it was the beginning of the process of de-colonization which was soon to engulf the overseas possessions of all the old colonial powers. Drastic frontier changes were imposed in Central Europe at the expense of defeated Germany, in favour not of the West but of the USSR and Soviet-dominated Poland. Germany was not made to cede any territory to the Western 'imperialists' but had to surrender to her 'socialist' Eastern neighbours more than one-fourth of what had remained to Germany under the Versailles Treaty.

All this must have been highly disturbing to the orthodox communist. There was no easy Marxist-Leninist explanation either for Soviet expansionism or for Western moderation. Why, having fought and won an 'imperialist' war, did the Western powers not impose an 'imperialist' peace? Could there be a flaw in Lenin's doctrine of imperialism? Or had this concept ceased to be valid just before or during the Second World War?

Theory and post-war reality

Such doubts were reinforced by what happened in the post-war period. The old colonial powers gave independence to their overseas possessions. This (largely voluntary) dissolution of empires did not accord too well with doctrinal anticipations; neither did the fact that the process was beneficial rather than harmful to the metropolitan economies.

Generally speaking, post-war economic and political developments contrasted starkly with Marxist-Leninist expectations. From the point of view of the theory the Second World War should have had a more powerful revolutionary impact on the capitalist world than the First. Over a period of a quarter of a century the decay of the system should have progressed anyway, even without a war. There was now also the destruction, dislocation and confusion which characterized the aftermath of the greatest war of all times; the loss to the Western countries of markets in Eastern Europe and later China, the incipient disintegration of the colonial empires and the erosion of Western political and economic influence in the developing world. Everything seemed to point to an early break-up of the existing order.

Yet history took a different course. The war changed a great many things but the downfall of capitalism was not one of its short-term or even long-term results. Communism spread to parts of Eastern and Central Europe, not through revolutionary working-class action but through Soviet military expansion. In parts of continental East Asia, where capitalism had not reached an advanced stage, some kind of oriental communism was substituted for the mixture of semi-feudalism and semi-colonialism that had marked the pre-war era. But in the highly developed industrial countries of the West, with their organized and politically conscious working classes, no communist or other left-wing party even attempted to seize power. The pattern of the years 1917–23 did not repeat itself. After 1945 a few years of unrest, turmoil and revolutionary tension in some capitalist countries were followed by a long period of political stability and economic growth. In the USA, Britain, France, Italy, the Low Countries, Scandinavia, West Germany, Austria and Japan, where recessions and mass unemployment had been endemic between the wars, these phenomena did not recur, contrary to the firm expectations of virtually all Marxists and many non-Marxists. Some five years after the end of the Second World War it was obvious that world capitalism, so far from collapsing, had acquired a capacity for progress and expansion it had not displayed for several decades. By the mid-fifties the chances of proletarian revolution were manifestly more remote than they had been throughout the inter-war period.

Thus the paradox of the late 1930s had, in a curious way, been reversed. The socialist cause had recovered from the disastrous defeats of the pre-war decade, but now it appeared that the Marxist predictions, seemingly confirmed by the events of that epoch and the outbreak of war, had after all been wrong. Fascist dictatorships had been toppled, parliamentary democracy and the rule of law re-established in most countries of the European continent. But what had happened to the messianic prophecies which appeared to have the ring of truth in the thirties? The senseless miseries of the Great Depression and the unleashing of another world war had not, after all, heralded the end of the capitalist world system. Armageddon had come and gone, Anti-Christ had lost the battle; yet what followed was not the socialist Millennium but a return to pre-war, pre-slump normality. Socialist parties and labour movements in Central and Western Europe had largely regained the positions they had lost before and during the war, but the cause of socialism had not advanced beyond the stage it had reached at the end of the First World War, and it did not seem set for early spectacular progress. This gradually produced some demoralization in the ranks of the Marxist faithful: confidence in the apocalyptic vision was shaken. The blissful twilight of the thirties had given way to a disappointing dawn.

The unexpected resurgence of the capitalist world economy after the Second World War should have made it incumbent upon Marxists to reappraise the situation in the capitalist world and the prospects of revolution. Yet for a long time they refused to acknowledge the fundamental changes in the socio-economic structure of the advanced industrial nations. For nearly two post-war decades the pro-Soviet communist establishment ignored, played down or disputed the existence in the major capitalist countries of such phenomena as state-sponsored planning, the adoption of *dirigiste*, Keynesian or New Deal economic policies, the (at least temporary and partial) invalidation of the classical trade cycle, comparative affluence in spite (or because) of decolonization, rising standards of living for nearly all sections of society, expansion and rapid economic growth, social security and the welfare state, and, in the political sphere, the comparative rarity of working-class upheavals such as abounded between the wars.

The dilemma which the gap between the theory of capitalist cataclysm and the reality of capitalist progress created for the leaders of world communism was reflected in the decisions and pronouncements of the Twenty-second Congress of the Soviet Communist Party (CPSU) in October 1961, when Khrushchev held undisputed sway in the Party and the state. The new Party programme adopted by this Congress proclaimed the continued validity of the assessment of world capitalism made by Lenin forty-five years earlier in his book *Imperialism as the Highest Stage of Capitalism*.[3] In 1916 Lenin had argued that by acquiring colonial markets for the export of goods and capital the imperialist countries had opened up, during the preceding forty years, sources of profits which at that stage could no longer be derived from investments at home, but on the eve of the (First) World War capitalism had reached its final phase of 'monopoly capitalist' decay; as the distribution of colonial territories among the great powers was substantially completed, there was little or no scope for finding further outlets for the surplus production resulting from the chaotic imbalance of a 'free enterprise' economy, and hence little or no scope for delaying ultimate catastrophe. In 1961 the Soviet Party leadership held that in all essentials this view of capitalism still applied to the contemporary scene. The 1961 Party programme also ridiculed 'bourgeois theories' which asserted that capitalism had changed its nature, had become more egalitarian and democratic, capable of averting cyclical fluctuations and slumps, or that the modern bourgeois state could be a welfare state. 'The vaunted welfare', the programme said, 'is welfare for the magnates of finance capital, and suffering and torture for hundreds of millions of working men.'

The programme spoke of the 'increasing decay' of capitalism, but added that this did not mean complete stagnation and a complete paralysis of the productive forces and did 'not rule out the growth of capitalist economy at particular times and in particular countries'. This was all the Soviet communist leaders had to say in 1961 about the unprecedented economic upsurge in the major industrial countries during the preceding dozen years. Yet while the Russian leaders pretended to stick to the Leninist analysis of capitalist decay and to the forty-five-year-old Leninist prediction of impending capitalist doom, their new Party programme used certain formulae which belied this show of confidence in an early world-wide victory of the communist cause. Thus great emphasis was laid on the need for peaceful coexistence with different social and economic systems. The programme described peaceful coexistence of the socialist and the capitalist parts of the world as 'an objective necessity for the development of human society' – an utterance not really indicative of firm belief in the imminent disappearance of the world capitalist system. More remarkable still is the statement, in the 1961 programme, that the chief purpose of coexistence, the prevention of nuclear war, could be achieved 'by the present generation'. The programme's authors clearly did not expect coexistence to be superseded, in the lifetime of the present generation, by the triumph of socialist world revolution. In the twenties and thirties communist leaders usually claimed to be certain that the revolution was, at most, only a few years away.

In 1961 the ideological fragmentation of world communism had not yet progressed very far. The Sino-Soviet rift was only just on the point of coming out into the open. In the previous year, eighty-one communist parties (virtually all except the Yugoslav) had agreed on a joint declaration giving their identical views of the state of the world and the struggle for socialism. In his speech at the 1961 CPSU Congress Khrushchev attacked the leadership of the Albanian Communist Party and the Chinese openly disapproved of this attack; but there was no Chinese criticism of the new programme's pronouncements about capitalism and peaceful coexistence. Hence it can be said that the appraisal contained in the 1961 Soviet Party programme was shared by all important sections of the world communist movement. It was, at that stage, generally accepted amongst communists that world capitalism, though doomed in the long term, was likely to survive for several decades to come.

Reappraising capitalism

Here was an incongruous situation for communists the world over. The Marxist-Leninist textbook insisted that capitalism in North America, Western and Central Europe and other highly developed areas was diseased, decrepit and moribund, and official communist strategy was based on this diagnosis. Yet at the same time the movement's leaders were clearly aware that no objectively revolutionary situation had arisen in any major capitalist country since the war, or at least since the end of the forties. They must also have noticed the absence of what their theory calls the 'subjective revolutionary factor': the heightened class consciousness of the proletariat, its determination to fight, under the leadership of a revolutionary party, for the conquest of state power and the socialist transformation of the economy. In the advanced capitalist societies the workers, while eager to attain higher standards of living, were evidently not in the mood for revolutionary action.

In the end the need for reassessing contemporary capitalism must have appeared overwhelming even to the conservatives and fundamentalists in the communist camp; from the mid-sixties onwards a fresh concept began to emerge in communist writings and discussions on socio-economic problems: the term 'state-monopoly capitalism' was used to denote a new phase – the ultimate stage in the evolution of the capitalist system. The phrase (often abbreviated to SMC in communist publications) is not in itself new. Lenin had used it to describe a feature sometimes to be discerned (in his opinion) in what he called the monopoly-capitalist or imperialist stage: a feature marked by *dirigiste* policies and selective nationalization. And in this sense the term had also appeared in the 1961 programme of the Soviet Communist Party and in communist theoretical journals between about 1950 and 1965. In those contexts the phrase had not been intended to refer to anything fundamentally new in capitalism, anything, that is, which would necessitate the elaboration of a new strategy in the fight against the existing order; it merely defined a trend which was aggravating the 'contradictions of capitalism'. However about half-way through the 1960s the intellectual élite of the international (pro-Soviet) communist movement began at last to acknowledge the appearance of novel features in modern capitalism, of structural changes which were seen to account for rapid economic growth and increasing prosperity, for the non-occurrence of revolutionary situations and for the unwillingness of the working classes to turn the struggle for higher wages and other economic and welfare targets into a campaign for power and socialism.

This new trend in communist ideology went largely unnoticed in the West. This is not as astonishing as it may seem at first glance. For several decades past Western observers had paid scant attention to the development of official communist theory, because in Stalin's day, and for some years after his death, the world communist movement was clearly only an adjunct of the USSR's international policy. The frequent and sudden changes in the Comintern parties' political line before and during the Second World War had convinced Western experts that any references in Party literature to new theoretical developments were merely designed to justify the Moscow-dictated twists and turns of the Party line. The result is that Comintern theory lost all credibility in the eyes of Western observers and students of communist affairs. Kremlinologists continued to analyse clashes of Soviet personalities and factions, and the motivation of Moscow's policy, but they understandably refused to take the *ad hoc* theoretical revisions and reappraisals seriously or to be interested in what then went under the name of 'Marxism-Leninism-Stalinism'. The result was that when a genuine and important shift did occur in the communists' theoretical approach to capitalist reality it was not immediately recognized as such in the West. Western experts in Soviet and communist affairs, in the late fifties and in the sixties, naturally took a keen interest in the incipient Sino-Soviet rift and other intra-communist conflicts; but they did not shed their indifference to the evolution of communist theory. The ingrained habit of regarding changes in communist ideology purely as reflections of fluctuating Muscovite policy persisted, and tended to obscure the fact that the new-found political autonomy of parts of the world communist movement was paralleled by the re-emergence of autonomous political thought. What in fact happened is that in the early sixties leading non-Soviet communists (mainly in the West, but also in some East European countries) began to take a fresh, independent look at the world scene, and to evolve opinions and theories which were not invariably in harmony with what Soviet statesmen considered to be the interest of their country and the communist camp.

This return to ideological independence went hand in hand with the elaboration and adoption, by the communist parties of some Western 'bourgeois democratic' countries, of policies of moderation and restraint in their opposition to the existing social order. Eventually some West European communist parties went to the length of deleting from their programmes the time-honoured watchword of the 'dictatorship of the proletariat' and of pledging themselves to respect, if they should obtain power by parliamentary methods, all traditional civil rights and liberties; they also committed themselves to the concept of pluralism and declared their readiness to give up governmental office if, after being voted into power, they should be defeated in a subsequent election.[4]

It must be emphasized that this communist conversion to legal, parliamentary methods in the transition to socialism shows every sign of being genuine. Communist moderation in word and deed, in programmatic pronouncements and political action, is in full accord with the communists' current assessment of modern capitalism, which has led them to the conclusion that their ends are more likely to be achieved by peaceful evolution than by violence and civil war. Consideration of Soviet policy and of Soviet interests do not enter into this: the new concept and the strategy that flows from it do not appear relevant to any particular line of Soviet diplomacy.

The deletion from the communist programmes of the 'dictatorship of the proletariat' highlights the theoretical reaction of the communists to the shift in their appraisal of world capitalism. An instructive example of a new practical approach to given situations is the behaviour of the French Communist Party and the communist-led trade unions of that country during the upheavals in May and June 1968, when spontaneous working-class actions reached general strike proportions. As their 'ultra-left' critics (to use Muscovite terminology) were not slow to point out, the communists not only failed to make the best of obvious revolutionary opportunities but actually strove to preserve the political *status quo*. Some left-wing extremists and other observers attributed this moderation to the Soviet Government's alleged wish to help de Gaulle, whose stance on NATO and the Middle East sometimes met with the Kremlin's qualified approval. The observers recalled in this connection the restraint shown by the French Communist Party more than thirty years before, in the spring and summer of 1936, when the Party – then only a junior partner in the 'popular front' alliance and not yet in control of powerful trade unions – supported the efforts of Léon Blum's centre-left administration to end the (largely spontaneous) strikes and factory occupations, and to curb revolutionary militancy. This was, indeed, a typical example of communist policy being dictated by the exigencies of Soviet diplomacy and, specifically, by the Soviet desire to ensure the continued efficacy of the Franco-Soviet alliance treaty of 1935. The French Party then gave some far-fetched explanations for its unwillingness to escalate the class struggle; the (covert) real motive was to restrain the French workers from jeopardizing the country's war potential.

Yet there was no real parallel between the events in France of 1936 and 1968. In 1936 Stalin's government was patently interested in the preservation of internal stability in France. In 1968, on the other hand, the survival of Gaullist rule was at best a dubious asset, from the USSR's point of view. De Gaulle had always been unpredictable. His policies had often embarrassed the Russians;

for instance, when he opposed Soviet designs on West Berlin or commended Rumania's semi-independent line in foreign affairs. In 1968, unlike 1936, Soviet security did not in any way depend upon France's political and economic stability and military strength. The Kremlin had no motive for urging the French communist leaders to exercise restraint; they did what they felt to be in their own party-political interest.

State-monopoly capitalism: the ultimate stage of capitalism

The basic difference between the French communists' policy in 1936 and in 1968 is that at the later date there was no discrepancy between theory and practice. Several years before adopting its Euro-communist stance and abandoning the 'dictatorship of the proletariat', the French Party ceased to be committed to the violent overthrow of the bourgeois government. The same goes for the communist parties in several other capitalist countries. Some of these parties have, during the post-war period, issued programmatic statements in favour of peaceful and gradual transition to socialism, the upholding of civil rights and liberties, *habeas corpus* and all the attributes of the rule of law. Sincere or not, these are now the declared principles of communist party policy in the major capitalist countries. Abstention from revolutionary action in France, and wherever else such action might have seemed to be indicated by traditional Marxist standards, is in keeping with these principles – principles deriving from the fundamentally new, and indeed revisionist, concept of state-monopoly capitalism (SMC) as a new phase in the economic and political development of the advanced industrial societies.

The subject of SMC was much to the fore in communist publications and discussions during the first five years after Khrushchev's fall. Its prominence declined in the 1970s, for reasons connected with the new crisis of world capitalism, but it has never been officially abandoned and, above all, the moderate policies which stem from the concept of SMC are still in full force. Contrary to what one might have expected, the troubles now besetting some of the capitalist economies have not led to a return to left-wing Marxist militancy, at least not in the parties with a Comintern background. The revisionist trend has, if anything, grown stronger in recent years. Thus the SMC theory, while less frequently invoked since the beginning of the seventies, has had a lasting impact on the evolution of communist strategy and tactics. As a theory it will probably regain topicality if and when capitalist stability is restored; at any rate it has not ceased to be of major importance. Economists may well find flaws in the communist analysis, that is to say, in the presentation of the facts, in the deductions, or both. But it is a consistent concept and seriously argued. Whether or not it is tenable, the emergence of the theory is a significant development which deserves a full appraisal.

Apart from being extensively debated in theoretical journals, state-monopoly capitalism has been the theme of several international conferences and round-table debates at which communist economists have discussed the problems of the class struggle in conditions of post-war capitalist affluence. Speakers at these meetings have differed on a number of points, but there is broad consensus that a new stage has been reached in the development of capitalism, beyond the imperialistic 'highest stage' defined by Lenin in 1916, which has necessitated the adoption of a new strategy: Communist policy in the advanced Western countries and in Japan should no longer be based on the expectation of capitalist collapse; armed insurrection, and revolutionary violence in general, is deemed both inappropriate and unnecessary.

The first major international event in the elaboration of the new theoretical concept took place in May 1966. A conference on state-monopoly capitalism was then held in the Paris suburb of Choisy-le-Roi under the auspices of the French Communist Party. It was attended by Marxist experts and economists from many capitalist and all European communist countries (except

Albania) including Yugoslavia. The conference material was subsequently published in a two-volume compilation of the French communist magazine *Economie et Politique*.[5]

A comprehensive picture of what communist theorists consider to be the chief characteristics of the new phase emerged from the debate and from a number of papers submitted at the conference. The upshot of this and of subsequent debates on the same subject is that SMC (which had its beginnings in the thirties and was fully developed after the Second World War) represents the phase of capitalist society which follows the ordinary 'monopoly capitalism' analysed by Lenin. SMC is marked by massive state intervention in the capitalist economy, by state-sponsored, centralized planning in some sectors, by the intertwining of the state machine and private monopoly, by the fusion of state and private monopoly in industrial production, transport and so on, in the form of total or partial nationalization, state control and direction, by public financing of production, regulation of savings and of credit, and by direct state intervention in the fixing of wages. These policies and methods are said to have worked structural changes in the economy of the countries concerned. By 'borrowing' socialist methods of economic planning, and thereby reducing the extent of anarchy in production, SMC has enabled the world capitalist system to survive; also SMC measures have partly invalidated the spontaneous operation of the economic laws which formerly produced recurrent and ever deepening depressions, and have succeeded in flattening, though not abolishing, the trade cycle. They have thus helped the capitalist system to experience a powerful revival of its productive forces.

The most important point about the virtually unanimous acknowledgement of this new SMC stage by the communists is that capitalism is no longer being described as 'stagnating' or 'decaying'. An age-old Marxist-Leninist tenet has been tacitly abandoned: the assumption that capitalism is doomed to self-destruction through its inability to develop the productive forces. At the Twentieth Soviet Party congress in March 1956 (at which Khrushchev delivered his famous secret speech), delegates had derided the notion of 'organized capitalism' and had insisted on the inevitability of capitalist collapse. At the Choisy meeting ten years later, prominent French communists stressed 'the momentous upsurge of the productive forces under the impact of the extraordinary scientific and technological revolution of our time', and 'the rise in industrial production and productivity' in contemporary capitalism.

Several speakers at Choisy raised the question of why Marxist experts had been so slow to recognize the symptoms of the new phase. It appeared that for certain unexplained reasons Stalin and the economists who took the cue from him had retarded the development of communist theory in this respect. (In his last book, *Economic Problems of Socialism in the USSR*, published in 1952, Stalin had completely ignored state-monopoly capitalism, although the book dealt with many aspects of post-war capitalist developments.[6]) It was also stated at the same conference that the formulation of a comprehensive theory on SMC had previously been prevented by obstacles which were eventually eliminated by the 1956 and 1961 Congresses of the Soviet Communist Party; in other words, reassessment of modern capitalism was impossible before de-Stalinization. Stalin came in for more criticism for his 'catastrophic vision' of the end of capitalism and for his tendency to oversimplify the role of the state under capitalism; speakers agreed that the state was not just a 'bourgeois agency' but often took up a mediatory position and fulfilled a positive economic function by raising collective demand in order to prevent or overcome stagnation. What makes these strictures on Stalin highly significant is that on both the role of the bourgeois state and the inevitability of capitalist collapse Stalin merely reiterated the teachings of Marx and Lenin.

Leninism revised

To appreciate, in general terms, the distance which communist theory has travelled since the early twenties in its interpretation of capitalism, one must go back to what Lenin regarded as typical features of 'imperialism'. Lenin declared decolonization and substantial improvements in living standards under capitalism to be impossible. In his book *Imperialism* he wrote, in 1916, that if capitalism could develop agriculture and raise the standards of living of the working masses, the need for imperialist expansion into underdeveloped territories would disappear; but, he added, 'if capitalism did these things it would not be capitalism'. To Lenin's mind a state of mass starvation was one of 'the fundamental and inevitable premises of this mode of production'. It is interesting that Stalin used a similar formula in his *Economic Problems of Socialism in the USSR*, at a time when, as John Strachey pointed out four years later, the majority of people in the capitalist USA enjoyed a higher standard of living than had ever previously been attained in any place at any time in the history of man.[7]

The implicit abandonment of the Leninist perspective of capitalist collapse, together with the explicit rejection of Stalin's 'catastrophic vision' (which in reality was shared by all Bolshevik leaders from Lenin to Khrushchev) would seem to pose the question of how the Socialist transformation of society was to be achieved. The SMC theorists' answer was that state-monopoly capitalism itself is, in a way, the beginning of the process of transition from capitalism to socialism. At a 'scientific conference' held in Moscow in March 1967 the Czechoslovak economist Ludek Urban argued that the successes achieved by the workers in the SMC countries – for example, rising incomes and social welfare – actually amounted to an 'accumulation in capitalist society of elements which no longer bear a purely capitalist character'.[8] Urban went on to say that capitalism would disappear, not as a result of economic collapse or revolutionary war 'as visualized by the present Chinese leadership', but as a result of the gradual transition which was already taking place. 'The disintegration and dying away of capitalism are possible only through the development of this capitalism, through economic growth. In the course of this development the necessary structural changes will take place, accompanied by the further growth of the working class and a change in the balance of forces; and this development will ultimately be consummated in the transition to complete socialist ownership.'⁹

This does not sound one whit more revolutionary than the views of Eduard Bernstein, the original German pre-1914 revisionist, or of the early Fabians in Britain. Yet no one at the Moscow conference seems to have pointed this out or to have denounced this heretical acceptance of gradualism. Some restrained criticism was, in fact, levelled at Urban's theses. The Soviet professor S. Menshikov doubted the correctness of Urban's formula of 'capitalism dying through prosperity' (this is how Menshikov summed up Urban's theory), but not one participant described this formula as a deviation from Marxism-Leninism. In Khrushchev's and even more in Stalin's day there would have been universal condemnation of such a thesis as a betrayal of the revolutionary Marxist vision.

It is worth noting that the various conferences and meetings on state-monopoly capitalism were marked by open controversy. Speakers not infrequently disagreed with one another; the published reports of the debates show none of the prefabricated unanimity that was typical of the movement's monolithic phase. Points of disagreement included the nature and the effects of state-monopoly capitalism. For instance, at Choisy-le-Roi in May 1966 the Yugoslav delegate Soskic suggested that the apparent stability of post-war capitalism was really due to the Cold War and the arms race; the end of the Cold War would see a return to instability and slumps. Other speakers rejected this as a relapse into the outdated theory of capitalist catastrophe. Thus a French delegate said that Soskic evidently underestimated the USA's ability to find other, non-military outlets such as space exploration. No one at any of the SMC debates was reported as having shared Soskic's interpretation, although his was, in fact, the generally accepted view among communists in the 1950s.

State-monopoly capitalism was again the chief topic of an international round-table discussion held in Prague in October 1967 – a few months before the 'Prague Spring' – to mark the centenary of the publication of Marx's *Das Kapital* and the half-centenary of Lenin's *Imperialism*.¹⁰ As on previous occasions, some speakers contemptuously dismissed bourgeois theories purporting to prove that Marxism was dead and buried. According to the Canadian communist Emile Bjarnason, every decade since the appearance of the first volume of *Das Kapital* had produced fresh disquisitions of this kind, but 'each time Marx arises like a phoenix, and all the theoretical exercises of his would-be destroyers are disproved by living reality'. Yet at the same meeting Bjarnason went on to disprove the theory of 'increasing misery', at least as far as his own country was concerned. It would be 'politically senseless', he declared, 'to try to convince Canadian workers that they face absolute impoverishment'. In Canada real wages had risen by about 65 per cent over the preceding twenty-five years, and 'the opportunities to buy a house, a car, various durables, coupled with the holiday and entertainment opportunities, are making an impression'.

At the same round-table debate another speaker, J. Zawadzki of Poland, went so far as to mention the higher performance of SMC economies as compared with 'socialist planning' in eastern Europe. He asked how it was that a worker in the USA earned more than a Polish worker. His explanation was the higher development of the forces of production and of labour productivity in the USA. The Polish speaker came very close to admitting openly the need for revising Marxism-Leninism in the light of post-war developments. He said Marxists should not 'try to prove, again and again, that Marx and Lenin were right, or that every word they uttered is still true today'; instead they should try 'creatively to develop' Marxism-Leninism 'in adaptation to our times'.

Another revisionist contribution (but not denounced as revisionist by any other speaker) came from A. Kolar of Czechoslovakia, who gave a brand-new twist to the view which Lenin claimed to have refuted, namely that the capitalists were, after all, capable of raising workers' standards of living. He said that there was a time when the bourgeoisie strove to keep wages, i.e. working-class consumption, at a minimum. But technological progress was now impossible 'without greater consumption by the working class and other sections of the population . . . In its own selfish interest, in order to keep the capitalist system afloat, the bourgeoisie can, indeed must, find solutions for social and economic problems affecting the whole of society.' The capitalists were no longer seeking to maximize profits by minimizing wages; they had had to agree to a redistribution of the national income in a way that would assure a relatively high level of consumption and investment.

The debate on state-monopoly capitalism which started within the pro-Moscow communist movement in the mid-sixties differs in some important respects from similar events in the past. This was clearly not a new general line decreed and imposed by the Kremlin, as was common in Stalin's days. In fact the concept of SMC seems to have emanated from non-Russian sections of the movement; German as well as French and Czechoslovak (pre-Spring!) communists were to the fore. Soviet economists took a conservative line in the debate; without rejecting the new theory, they sometimes criticized the more daring views expressed by Czechoslovak and French contributors. There was genuine controversy, in stark contrast to the sham discussions of the past; and communists from Western countries or from the East European satellites openly disagreed with their Soviet colleagues, whose opinions were not treated as authoritative. Perhaps the most striking feature of the debate was the detached tone in which contributors described and assessed the novel elements in world capitalism. The familiar, crude polemical clichés were not entirely absent, but the general atmosphere was one of cool analysis rather than of anti-capitalist propaganda tirades.

Revisionist strategies

The intra-communist discussion about state-monopoly capitalism has been marking time since the end of the sixties, probably because round about that time the situation in the capitalist world began to look less settled. The student unrest in France in 1968 sparked off a general strike which at times appeared to assume a revolutionary character. This crisis gave the French Communist Party an opportunity for demonstrating the moderation inherent in the SMC concept; but at the same time it may have aroused doubts among communists, in France and elsewhere, as to whether the possibility of capitalist collapse was really as remote as they had believed it to be. Other elements of instability have since appeared in a number of capitalist countries, culminating in the world-wide economic recession and in periodic outbreaks of terrorist action against the establishment and its representatives. Yet while the Moscow-oriented communists seem to talk and write less than before about the 'ultimate stage', they have never revoked their assessment of post-1945 capitalism; in fact they have continued to define and apply the gradualist, 'revisionist' strategy and tactics which follow from this assessment.

In the SMC debate the communist parties in the highly developed capitalist countries in Western Europe, North America and Japan were exhorted not to expect a cataclysmic end to capitalism.[11] They were also advised, by many delegates to those conferences, not to aim at the 'smashing of the capitalist state machine' – described as essential by Marx and Lenin – but to strive instead for the gradual transformation of the socio-economic system on a democratic-parliamentary basis, in a broad alliance with the progressive non-communist left. The SMC theorists outlined a 'short-term programme' for an 'intermediate democratic phase' between state-monopoly capitalism and socialism, which included the nationalization of key enterprises, industrial democracy (workers' control, co-determination), democratic planning, measures to speed up economic growth and ensure full employment, peaceful evolution towards more social justice and equality.

To this gradualist approach and to the avoidance (if possible) of revolutionary violence and civil war the bulk of the communist parties in the West, not only the so-called Euro-communists, remain committed. This is worth emphasizing because Western commentators on the communist scene sometimes tend to convey the impression that peaceful parliamentary evolution is the specific tenet of Euro-communism but is rejected by the old-style communists. In fact the principle of peaceful transition was sanctioned by the Soviet Communist Party in its 1961 programme – several years before the start of the SMC debate – and it later received the approbation even of such a conservative, hard-line party as the West German Communist Party, which has never yet deviated from the Kremlin line and has never uttered a single word of criticism of Soviet attitudes and policies.[12] The 'Euros' may have gone further than other communists in officially discarding some old-established Marxist axioms and in agreeing to compromise on domestic issues; but the basically revisionist strategy of modern communism emerged in the context not of Eurocommunism but of the theory of state-monopoly capitalism. This is why the discussions leading to the formulation of the new theory have not been rendered obsolete by the change of climate in the non-communist world.

The concept of peaceful transition is not an innovation of the post-Second World War era. It even played a part in the original Marxist system. Karl Marx believed that violent revolution would be the rule, but that a peaceful (though not gradual) take-over was conceivable in some bourgeois democratic countries, notably Britain and the USA. In subsequent discussions among Marxist-Leninists about the peaceful take-over it was always understood that the capitalist class, when faced with the threat of a genuinely socialist electoral victory, was likely to break the rules of the parliamentary game and oppose the socialist transformation by force, thus making revolutionary violence inevitable and civil war probable. The new element in the SMC theory is that its protagonists expect peaceful change to be the rule rather than the exception, and some of them actually maintain that gradual transition towards socialist production relations *is already in progress*. From this point of view communist party policy at present appears to have two main objectives: to promote and expedite the process of economic transition and to secure the replacement of bourgeois rule (which includes rule by labour or social democratic parties) by a coalition of communists and left-wing socialists. If we were to express this perspective in a brief, over-simplified formula, modelled on Lenin's famous post-1917 equation for Russia ('Socialism equals electrification plus Soviet rule'), we might say that in the opinion of most communist economists and political leaders socialism equals SMC plus a left-wing government with effective communist participation.[13]

The theory of state-monopoly capitalism as a new stage of imperialism is the latest variant of an old theme: how can it be explained that the socialist revolution has failed to materialize where it should have occurred in the first place, in the advanced capitalist countries of the western hemisphere? The history of Marxist thought since the days of Marx is largely the history of attempts to explain this phenomenon.

Marx himself regarded the overthrow of the existing order as something likely to occur in his own time. In his view the mid-Victorian capitalist system (analysed in *Das Kapital*) was ripe for revolution, which might be sparked off by any severe economic crisis. Yet the trade cycle did not fulfil his expectations. Booms and slumps came and went, but capitalism survived. When the revolution was still not in sight at the time of the outbreak of the First World War Lenin furnished the Marxist explanation with his theory of 'imperialism'.

According to Lenin, the ruling classes of the leading capitalist powers had been able to prevent the collapse of the system by imperialist expansion into overseas markets and by acquiring cheap sources of raw materials in colonial territories. Furthermore they had used the extra profits derived from colonial exploitation to bribe, and buy the support of, right-wing labour and trade-union leaders and a section of *embourgeoisés* workers; these renegade supporters of imperialism Lenin called the 'labour aristocracy'. Thus profitable colonialism delayed (according to Leninist theory) the ripening of the objective conditions for proletarian revolution, while the rise of a corrupt labour aristocracy held back the development of the workers' revolutionary consciousness. The subjective side of this theory could also, it seemed, account for the failure of revolution between the two world wars. Marxists believed that revolution was then objectively on the agenda in all capitalist countries, since capitalism was clearly bankrupt. The reason why revolution did not break out, and why attempted uprisings in Germany, Hungary and Estonia remained abortive, was to be found in the treachery of the right-wing social democratic and trade union leaders; these, the theory maintained, enjoyed the active support of a stratum of skilled, highly paid workers and the passive support of masses of ordinary workers and unemployed who had not yet seen through their leaders' treachery.

The years between the wars saw the rise and triumph of Fascism in Germany and Italy, and of semi-Fascist, dictatorial regimes in other capitalist countries. Communist theory again linked this development with the non-occurrence of the overdue revolution. Marxists had always doubted the authenticity of parliamentary democracy in a bourgeois country, on the grounds that the capitalists invariably controlled the media of mass communication as well as the hierarchies of the civil service and the armed forces. In a grave economic or political crisis (and the former would inevitably produce the latter) the bourgeoisie could no longer allow the working people such limited democratic freedoms as free speech, the right of assembly, the right to join political parties or independent trade unions. According to the communist textbook,[14] Fascism, which abolished these rights and freedoms, was the last refuge of the dying bourgeois order, its desperate answer to the growing threat of collapse and proletarian revolution. In an attempt to contain this threat the capitalist class would shed the trappings of formal democracy, of human rights and the rule of law; it would try to defend its rule by resorting to an openly dictatorial system of absolute coercion.

A new situation arose when the Second World War ended and the proletarian revolution, which all true Marxists had confidently expected, was apparently still not imminent. All that had happened up to that point could somehow be shown (albeit not always convincingly) to be consistent with the nineteenth-century doctrine as amplified by the twentieth-century *epigoni*. Marx had been right (the argument ran) in predicting the self-destruction of capitalism, but by imperialist expansion, by bribing right-wing labour leaders and by installing Fascist dictators the bourgeoisie had been able to postpone the day of reckoning. Explanations of this kind clearly did not fit the developments of the fifties and sixties. The momentous economic progress in all major capitalist countries during those two decades could not possibly be explained by the theory of imperialism, by the concept of the 'labour aristocracy' or by the communists' interpretation of the Fascist phenomenon. Hence either the Marxist vision of capitalism was wrong or else there must be some other reason, not previously established, why capitalism proved able not only to survive but to prosper, which it could not in the inter-war period. This is the problem which the theory of state-monopoly capitalism tried to resolve.

The new theory purported to supply the ideological armoury of the world communist movement with an essential weapon – knowledge of the structure and the functioning of contemporary capitalism, and based on this, the economic, social and political strategy for achieving the movement's objectives. The theory of state-monoply capitalism, in other words, was intended to do for present-day communists what Lenin's writings such as *Imperialism* or *The State and Revolution* did for his own generation of left-wing socialists. In communist eyes Lenin's contributions are a logical development of Marxist theory, the successful adaptation of the doctrine to the situation prevailing during the first two decades of this century. The protagonists of the SMC concept would make an analogous claim for their theory which, in their view, has brought Marxism-Leninism (i.e. the product of Lenin's adaptation of Marxism) up to date, and has devised the appropriate communist strategy for what they consider to be the last stage of capitalist development.

There are, however, important differences between these two attempted adaptations. Lenin's analysis of 'monopoly capitalism' on the eve of the First World War and his political conclusions did not contradict the basic premises of Marxism. Non-communist Marxists have emphatically, and with much justification, disputed Lenin's and the Leninists' claim that his theories (or, for that matter, his practice) were in harmony with Marxist teachings. Yet Lenin's *Imperialism* certainly accepted and developed the Marxist doctrine that capitalism is bound to succumb to its own inherent contradictions.

The approach of the SMC theorists is altogether different. They reject, without explicitly admitting it, the fundamental Marxist tenet of the inevitability of a catastrophic end to world capitalism. They have also abandoned the doctrine of ever-increasing misery which Lenin in 1916 (and Stalin in 1952!) specifically reaffirmed. And there is another difference. Whilst no recasting of revolutionary strategy and tactics followed from Lenin's 1916 analysis of the imperialist phase of capitalism, the emergence of the SMC concept fifty years later did necessitate a strategic reappraisal; not because of the thesis of a peaceful change-over – that possibility had been envisaged by Marx himself – but because the idea of a gradual transition, with intermediate stages, from state-monopoly capitalism to socialism has little in common with original Marxism but a great deal with the revisionists' belief in evolutionary socialism. It is only logical that the strategies recommended by the SMC theorists – parliamentary methods, alliances with other progressives, a fight for industrial democracy, economic growth, full employment, democratic planning, social justice and equality – are also in keeping with traditional revisionist and reformist strategy.[15] Yet while Bernstein and his friends never denied their intention to revise Marxist theory and strategy, the SMC concept is stated by its upholders to have no affinity with revisionist theory of practice.

Euro-communism

The *Agitprop* machine of world communism has had some hard knocks since the end of the Second World War. Splits and defections, together with the Soviet Government's bullying and aggressive foreign policies and evidence of repression and intolerance inside the USSR, have inevitably weakened the Kremlin's appeal to Western workers. It remains true, nonetheless, that in the major capitalist countries most parties with roots in the working class and with positions to the left of the social democrat or labour parties are still communist in the sense that they are loyal to

Moscow, though no longer invariably subservient to, and uncritical of, the Soviet leaders' pronouncements and actions. This goes not only for France and Italy, where Moscow-oriented parties enjoy mass support, but even for countries where communism as a movement is weak. The British Communist Party, which has no mass following and no seats in Parliament, is still, in terms of active membership, much stronger than any other group to the left of the Labour Party and probably stronger than the entire 'ultra-left' combined.

The resilience of old-fashioned communism may have something to do with the movement's realistic conversion to evolutionary strategies. With the beginning of the world economic recession in 1974–5 the communist parties of the West might have felt tempted to return to a more radical revolutionary line in order to avoid being outflanked on the left by Maoists, Trotskyists and other extremist groups. They withstood this temptation, partly because of the reassessment reflected in the SMC concept and partly, it may be assumed, because they felt that the ultra-left argument, while persuasive to a certain type of intellectual, would fail to impress the ordinary manual worker.

Yet while the international communist movement has continued to be a significant factor in world affairs it has been transformed by a process which began in the late forties but really got into its stride about a decade later: the gradual erosion of Moscow's position as the ideological and power centre of world communism.

There are two aspects to this process. The first is a tendency towards rupture, or at least estrangement, between the Soviet communist leadership and the (East European or Asian) communist parties in power, the second a loosening of the ties linking the Kremlin to the communist parties in the non-communist countries, i.e. to the parties which used to give unconditional and unqualified support to the USSR and her policies.

The first breach between the Kremlin and a non-Soviet communist regime occurred in 1948 when the Yugoslav party and government renounced Soviet tutelage and asserted their right to choose their country's own 'road to socialism'. This led to a fierce propaganda war between the Yugoslavs on the one hand, and Moscow and its loyal satellites and friends (including Red China and Albania!) on the other. Yet in 1955 the Soviet rulers suddenly offered peace. They acknowledged Yugoslavia's real independence (as distinct from the purely nominal independence enjoyed by the satellites) and resumed diplomatic and inter-party relations, without insisting on Moscow's predominance. Tito's success in defying Moscow's monocentric position provoked the efforts then made by other East European governments to attain the autonomous status Yugoslavia had achieved: the partly successful attempt by the Polish leaders in 1956 and, from the early 1960s onwards, by those of Rumania, and the unsuccessful attempts – crushed by Soviet tanks – in Hungary in 1956 and in Czechoslovakia in 1968. The year 1961 saw Moscow's open break with Albania; rupture with China became official in 1963. In the following years some Asian communist parties and regimes took up a stance of ideological neutrality between Soviet Russia and communist China, while others sided with China.

The impact of these dramatic events was not confined to the communist world. Leading communists in Western Europe and North America, while still professing loyalty to the Soviet Union, began to recover their critical faculties and to shed the proclivity to endorse, as a kind of automatic reflex, all Soviet actions and pronouncements. When in November 1956 Soviet troops marched into Hungary, the bulk of the world communist movement still approved, but only after much heart-searching and bitter debate. Communist newspapers in the West, including the British *Daily Worker*, published letters from party members and followers attacking Soviet intervention. The accustomed monolithic unanimity had gone. Centrifugal tendencies were strengthened by the Sino-Soviet split and the ensuing acrimonious polemics. Western communists also began to criticize the Soviet government's illiberal cultural policies. In the late 1960s the debate on 'state-monopoly capitalism' reflected a process of incipient ideological emancipation on the part of some non-Soviet communist parties and prominent individuals. International communist reaction to the Soviet invasion of Czechoslovakia in

August 1968 reflected the new mood. There was not even hesitant general approval, as after the Hungarian showdown nearly twelve years before. Several communist parties, including the Italian, French and British, openly denounced the action of the USSR and her partners.

A few years later the two strongest communist parties in the capitalist world, the Italian and the French, began to voice open criticism of Soviet dictatorial methods; they also proclaimed new programmatic and strategic principles without soliciting and obtaining the Kremlin's sanction. The smaller but important Spanish party followed suit, and went even further in denouncing dictatorial practices inside the USSR. The Spanish communist leader Santiago Carillo actually used the term 'Euro-communism' and applied it to his party's political position; he also cast doubt on the socialist character of the Soviet state. Some (but not all) of the minor European communist parties adopted a similar line of critical independence from Moscow, including the British party, whose official espousal of certain 'Euro-communist' positions (such as renouncing the 'dictatorship of the proletariat') provoked the breakaway of a group of hardline Stalinists and the formation of a 'New Communist Party'.

In his book *'Eurocommunism' and the State* Carrillo describes and explains the genesis and the evolution of the new intra-communist trend.[16] When the anathema was pronounced against Tito and his friends in 1948, the Spanish communists, Carrillo writes, true to 'the tradition of unconditional support for the Soviet Union . . . followed like a flock of sheep the condemnation levelled against comrade Tito and the other Yugoslav leaders. . . . When Khrushchev had the courage publicly to dismantle the whole edifice, we felt that we had been cruelly deceived and vilely manipulated'.[17] Many members of other communist parties probably reacted in much the same way. It must be remembered that between 1948 and 1955 Tito was not just a comrade gone astray, but, in the eyes of Soviet and satellite propaganda, a deviationist pursuing mistaken policies: he was a vicious enemy, and his regime was a treacherous, counter-revolutionary, neo-fascist dictatorship. In Stalinist demonology Tito was cast for the role which Trotsky had

been made to play in the 1930s. In Hungary, Czechoslovakia and
Bulgaria leading communists had been convicted and put to death
as Titoite spies and agents. Now suddenly, in 1955, the Soviet
leaders proclaimed that this devil incarnate was and always had
been an upright communist, deserving of fraternal relations with
the soviet leadership and with communists throughout the world.
It is not difficult to imagine what a shock this must have imparted
to all but the dullest and most mindless of rank-and-file
communists.

If Tito was execrated as a devil from 1948 to 1955 Stalin had
been revered, from the late twenties until his death – and a little
longer – as a kind of demi-god, or at any rate as a superhumanly
wise, good and efficient leader. Coming on the heels of the
rehabilitation of Tito, the relegation of the dead Stalin, in 1956, to
the status of (almost) an un-person, must have seemed the end of
the world as they knew it to the militant faithful in the capitalist
countries. Many of them surely felt that this (to quote Carrillo
again) 'completed the demolition of what remained of the
mythical and almost religious element in our attitude towards
the Communist Party of the Soviet Union'.[18]

Some Western observers have interpreted the emergence of
Euro-communism as primarily a switch by some communist
parties to a milder, more moderate version of the creed and of
practical strategy. It is true that most if not all Euro-communist
parties have adopted flexible policies. They have not only expressed
preference for the peaceful parliamentary road to power (so
have a number of non-Euro parties), but have also pledged
themselves to surrender governmental power if, after winning an
election, they should be defeated in a subsequent poll. But there
is, as was pointed out before, only a difference of degree between
the views of the Euro-communists and the theses expounded,
during the debates on state-monopoly capitalism, by the spokesmen of a very large number of communist parties.[19] Besides, the
Euro-communists' strategy is no more moderate, no more at
variance with Marxist-Leninist orthodoxy than was the policy of
the Comintern sections in several capitalist countries between 1934
and 1939, when they were committed to 'Popular Front' tactics,

i.e. to forming alliances not only with Social Democratic but also with those anti-socialist 'bourgeois' parties which, in international affairs, favoured some kind of accommodation or co-operation with the Soviet Union.

The kernel of Euro-communism is not its moderation in the everyday struggle or the shedding of Marxist shibboleths but the attitude towards the leadership of the USSR and the Soviet Communist Party. The new heresy stems largely from the conviction of leading West European communists that their chances of success in the domestic arena depend on autonomy vis-à-vis the Kremlin, on their right to hammer out their own strategies without interference from Moscow. They have reached the conclusion – probably a correct one – that without denouncing some of the Kremlin's more repulsive methods (e.g. the treatment of dissenters), and without criticizing such clearly aggressive actions as Soviet intervention in satellite countries, they would be likely to forfeit working-class sympathies at home. This critical stance has nothing to do with the degree of militancy in the general policy of the party concerned. Actually some of the Euro-communist strictures are levelled against the very targets which have been attacked, from the 1920s onwards, by the *left-wing* communist opponents of Stalin and his successors; for example, the bureaucratic ossification of the Soviet state and party apparatus, the lack of democratic decision-making and/or democratic rights at all levels, the disfranchisement of the working masses, etc.

The outcome to date of the confrontation between Moscow and Euro-communism is that the policies of each of the parties concerned depend on what the leaders consider to be in the party's interests, and no longer on what the Kremlin leadership, for reasons of its own, wishes that party to do. The 'moderate' policies of the Popular Front era were framed at international level, under Muscovite auspices. When the French and British communists switched from calling for war with Germany in August 1939 to calling for peace a few weeks later they acted on Stalin's orders, or at any rate did what they thought he would want them to do. The Comintern sections at that time did not bother to revise Leninist theories about 'revolutionary defeatism' or 'transforming the imperialist into civil war'; they ignored the theory and toed the line laid down in Moscow. But when later the French and Italian ('Euro'-) communists renounced the dictatorship of the proletariat, or promised to respect the rules of the parliamentary game, or criticized the suppression of dissent and the abuse of psychiatry in the USSR, they did what they thought would enhance the popularity and the electoral appeal of their respective parties, and increase their prospects of gaining state power. The Russians naturally resent the criticisms coming from foreign communist parties, and the refusal of these parties to heed the Kremlin's ukases on points of theory or practical politics; but this resentment, whether explicit or not, has no effect on the Euro-communists' actions.

Moscow's monocentric position in its evanescent phase is being succeeded not by a bicentric set-up but by polycentrism. The defecting regimes have not founded a rival international. Yugoslavia is not on friendly terms either with China or Albania. After nearly fifteen years of concord, the Chinese-Albanian partnership has also come to grief. More and more communist regimes tend to decide to go their own way. This contrasts starkly with the situation in the late forties and the fifties, as well as with Leninist theory. Between the wars, when the Soviet Union was the only communist state in the world, communist theorists took it for granted that the spread of communist revolution to other countries, and especially to countries adjacent to Soviet Russia, would lead not only to a close alliance between Russia and the newly converted nation but to full-scale union; it was assumed, in other words, that there would not, for any length of time, be more than one communist state in the world. This was clearly in the mind of the Bolshevik leaders when they named post-revolutionary Russia the 'Union of Soviet Socialist Republics': they deliberately chose a title containing constitutional and ideological elements, but no reference to nationality – a title which would permit the accession of other revolutionary countries without a change in their designation.

Union with the satellite countries of Eastern Europe or, to put it differently, annexation of these countries by the Soviet Union was apparently Stalin's aim during the immediate post-Second World War period. The appointment of Soviet 'advisers' to key positions in the satellite state and military apparatus was obviously intended to pave the way to annexation.[20] Yet the process had to be reversed from the mid-fifties onwards, and especially after the 1956 upheavals in Poland and Hungary. National consciousness proved too strong to permit the peaceful abrogation of nominal independence – too strong in fact, in some cases, to permit the maintenance of full satellite status.

The rise of Euro-communism in the mid-1970s threatens Moscow-based monocentrism within what is still the Soviet-oriented branch of the world communist movement. One of the reasons for the emergence of the new tendency at this particular juncture is again, most probably, the world-wide upsurge of nationalism – more pronounced now than in the fifties. Like the splits, defections and near-defections which have plagued world communism since the end of the forties, Euro-communism is a facet of the universal growth of national consciousness; it reflects the unwillingness of non-Russian communists, both the leaders and the led, to bow to the dictates of an ethnically alien centre and to carry loyalty to the Soviet Union to the point of damaging their own interests and prospects.

There is an historic parallel between intra-communist developments in our days and the situation existing in Western Christendom before and during the Reformation. The problems of the European Church too, were strongly influenced by the awakening of national consciousness in the fourteenth, fifteenth and sixteenth centuries. This became apparent, for example, in the 'Great Schism' at the end of the fourteenth and the beginning of the fifteenth century, when the various parts of Central and Western Europe lined up on the side of either of the rival Popes on strictly national lines.[21] Czech nationalism proved an elemental force in the fifteenth century, in the militant Reformational movement and the bellicose ventures sparked off by the teachings, and the death at the stake, of John Hus. National aspirations also played a major part, in the sixteenth century, in the readiness of European peoples to endorse the Reformers' repudiation of the doctrinal claims and the practices of a degenerate Roman Curia, and in their support for ecclesiastic independence. Emergent nationalism thus contributed to the end of the monocentric religious unity that had been a perennial feature of Western Christianity in the Middle Ages, just as resurgent nationalism in our time seems incompatible with the survival of a communist monocentrism which presupposed the subordination of national movements to a supreme authority situated in a foreign capital.

The progress of Euro-communism has not so far reached the 'Protestant' stage, the point of rupture with Moscow. The USSR is still, in the eyes of the French, the Italian and even the Spanish communists, superior to any capitalist country. The Euro-communists still denounce American imperialism, and they generally side with the Soviet Union against Communist China, although there are differences in this and in other respects within the Euro-communist camp. They favour the dissolution of all military blocs, including both NATO and the Warsaw Pact. They have not renounced the basic tenets of Marxism-Leninism. There is no Euro-communist equivalent as yet to the Reformation. But the heresy is still young, and the break with established authority is not usually an immediate or even early event in the development of a schism.

The Soviet leaders must wish to avoid open conflict with the West European parties, seeing that they have no weapon against the heretics except verbal condemnation, which would not necessarily be endorsed by all communists outside the Euro-camp. The Kremlin cannot, after all, do to Carillo, Berlinguer and Marchais what it did to Imre Nagy after the Hungarian 1956 revolution, or to Dubček in 1968-9 – or what medieval Christianity did to Hus and Savonarola. To provoke a showdown might mean, from the Russian leaders' point of view, to initiate the kind of development which, over 400 years ago, ended the unity of Western Christendom; and the consequences might well be more pernicious for Soviet communism and for the coherence of the multi-national Soviet state than they proved to be, on the earlier occasion, for the Catholic Church.

Whatever happened to the imperialist war?

The conclusions derived from Marxist-Leninist analysis have, on numerous occasions, been disproved by actual developments. Communists at first tried to ignore this gap between theory and reality, but eventually felt constrained to modify their doctrines and bring them into line, as far as possible, with practical experience. Communist parties, especially in the capitalist West, have 'revised' – without necessarily agreeing among themselves – one or the other tenet of the common creed. Beliefs that have fallen by the wayside include the necessity of capitalist collapse, the inevitability or near-inevitability of violent revolution and civil war, the 'increasing misery' of the working masses, the compulsion (for capitalist powers) to acquire colonial territories and hold on to them. The positions and formulae emerging from this development of communist theory are often indistinguishable from the opinions expressed, throughout the present century, by social democrat 'revisionists' – although the communist revisionists, of course, never admit this.

A significant aspect (not so far mentioned) of the revisionist trends in present-day communism is the lack of emphasis on a phenomenon that used to be a central issue in communist speeches and writings in preceding decades: imperialist war. The inevitability of imperialist wars, that is to say of predatory wars for the redistribution of the world among the great capitalist powers, was a communist axiom in the days of Lenin and Stalin. It was taken for granted that such wars would occur again and again, until capitalism was finally vanquished by socialist world revolution. In his last published work, *Economic Problems of Socialism in the USSR* (1952), Stalin reiterated that 'the inevitability of wars between capitalist countries remains in force': only the abolition of imperialism would eliminate this inevitability. The danger of the 'imperialists' plunging the world into war still loomed large in Khrushchev's speeches at the Twenty-second Congress of the Soviet Communist Party in 1961, although he no longer stressed the *inevitability* of war. In any case neither Stalin nor Khrushchev appeared to think that the mutual threat of nuclear extinction would render a major war extremely unlikely.

Today it is the Chinese communists who keep preaching the gospel of the inevitable war; to be precise, it is nuclear war between the superpowers, the USA and the USSR, which the Chinese consider to be certain. This view, which possibly contains an element of wishful thinking, is not shared by the Soviet-oriented communists, neither the orthodox nor the 'Euros'. From the debates and publications on state-monopoly capitalism in the late sixties war was almost completely absent, and it has not since come back into intra-communist discussions and arguments. The large Euro-communist parties of the NATO countries, the Italian and the French – parties hopeful of entering coalition governments in the foreseeable future – have declared their readiness to respect NATO and other defence treaties; they have done so partly (and they admit this) on the grounds that war between the NATO alliance and the Warsaw Pact countries seems a very remote contingency.

The possibility of 'imperialist' war or, practically speaking, of a third world war, is not being disproved in present-day communist literature. It is simply that war does not figure as a contingency in analyses of the transitional process which is supposed to lead to socialism. It could be said that imperialist war is as irrelevant to modern (pro-Soviet) communist doctrine as God is to the theory of evolution, which does not prove the non-existence of a supreme being but refuses to assign to him the role of creator. The revisionist communism of our days does not explicitly deny the possibility of war, but (unlike the Marxist-Leninist concept which was considered valid until recently) it has no need of this hypothesis.

The omission of 'imperialist' war from modern communist theory is consistent with the views about post-war capitalism which Labour theorists like Strachey, Crosland and Douglas Jay expounded in the fifties. It was above all the ex-communist John Strachey who showed, in books like Contemporary Capitalism and The End of Empire,[22] that modern capitalism can avoid collapse and can expand without acquiring or retaining colonial territories for exploitation. Most present-day communists have accepted this;

it is implicit in their assessment of contemporary reality that economic and political developments since 1945, together with the military technology of the nuclear age, have invalidated Lenin's axiom of the inevitable 'imperialist' war. They do not explicitly say that this is so; they have not yet reached the stage in their involvement with revisionism at which they will openly declare that any of Lenin's fundamental theses has been falsified by history.

Notes

Farewell to Revolution: Revisionist Trends in
Contemporary Communism

1 Marxists have nearly always been at odds about the 'correct' attitude in a particular war. In 1870 Marx and Engels favoured Prussia until the battle of Sedan in September, then sided with republican France: but their German followers August Bebel and Wilhelm Liebknecht, both members of the Prussian Diet, opposed the war from the start. In 1904–5 Lenin and his friends, unlike other Russian solialists, welcomed Japan's victories over the Tsar's forces. In the 1914–18 war most socialist leaders in the various belligerent nations believed their own government to be in the right and supported the war effort; these 'social imperialist' leaders were denounced as traitors by the Bolsheviks and other left-wing sections of the Second International.

2 This is still the view of official historiography in the Soviet Union and the other communist countries.

3 *Imperialism as the Highest Stage of Capitalism* in *Collected Works* (Moscow 1964), XXII, pp. 185–304.

4 For more about this Euro-communist heresy, *see* pp. 235ff.

5 I, 143–4 (1966); II, 145–6 (1966).

6 *Economic Problems of Socialism in the USSR* (Moscow 1952).

7 In *Contemporary Capitalism* (London 1956), p. 155.

8 Reported in *World Marxist Review* (May 1967), p. 42.

9 Reported in *World Marxist Review* (May 1967), p. 43.

10 Reported in *World Marxist Review* (December 1967) and (January 1968).
11 Cf. pp. 223ff. above.
12 It is completely under the control of the East German Socialist Unity Party, i.e. the East German Government.
13 Lenin himself wrote in 1917, in his pamphlet *The Impending Catastrophe and How to Combat It*: 'Socialism is merely state monopoly which is made to serve the interests of the whole people and has to that extent ceased to be capitalist monopoly.'
14 Post-Lenin editions, of course, but well in the spirit of Lenin's own teachings. Lenin lived to see the opening phase (in Italy) but not the perfection of Fascist dictatorship.
15 Cf. p. 230 above.
16 *Eurocommunism and the State* (London 1977).
17 *Ibid.* p. 112.
18 *Ibid.*
19 Cf. p. 231 above.
20 Cf. the essay 'The Decline and Fall of the Soviet Empire' in this volume, pp. 194ff., especially p. 196.
21 For greater detail *see* K. Scott Latourette, 2 vols, *A History of Christianity* (New York 1975), p. 627.
22 London 1959.

Index